Dual-Earner Families

To

To our own dual-earner partners:
David, Dove and Norbert

DUAL-EARNER FAMILIES
International Perspectives

edited by
Suzan Lewis
Dafna N. Izraeli
Helen Hootsmans

SAGE Publications
London • Newbury Park • New Delhi

First published 1992

SAGE Publications Ltd
6 Bonhill Street
London EC2A 4PU

SAGE Publications Inc
2455 Teller Road
Newbury Park, California 91320

SAGE Publications India Pvt Ltd
32, M-Block Market
Greater Kailash – I
New Delhi 110 048

British Library Cataloguing in Publication data

Dual-earner families: International perspectives
   I. Lewis, Suzan   II. Izraeli, Dafna N.
   III. Hootsmans, Helen
   306.85

   ISBN 0-8039-8382-4
   ISBN 0-8039-8383-2 pbk

Library of Congress catalog card number 91-50851

Typeset by Contour Typesetters, Southall, Middx.
Printed in Great Britain by Biddles Ltd, Guildford, Surrey

Contents

PART 3   WORK AND THE FAMILY: IMPLICATIONS FOR ORGANIZATIONAL POLICY

Preface

The original idea of putting together this volume, to place the discourse on family and paid work within a cross-national context, was conceived at an international industrial relations conference in Israel in December 1987. Here five women, all of them feminists, from different countries and different disciplines, shared a panel on work and the family. Inevitably we continued comparing notes outside the conference halls. We discussed the ways in which the problems and the solutions, the constraints and opportunities, the price and the promise, for dual-earner couples, and especially for women, were the same and the ways in which they differed in our respective countries. Three of us – Sue Lewis, a British psychologist, Dafna Izraeli, an Israeli sociologist and Helen Hootsmans, an American management consultant resident in the Netherlands – joined forces to develop the project. We invited others whom we knew were researching and writing about dual-earner families around the world to join us. They responded enthusiastically and working with them has been one of the pleasures of making this book happen.

A book of this nature is indebted to numerous people with whom we have discussed ideas and who have provided support, including our families, friends and colleagues. Individual authors have made their own acknowledgements at the end of each chapter. Special mention must be made, however, of the contribution to the entire book of Sue Jones, our friend and guide at Sage, whose patience, insight and encouragement have been invaluable.

Notes on the Contributors

Julia Brannen is Senior Research Officer at the Thomas Coram Research Unit, Institute of Education, University of London. Much of her work is on families and households, including past longitudinal research on dual-earner households in the period following the first birth and a current project about parental responsibility and adolescent health. She is co-editor of *Give and Take in Families* (1987) and co-author of *Marriages in Trouble* (1982), *New Mothers at Work* (1988) and *Managing Mothers* (1991).

Jeanette Taudin Chabot, MA, University of Washington, combines three cross-national perspectives in her consultancy and interpreting service, which specializes in facilitating Japanese cultural and economic relationships. A PhD candidate at the University of Leiden, her publications include a handbook on doing business with the Japanese and articles on the position of women in Japanese literature and in the Japanese labor market and on commuter marriage.

Christine E. Clason is Associate Professor of Sociology at the University of Groningen in the Netherlands. Born in Indonesia, she was raised in Indonesia and the Netherlands. She studied sociology at the University of Groningen and the University of the Pacific in California. In 1986 and 1987 she organized two Dutch–Hungarian socioeconomic seminars in Budapest and Groningen as part of government bicultural exchange programs. She is currently engaged in multifaceted research on the interaction of gender, work and family. She is married to a Hungarian-born biologist.

Alice H. Cook is Professor Emerita of Industrial and Labor Relations at Cornell University, Ithaca, New York. In recent years she has worked primarily on issues of social policy, support systems and the role of trade unions in relation to the needs of women in the labor force. She has written comparatively on these matters as they have developed in industrialized countries. Among her publications are: 'Pay Equity: theory and implementation,' in *Public Personnel Management*, ed. C. Bose and N. Riccuci (1991); 'Public policies to help dual-earner families meet the demands of the work world,' *Industrial and Labor Relations Review*, Winter 1989; 'Family and Work,' Canadian Industrial and Labor Relations Association *Proceedings* (1987); 'Policies affecting women's employment in industrial countries' (with Ronnie J. Steinberg) in *Women Working: Theories and Facts in Perspective*, ed. Stromberg and Harkness (1987); *Women and Trade Unions in Eleven Industrialized Countries* (ed. with Val R. Lorwin and Arlene Kaplan Daniels, 1983); *Working Women in Japan: Discrimination, Resistance and Reform* (with Hiroko Hayashi, 1980).

L. Suzanne Dancer is Assistant Professor in the Department of Educational Psychology at the University of Wisconsin-Milwaukee where she teaches courses in statistics and research methodology. She has been a Postdoctoral Fellow in the Sociology Department at Indiana University and has worked with the late Louis Guttman at the Israel Institute of Applied Social Research in Jerusalem. Her major area of research involves the application of newer measurement techniques and research methodologies, including nonmetric multidimensional scaling and log-linear models, to current social problems.

Lucia Albino Gilbert is Professor of Educational Psychology at the University of Texas at Austin and teaches in the department's doctoral program in counseling psychology. Two of her major research interests are dual-career families and gender issues in counseling and psychotherapy. She is the author of *Men in Dual-career Families: Current Realities and Future Prospects* (1985) and *Sharing It All: The Rewards and Struggles of Two-career Families* (1988). She has also authored a number of chapters and articles in the area of gender and mental health including a chapter on this topic for the second edition of the *Handbook of Counseling Psychology* (forthcoming). She is associate editor of *Psychology of Women Quarterly* and serves on the editorial boards of *Journal of Family Issues* and *Professional Psychology*.

Rosanna Hertz is an Associate Professor of Sociology at Wellesley College and a Research Fellow in the Department of Psychiatry at Harvard Medical School. Her research focuses on understanding the relationship between work, family and gender in various organizational and community contexts. She has recently published a series of articles on the effects of shiftwork on family life and she is presently working on an in-depth study of the meaning of money and financial arrangements among couples. She is the author of *More Equal than Others: Women and Men in Dual-Career Marriages* (1986). During 1991 she gave birth to her first child and she was named the co-editor of *Qualitative Sociology*.

Helen M. Hootsmans is a consultant specializing in work and family issues and a facilitator of cross-cultural exchanges. An American married to a Dutch engineer, she has been an equal opportunities consultant in the Dutch National Women's Project, co-ordinator of national and international interdisciplinary women's studies conferences and seminars, co-organizer of the Council of Europe's European Women's Studies Network and director of the Partners and Life/Career Guidance Project. Her recent publications focus on dual-career couples, relocation and the development of work-time options in support of a more equitable work and family interface.

Dafna Nundi Izraeli is an Associate Professor of Sociology at Bar-Ilan University in Israel. She is editor of *Women in Israel* (1987); *Women in Management Worldwide* (1988, with Nancy Adler); *Women in Israel: A Sociological Perspective* (forthcoming, with Yael Atzmon) and author of 'An international comparison of women in management: women managers in their homelands and as expatriates', in *Women in Management*, ed. E. Fagenson

(Women and Work, Vol. 4) (1992, with Ariane Berthoin Antal). Her current research focuses on public policy, work, family and gender in Israel.

Suzan Lewis is a Senior Lecturer in Psychology, and co-director of the Elizabeth Gaskell Centre for Interpersonal and Organisational Development, at Manchester Polytechnic. Her research interests and publications are in the areas of dual-earner families, occupational stress and women and work and she is co-author, with Cary L. Cooper, of *Career Couples: Contemporary Lifestyles and How to Manage Them* (1989). She is the mother of three sons.

Vivien Lim is a Senior Tutor in the Department of Organizational Behaviour, National University of Singapore. She is currently on study leave as a doctoral candidate in the Joseph M. Katz Graduate School of Business, University of Pittsburgh.

Peter Moss is a Senior Research Officer at the Thomas Coram Research Unit, London University Institute of Education, where he has undertaken research on under-fives services and dual-earner households with young children. He is also co-ordinator for the European Commission Childcare Network. He has three children aged 18, 16 and 10.

Karin Sandqvist obtained her MA in the USA and PhD in Sweden and has worked with teaching and childcare in these two countries. Her cross-national family research has been conducted within the International Group for Comparative Human Ecology. In her current post as Educational Researcher at the Stockholm Institute of Education, her research focuses on the father's role in the family, gender equality and child development. She is married to a Danish-born Canadian living in Sweden and they have three children. She finds that examination of unconscious cultural assumptions is frequently necessary both in her private and professional life.

Uma Sekaran is Professor Emerita of Management at Southern Illinois University at Carbondale (SIUC) and Adjunct Professor at St Mary's College, Moraga, California. Her research interests are in the areas of dual careers and cross-cultural management. She is the author of five books, and author or co-author of numerous book chapters journal articles, and papers presented at national, regional, and international conferences. She is on the editorial board of the *Academy of Management Review*. Her book titled *Dual-Career Families: Contemporary Organizational and Counseling Issues*, published by Jossey-Bass, was selected as one of three best books of 1986 by the Behavioral Science Book Club. She was the Director of University Women's Professional Advancement at SIUC.

Edith Yuen obtained her PhD from the University of Sydney, Australia. She is currently a Senior Lecturer in the Department of Organizational Behaviour, National University of Singapore.

1
Introduction: Dual-Earner Families in Context

Suzan Lewis

Family structures are changing throughout the industrialized world. The once traditional pattern of male breadwinner and female home-maker is giving way to alternative roles and relationships. Prominent among these is the dual-earner family pattern in which both spouses share the provider and homemaker roles, albeit rarely equally. The dual-earner family, with its inherent conflicts, pressures and rewards is the focus of considerable research by social scientists. Much of this interest stems from the possibilities that this family pattern represents in evolving away from gender-based family and employment roles and from the family as a pivotal system in the oppression of women. However, family, employment and gender roles do not develop in a vacuum. They are an integral part of wider systems of social relations and institutions and need to be understood within that context. The nature and pace of change in gender roles associated with the growth of dual-earner families differ with the specific cultural and institutional context of national societies. Culture, the historically evolved, learned values, attitudes and meanings shared by members of a given community (Tayeb, 1988) is internalized and also reflected in state and organizational policies. These in turn inevitably shape and constrain the lives of individuals and families.

The majority of dual-earner family research has been conducted within North America, by researchers who have often ignored or underestimated issues of cultural bias and generalizability. Research taking place elsewhere in the world is less well known beyond the country of origin. American reviews of dual-earner family and work/family research rarely cite literature from other countries. This phenomenon of course is not restricted to research on dual-earner families. Other authors, in making a plea for a more cross-national spread of ideas, have noted that although many European journals routinely publish in English in an effort to reach a wider English-speaking readership, European writers often express disappointment that their research is seldom read or cited by American researchers (Gutek et al., 1988; Antal and Izraeli, 1992). New concern about assumptions of cross-national generalizability is now emerging, however, and the exchange of ideas and findings by researchers in different countries is being encouraged. This concern is demonstrated by the inclusion of sections on international perspectives in recent American edited collections on women and work, work and the family and related topics (for example Fagenson, 1992; Gutek et al., 1988; Goldsmith, 1989; Zedeck, 1992).

This volume presents some cross-national perspectives on dual-earner families. It includes contributions from a range of countries and continents. Current issues emerging from the dual-earner family literature are examined within this wider context. Contributions have been selected to represent different cultural, political, religious and economic systems. Inevitably, the selection is not exhaustive. In the early chapters, authors highlight the impact of national history, institutions and cultural ideology, both directly on the lives of dual-earner families, and via their impact on social and organizational policy. The perspectives are those of authors who live in or are closely associated with the countries they write about and whose own lives are constructed within their culture. As such, each chapter is written by an 'insider', and cannot claim to be entirely 'objective' or 'value free', were such a position to be possible. The cultural values of sub-groups within a national community also impact on dual-earner families (Thomas, 1990), and to the extent that such values conflict with the dominant ideology, they may create additional pressures for specific ethnic groups. The authors in this volume, who live in multicultural societies, are sensitive to this issue, but focus on the impact of the dominant majority groups whose influence on policy is greatest. Issues of ethnic cultural difference for dual-earner families are relatively underexplored, as is the interplay of social class and gender, and should be the subject of future research.

Despite the spread of dual-earner families, most industrialized societies continue to be structured around the traditional single breadwinner family. This social myopia is the source of considerable pressure for dual-earner partners attempting to transform family roles and relationships. Later chapters in this volume examine issues relating to the impact of social expectations and the reconstruction of gender roles within dual-earner families, and consider some of their implications for the organization of work in the 1990s and beyond.

Dual-earner or dual-career families?

Traditionally, level of commitment, mobility and occupational status have been the criteria which distinguished a career from a job, and hence dual-career from dual-earner families. A substantial literature on dual-career families developed from the pioneering work of British researchers, Rhona and Robert Rapoport (1969, 1971) who defined careers as occupations with a developmental sequence, which require a high level of commitment and are highly personally salient to the occupants. The Rapoports studied families in which both partners displayed a high level of commitment to both family and career, and who, they maintained, were thereby in the forefront of social change. The belief that highly educated, well paid women have the potential to transform families and create more egalitarian options for other women, focused attention on middle-class professional and managerial dual-career families (Epstein, 1971; Paloma and Garland, 1971; Hertz, 1986; Sekaran, 1986; Gilbert, 1985; Izraeli, 1989). This focus has been criticized for being elitist (Hiller and Dyehouse, 1987; Lewis and Cooper, 1988) and for overlooking the special problems faced by other dual-earner families (Keith and Schafer, 1980; Lein, 1979).

Examination of the criteria used in the literature to distinguish dual-career from dual-earner marriage reveals a confusion between psychological, subjective variables, particularly job commitment, on the one hand, and structural objective variables, notably occupational status on the other (Hiller and Dyehouse, 1987). This confusion may be attributed to the assumption of a strong relationship between high occupational status and high job commitment among dual-earner spouses, a relationship which is not borne out by empirical evidence (Hiller and Dyehouse, 1987). In view of the confusion concerning the definition of career, and the narrow focus of much of the dual-earner family literature, Greenhaus (1989) proposes that the distinction between dual-career and dual-earner families be abandoned. He argues that this will broaden research beyond elite, professional couples and hence provide evidence generalizable to a wider section of the population.

While agreeing with the need to address issues pertaining to more than an elite minority, we argue that it is nonetheless necessary in some situations to emphasize heterogeneity among couples in which both spouses work, in order to avoid unwarranted generalizations. Hence we have retained the distinction between dual-earner and dual-career families in this volume. We use the term dual-earner in the broader sense, to apply to all families in which both spouses are employed. However, we also retain the term dual-career family to refer deliberately to more elite groups of middle-class couples in high-status occupations with an opportunity structure, who may or may not be more highly committed to their jobs than other dual-earners. The distinction is particularly important in societies where social class divisions are very apparent, and generalization from elite groups to an entire population would be inappropriate. In addition, Lucia Gilbert and Suzanne Dancer (Chapter 9) stress that it is important to emphasize the heterogeneity amongst dual-earner families, including differences in behaviours and attitudes, in order to understand the impact of family pattern on family members. They distinguish between dual-career and other dual-earner families, using criteria similar to those employed by the Rapoports, but also demonstrate considerable variations within each pattern, particularly in terms of role behaviours within the home.

Theoretical frameworks

The dominant theoretical framework in the dual-earner family research literature is a role theory approach, with particular emphasis on gender roles. Gender attitudes and expectations are crucial determinants of the experiences and conflicts of dual-earner spouses (Lewis and Cooper, 1988). Beliefs about gender relationships, furthermore, are inextricable from the ideology of the family. Statements about the ideal family within any culture indicate the roles and behaviours deemed appropriate for women and men (and also children and elders). The culturally defined behavioural expectations of gender are therefore central to our understanding of dual-earner families. However, these values, and the extent to which they are embedded in social structures, differ across nations. For instance, Karin Sandqvist (Chapter 5) demonstrates that gender differences, at least in terms of values and personality, are relatively blurred in Sweden, in comparison with other countries. This is reflected in social policy which recognizes that women and men have equal responsibility (and by implication, aptitude) for both parenting and breadwinning. In countries which emphasize gender role differences, social policies are less supportive of the dual-earner lifestyle and of gender equality in the family. A limitation of a role theory approach is that this wider context is often neglected.

Much of the recent research on dual-earner families is also conducted within an open systems framework (Barling, 1990). This perspective is useful because it acknowledges the interdependence of family and work, the two central systems for dual-earner couples, and proposes that a change in one system requires a change in the other if equilibrium is to be maintained (Pleck, 1977). Dafna Izraeli (Chapter 2) points to the need to extend the systems boundaries studied, to incorporate state institutions and public policy. Systems models are circular process models and therefore view the work, family and wider social systems relationship as an ongoing process, changing over time. Thus while a role theory approach is useful in highlighting the impact of changing social expectations, particularly within the family, an open systems approach highlights the work/family interfaces and also the relevance of forces beyond work and family, including patterns of industrialization, labour supply, war and peace, which indirectly impact on gender roles and relationships.

Similarities and differences of experiences across nations

This book explores the ways in which dual-earner couples are reconstructing gender and family roles to balance work and family, in societies which range from the more traditional to the very liberal. The national cultures represented in this volume differ in terms of the recency of industrialization, economic conditions and political and religious ideology. They differ in the ways in which gender divisions are embedded in social institutions, in the value they assign to work and family life in general and to women's participation in the labour force in particular, and in their receptivity to change. However, a common strand which permeates cultural diversity is that of continuing gender inequality. The extent of inequality and the way in which it manifests itself, depend on structural and ideological contexts. A universal baseline, however, is that most dual-earner women retain the major (and sometimes sole) responsibility for childcare and domestic work in addition to paid work, family roles are more salient for mothers than fathers, and it is more legitimate for women than men to modify work schedules for family. Women's income remains lower than men's, but women's financial contribution to the household, even when this is considerable, does not necessarily increase their authority within the family (Hertz, Chapter 8; Sekaran, Chapter 3). In the workplace, sex segregation, both vertical and horizontal is widespread, and women find it more difficult than men to advance in their careers, particularly into the most senior positions (Adler and Izraeli, 1988). In deviation from this baseline, some men in dual-earner families in some countries are participating more equally in family work, especially childcare (Sandqvist, Chapter 5; Yuen and Lim, Chapter 4; Gilbert and Dancer, Chapter 9) and the reallocation of gender roles within some families, at least in the USA, is giving rise to the possibility of a new generation who may be less closely attached to stereotypical gender roles (Gilbert and Dancer, Chapter 9). Some dual-earner women, in some societies, are making strides in their careers, although few pierce the glass ceiling. Ambition and striving are less characteristic of both women and men in certain societies (Sekaran, Chapter 3; Sandqvist, Chapter 5) than in others, and power and career success are less sought after (although most positions of power are still occupied by men in these countries, as elsewhere). Where women's work is highly valued, the gender gap in income level may be narrower, despite occupational segregation (Sandqvist, Chapter 5). Dual-earner families are changing the structures of families, organizations and wider societies, but the process is slow and uneven.

A number of interrelated aspects of the socio-cultural contexts explored in this volume emerge as significant in determining the rate of change, the ease or difficulty with which work and family are balanced, and the progress, or otherwise, towards gender equality within the family. In all the countries represented here, the need for women's labour in the context of a tight labour market was a major impetus for social change, and for the implementation of public policies to support dual-earner families. Singapore, for instance, provides an example of public policies aimed at shaping family behaviour in line with perceived changes in the country's economic needs (Yuen and Lim, Chapter 4). Japan, in contrast, has been able to industrialize, until recently, without facing any economic imperative to develop women's labour force potential. It remains therefore a very traditional society in this respect, despite being economically advanced (see Chabot, Chapter 10). So economic factors are paramount, but the ease with which governments can respond to perceived economic needs by implementing social change is also influenced by cultural attitudes to the roles of women and men.

Ideology and gender equality
Countries differ in the extent to which they are ideologically committed to a notion of gender equality which incorporates the ideal of modifying gender roles within the family. At one extreme, Sweden endorses the 'equal roles paradigm' (Sandqvist, Chapter 5) and this is translated into social policies that encourage equal responsibility for parenting as well as equal opportunities in the public sphere. Equality was also a basic tenet of the socialist regimes in Eastern Europe. Influenced by Marxist and Leninist theory, Soviet and other Eastern European governments encouraged women's labour force participation. Equality of opportunities for women was pursued through a shift of domestic functions such as childcare from the private to the public domain, but less attention has been paid to the issue of the reallocation of male and female family roles (Clason, Chapter 6; Lapidus, 1988).

In other cultures a commitment to true gender equality is not easily compatible with cultural traditions and beliefs in which the subordination of women is deeply embedded. This creates dilemmas for women in dual-earner families. In these contexts women find ways of coping with work and family which avoid challenging existing gender roles and relationships, and thus minimize potential tension. In India, for instance, this involves devolving domestic responsibilities to hired help or female relatives, rather than expecting men to be more involved in family work (Sekaran, Chapter 3). In Israel the tension between women's groups with a commitment to equality, and traditional ideology is resolved by the perpetuation of a modified version of family equality. Men are encouraged to 'help' with family work but the ideal of role sharing is not articulated (Izraeli, Chapter 2).

The relationship between ideology and behaviour, however, is rarely straightforward. Although Swedish men are increasingly involved in childcare and family work, women continue to perform most of the domestic work and to make more modifications to their work schedules for family reasons. Karin Sandqvist (Chapter 5) points out that behaviour in Sweden lags behind ideology in this respect. Elsewhere the reverse is often true: ideology tends to lag behind behaviour. In Britain, for instance, a growing number of mothers of young children are employed, but the ideal of the stay-at-home mother persists (Brannen and Moss, Chapter 7). As women's and men's behaviours change, however, cultural elements, including socially acceptable and defined attitudes, may also change. Lucia Gilbert and Suzanne Dancer (Chapter 9) demonstrate that this is occurring in the USA, where paternal participation in families has increased and is also socially acceptable and expected.

The social construction of masculinity

The social representation of masculinity in terms of the primacy of the breadwinner role, and of men's lack of 'aptitude' for domestic work serves to perpetuate inequalities in the family and ultimately in the workforce. Where masculinity is socially constructed in this way, women have low expectations of assistance from their partners. Rather than expecting spousal support as of right, women are grateful for any instrumental or emotional support they do receive from partners who, by virtue of their maleness, are not expected to provide either (see Brannen and Moss, Chapter 7; Sekaran, Chapter 3). Men and women in many cultures and subcultures subscribe to the view that men are inept or incapable of domestic work and this serves to excuse men's non-participation in family work, and to avoid confrontation (see, for example, Chabot, Chapter 10; Sekaran, Chapter 3). In Sweden, and other Scandinavian countries and to some extent, America, there is a recognition that men's roles must change (see Sandqvist, Chapter 5). The routine practice of sharing childcare and ongoing marital discussion of this subject help parents to construct an image of the father as a competent caregiver (Coltrane, 1989). Without modifications to behaviour and explicit discussion of what it means for men to share what is traditionally women's work, there is little opportunity for significant social change. Similarly, Rosanna Hertz (Chapter 8) argues that lack of discussion and information-seeking, and the lack of explicit articulation of rules about the handling of money help to perpetuate the male breadwinner myth and male authority in dual-earner families, despite women's increased earning power.

The myth of women's choice

Myths about women's 'choices' of work and family balance also serve to disadvantage dual-earner women at home and in the workplace. Women's right to employment (although not necessarily to a career) is now widely accepted. However, the authors in this volume attest to the fact that most women work for economic reasons, to contribute to the family income. The emphasis on the right to work implies a choice while in reality wives' employment is more often a necessity. Julia Brannen and Peter Moss (Chapter 7) demonstrate that the decision for new mothers in Britain to return to employment tends to be constructed as the woman's individual choice, even though her continued income is essential. In a society where the employment of mothers of infants is not normative, this construction serves to absolve men from having to share in family work.

Even in countries where women are expected to play a part in the labour force, women's decisions about their level of commitment or involvement in a career and the priority assigned to family work are constrained by prevailing social and organizational values, by the level of their partner's involvement in family work and by the availability of occupational opportunities. In societies where women's family responsibilities are accommodated by the workplace and men are protected against the intrusion of family into work, women's labour force participation fails to expand women's (and men's) choices or to contribute to gender equality (Izraeli, Chapter 2; Clason, Chapter 6). In Israel, for instance, the belief that women choose to work part-time and give priority to family legitimizes employer discrimination as a rational response (Izraeli, Chapter 2). Similarly, in communist Hungary public provisions enabling women to combine family and employment reduced women's burden, but also reduced their occupational opportunities. Christine Clason (Chapter 6) argues that the consensus that childcare and household work are women's responsibilities is so strong in Hungary that even when concessions became available to both parents, the men's rights to parental leave were regarded as irrelevant.

The belief embedded in many cultures that women have a free choice of family and employment roles assigns responsibility for the inferior position of women in the workforce, their lower income in comparison to men, and their domestic overload, to women themselves and serves to conceal the structures of power which constrain them. Alice Cook (Chapter 12) suggests that this belief may be a feature of cultures emphasizing individualism. This was certainly a feature of Thatcherite Britain, where the Prime Minister was famous for her belief that there is no such thing as society, only individuals (see Brannen and Moss, Chapter 7). The structures of power which constrain women's choices are illustrated by the fact that women's preferences about how work in general should be restructured have had less impact on the workplace than the demands of men, who dominate the trade unions, and who prefer longer holidays to the shorter working days which would benefit parents (see Sandqvist, Chapter 5; Cook, Chapter 12). Thus women's choices and preferences continue to be marginalized.

Beliefs about the needs of children

A powerful ideology helping to maintain a fairly traditional sexual division of roles among dual-earner parents is the belief that infants need full-time maternal care. The social constructions of the ideal mother in many cultures as one who provides full-time mothering creates guilt and conflict for women, and is particularly pernicious in the context of the increasing need for two incomes. This belief, influenced by John Bowlby's theory of maternal deprivation, is strongly held in Britain (Jowell et al., 1988). It underpins the provision of maternity, but not parental, leave in many countries. In much of Europe however, there is a recognition that infants benefit from close attachments with fathers as well as mothers, giving rise to the provision of parental leave rights for either parent (see Sandqvist, Chapter 5; Hootsmans, Chapter 11). This provision is also available in Israel, where the legacy of socialist ideology, and particularly the Kibbutz movement, stresses the importance of children having social experiences from an early age, to foster independence from parents. Mothers who do not send children to nurseries are criticized as overprotective. The recognition that parental care need not be full time is also related to the belief characteristic of most Eastern and Western European countries that childcare is a public rather than a private responsibility. The role of the mother in the care of infants also receives less emphasis in many Eastern countries, although childcare often remains a private responsibility. So it is socially acceptable for parents to leave young children for substantial periods of time with grandparents (Sekaran, Chapter 3) or, in Singapore, with foster parents (Yuen and Lim, Chapter 4).

Beliefs about the needs of school-aged children also vary between cultures, and these too impact on the experiences of dual-earner parents, especially mothers. Cross-nationally, factors such as the normative role of parents in their children's education, and the length of the school day affect the amount of time spent in family work. Where a high premium is set on education, it is the mother's role which again tends to be emphasized, with the crucial role of mothering being constructed as extending well into the school years, thus constraining women's participation in the labour force. This is particularly the case in the Far Eastern countries represented here: Singapore and Japan. In Singapore the traditional emphasis on the mother's substantial role in the education of her children conflicts with the government's policy of encouraging women's labour force participation. The emphasis on the importance of education in Singapore also extends to a belief that well-educated mothers produce the most intelligent children, a belief which informs a selective pro-natalist policy.

The short school day in Singapore, Japan and Israel also constrains the labour force participation of mothers. While half-day schooling may be based on beliefs about children's needs for rest and recreation, it is significant that the conversion to full-day schooling is occurring in the context of a tight labour market in Singapore, and pressure from ethnic-based political groups in the weaker sectors of the economy in Israel.

Interestingly, in Israel, where the notion of a good mother does not preclude an employment role, guilt and anxiety are invoked in mothers at a later stage. Dafna Izraeli (Chapter 2) describes the tensions associated with mothering a soldier. The perception that sons and daughters in the army need extra care and pampering is translated into the need for extra maternal care at a time when maternal responsibilities are declining elsewhere. This nicely illustrates the impact on dual-earner spouses of the interrelationship of cultural expectations with essentially non-cultural, in this case military, conditions.

Social class divisions
In societies with a clear-cut class system, a substantial immigrant population and few employment opportunities for lower-class women, the solution to childcare and domestic problems for more privileged dual-earner spouses is to employ domestic help. In India and Singapore, for instance, paid domestic help alleviates overload for middle-class women, enabling them to devote time to a career, but perpetuates class inequalities. The delegation of family work to servants or to female relatives fails to challenge the basic sexual division of labour. The potential for more privileged women to change the structure of families and to create egalitarian options for other women is much diminished, therefore, in the context of continuing class and gender inequality. In Sweden, commitment to class equality as well as to gender equality renders this type of solution for dual-earner families ideologically unacceptable (see Sandqvist, Chapter 5). Hence the need for their involvement, together with ideological commitment, propels men into being more involved in family work. A

similar process has occurred in the USA, albeit due more to practical need than to any explicit public commitment to gender equality. Nevertheless, many Americans still use lower-class or immigrant women as domestics (Hertz, 1986).

Class divisions and a readily available pool of paid help may hinder the transition to more egalitarian family roles, but a homogeneous population does not guarantee such a transition. In Japan there is no underclass but the issue of equal roles within the family has not yet been deliberately addressed in terms of policy changes and hence women are particularly overburdened (Chabot, Chapter 10).

Extended family structure

While the forging of new roles and relationships is taking place more or less slowly within the nuclear family in the West, the extended three-generational family is still prevalent in the East. Extended family, especially grandmothers, provide an important source of childcare in the context of strong family ties and shared accommodation or close proximity. Relatives remain the main source of day-care in other countries lacking a comprehensive public provision of childcare, but in the context of the nuclear family such assistance is not automatically forthcoming (see Brannen and Moss, Chapter 7).

Family support systems are deeply embedded in family structure in India, Japan and Singapore, and this considerably reduces the pressure on dual-earner couples with young children. At a later stage, however, the roles are often reversed, with the elderly relatives requiring care. In all countries represented here, it is female relatives who are expected to take on this task, relinquishing their jobs if necessary. Indeed, cultural norms may militate against construing the elderly as a 'problem' in traditional societies. In India, seniority is a source of status, both in the family and the workplace. Grandparents become heads of family, to be respected and, when the time comes, cared for (Sekaran, Chapter 3). Jeanette Chabot (Chapter 10) demonstrates that eldercare creates particular problems for dual-earner families in Japan, which has a strong tradition of care by the eldest son (or rather, his wife). However, the population is ageing almost everywhere, and this may become a widespread issue on the scale of childcare, in the future. It will be particularly problematic in countries, such as Britain and Israel, with a strong commitment to limiting public spending and to encouraging caring in the community, as well as those such as Japan and India, where there are strong cultural constraints against non-family care of the elderly.

The structure of the family and relative importance of inter-generational relationships are also significant as background to changing power relations within dual-earner families. This can be illustrated with regard to the significance of money in family relations. Within the nuclear family, wives who earn as much or more than their husbands are in a strong position to negotiate a more equal division of labour in the home (see Izraeli, Chapter 2; Feree, 1987). Rosanna Hertz (Chapter 8) points to mechanisms devised by spouses to deal with money as important indicators of power relations between American husbands and wives. In India, however, where conjugal relationships tend to be submerged within the wider family, the wife's income is constructed as a contribution to the wider household and any power attached to this income operates within this context, rather than in the husband and wife dyad (Sekaran, Chapter 3). A wife's earnings provide her with bargaining power with her mother-in-law in relation to domestic work, but less so with her husband.

Social and organizational policy

Public provision of childcare and eldercare as well as legislation for maternity and parental leave, leave to care for a sick relative, the protection of part-time workers and progressive tax systems all serve to support the dual-earner lifestyle. There is considerable national variation in these policies, as a consequence of different ideologies, and varying economic conditions. Governments vary too, in their level of interventionism. Sweden, Singapore and Hungary provide examples of policies which deliberately aim, or have aimed, to influence families, although their primary motives differ: egalitarian ideology in Sweden (but with economic factors playing a part), economic growth in Singapore, and the creation of a socialist state, as well as modernization, in Hungary. At the other end of the scale of interventionism successive British governments, of different political persuasions, have declared themselves reluctant to 'interfere' in the family (Brannen and Moss, Chapter 7; Lewis, 1992). Reluctance to interfere translates into reluctance to support public provision of childcare or parental leave rights.

Social policies to support the combining of family and employment can be instrumental in facilitating the development towards equal family roles. Nevertheless, while government policies may produce some changes in behaviour and attitudes, certain traditions, especially the sexual division of domestic labour, are slow to change, whatever the level of interventions and provisions. The fact that gender inequalities persist, albeit to varying extents, among all the countries represented here, including those with well developed social support structures, demonstrates that development is a slow process. In this respect all countries, and not just those in the Third World, can be construed as developing, rather than developed nations.

Cross-national variations as well as similarities in organizational culture are well documented (Hofstede, 1980; Tayeb, 1988). National organizations in all industrialized countries have been constructed by men for men and notions of organization remain patriarchal (Hearn and Parkin, 1988). However, organizations are inevitably influenced by cultural factors such as attitude to gender roles and the value placed on competitiveness and seniority.

Women's primary responsibility for childcare is assumed in most countries, but countries differ in the extent to which work organizations are expected to consider family needs. The rhetoric of individual choice and responsibility in Britain, for instance, sustains the view that employed mothers are responsible for their own 'predicament' and therefore should not expect any special consideration from employers (Brannen and Moss, Chapter 7). Consequently little support has been forthcoming, except in times of acute labour shortages. Israeli mothers, in contrast, are expected to be employed, but are simultaneously expected to prioritize their family commitments. The legitimacy of mothers asking for concessions at work, in the interest of family, are embedded in Israeli work culture (Izraeli, Chapter 2). This eases the stress of managing multiple roles for women, but consequently it is men, who do not allow family to spill over into work, who are the preferred employees (despite their periodic absence for military service). Hence, whether employers ignore the reality of women's family responsibilities forcing them into less demanding or fulfilling work, or take the more paternalistic approach of allowing women concessions to care for family, as long as issues concerning the balance of work and family are constructed as issues for women rather than families, the consequences are the same; women remain in a secondary position in the workplace, as in the family.

Women's assumed prior responsibility for family also underpins other paternalistic organizational policies. In India, for instance, it is often thought inappropriate to transfer women employees away from their families or to expect them to travel on overnight assignments. Uma Sekaran (Chapter 3) suggests that this attitude is beginning to change, but that meanwhile it can be damaging to the careers of women who would choose to be involved in such activities. While some protective legislation is common to most countries, ongoing paternalistic policies such as those described in the chapters on India and Israel aim to protect women by enabling them to fulfil their family obligations, and consequently to protect men against family demands. Many women welcome such protection. Nevertheless, such policies, while protecting women against pressure and conflict, also reinforce their economic dependence on men, their protectors.

Equal opportunities legislation in its various forms has had only a limited impact on organizations to date because, as Alice Cook (Chapter 12) points out, it generally aims to give women equality with men in the workforce, under conditions established for men, without family responsibilities. The male model of work requires full-time, continuous work involvement, without concessions to family life. It is difficult for both parents of young children to conform to this ideal, although it is made feasible in some countries by the delegation of childcare to employees or female relatives, or by the provision of nurseries. Part-time work for one parent, invariably the mother, is regarded as a solution in some countries. Alice Cook (Chapter 12) describes how women in Eastern Europe regarded this option with envy before part-time work became available. However, while the ideal of the male model of work persists, part-time work for women is generally career limiting. Only in Sweden has the ideal of a shorter working day for both parents been articulated, but even there it is primarily women who take up this option.

In countries where professional advancement is based on competition, careers are expected to conform to a male pattern of uninterrupted work, which handicaps those who take breaks for childcare or other family involvement. Competition and individualism, however, are not valued uniformly cross-nationally. In India, seniority is a criterion for promotion, at least in the public sector. Similarly, the 'masculine' values of recognition, advancement and challenge are less important and 'feminine' values such as co-operation are more important to men in Sweden than elsewhere (see Sandqvist, Chapter 5). This reduces the pressure on employed women to remain on a career track, to 'compete' with men, and makes it possible to envisage alternative career patterns for men as well as women, although other factors may militate against this occurring.

Helen Hootsmans (Chapter 11) and Alice Cook (Chapter 12) argue that organizations need to take account of the needs of dual-earner families by rethinking the male model of work and organizations. Such change is necessary if equilibrium between family and work systems is to be maintained. This involves viewing alternative patterns of work and alternative career routes as acceptable for women and men at all levels of seniority. It involves a questioning of basic assumptions about gender and about the nature of work, especially the assumptions that women and not men have prior responsibility for family, and that 'good' workers do not allow family to impinge on work. The legitimization of family involvement for men as well as women may be more difficult to achieve in highly competitive organizational contexts and so the extent of organizational change required will be greater in these circumstances. Nevertheless, Alice Cook argues that the real test of whether organizations are adapting to their changing workforce is the extent to which they achieve thorough accommodation of work to family and also contribute towards gender equality in the home. As in any aspect of the management of change, managers will have to pay attention to environmental and cultural contingencies and constraints in working towards these goals.

Charting future developments
This chapter has discussed the importance of locating dual-earner families within their national socio-political context. The impact of wider social changes which transcend national boundaries is also considered by Alice Cook and Helen Hootsmans, who refer to changes taking place in Eastern and Western Europe as presenting challenges and opportunities for real changes in the nature of work, and the work/family relationship. Society is never static. Research is needed to chart the impact of changing social and organizational policies on dual-earner families, as well as the impact of dual-earners on social structures and policy. A systems approach is indicated to encompass the circular process of the interface between the family, the organization and wider social structures. In addition we must be aware of the limits of existing research methodology for charting change. Both Rosanna Hertz (Chapter 8) and Karin Sandqvist (Chapter 5) remind us that failure to detect changes in family structures and behaviours may be a function of inadequate measures of change. We must beware the pitfall of believing that what we cannot measure does not exist.

Outline of the book

The book is divided into three parts. Contributors to Part 1 explore the impact of national culture and socio-political context on dual-earner families within five countries differing in political ideology, family policies, religion and economic and social conditions. Dafna Izraeli (Chapter 2) discusses the ways in which social policy and cultural legacies in Israel shape women's options and reproduce gender inequalities in the family and the workplace. She demonstrates that the high value placed on women's family work, together with protective employment legislation, have simultaneously reduced the strain on employed women and diffused the tension which is a precondition of social change. In Chapter 3 Uma Sekaran explores the complexity and paradoxes of Indian society, where cultural traditions provide support for dual-career women and yet also constrain them from breaking away from ascribed gender roles. She confines her discussion to urban middle-class couples. Trends among dual-earner families in Singapore in the context both of government policy, which has, in the interest of economic growth, deliberately set out to shape the family and labour force, and of persisting cultural legacies are examined by Edith Yuen and Vivien Lim in Chapter 4. Karin Sandqvist in Chapter 5 discusses concepts of gender in Sweden, in the context of ideological commitment to equality and progressive social policies. She demonstrates that while gender distinctions in terms of values and personality tend to be blurred, they remain sharp in terms of tasks performed in the home and the workforce, and suggests that these gender similarities and differences are rooted in Swedish tradition and culture. This part of the book is completed by a chapter on Hungary in which Christine Clason briefly traces the vicissitudes of dual-earner families from pre-communist times to the present day. She describes an enforced experiment in social transformation imposed under the communist regime and argues that rather than resulting in changes in traditional values and norms, the experiment strengthened the attachment to old forms of behaviour. Women are now retreating to traditional family roles.

In Part 2 of the book, we explore specific issues arising within the family, as dual-earner couples attempt to reconcile evolving gender roles and identities with social expectations. The transition to parenthood is a particularly significant time in the dual-earner family life cycle, requiring substantial adjustment to changing roles. Julia Brannen and Peter Moss (Chapter 7) discuss this in the UK context. Drawing on a longitudinal study they explore the negotiation of gender roles within the household and the sources of support available to dual-earner mothers after maternity leave. According to Rosanna Hertz (Chapter 8), a crucial issue for helping us to understand the dynamics of dual-earner families, and especially the persistence of traditional patterns of family authority, is the way in which families deal with money. She draws on Anglo-American literature and her own research with American families to explore what is known and what needs to be known about household financial management in dual-earner families.

It is likely that it will take more than a single generation for gender roles to change within dual-earner families. It is therefore particularly important to look at gender identities, aspirations and self-concepts of adolescents brought up in dual-earner families, to chart developments and identify factors which contribute to change. In Chapter 9 Lucia Gilbert and Suzanne Dancer discuss the impact of family context and involvement of fathers and mothers in household work, on young women and female adolescents in the USA, where the dual-earner family now represents the modal form of family context.

The problems experienced by dual-earner women in Japan, with particular emphasis on the emerging issue of eldercare, are vividly illustrated in a case study in Chapter 10 by Jeanette Chabot. The issue of eldercare is also touched upon by other contributors, and poses a potentially explosive problem for dual-earners in the future.

In the final part of the book we explore some of the implications of issues faced by dual-earner couples, for the organization of paid work. Helen Hootsmans (Chapter 11) examines social policy and corporate practice in the context of preparations for a single European Market. In the penultimate chapter Alice Cook points out that, to date, all accommodation to the needs of the workplace has been done by families and especially women, with their double burden, and explores strategies by which employing organizations can now begin to adapt to the needs of families. We end with some thoughts about potential agendas for working towards balanced lives and gender equality in dual-earner families.

Note

I wish to thank Dafna Izraeli, Helen Hootsmans, Carolyn Kagan, Jeremy Lewis and Karin Sandqvist for their ideas, support and other contributions to this chapter.

References

Adler, Nancy J. and Izraeli, Dafna N. (eds) (1988) *Women in Management Worldwide*. New York: M.E. Sharpe.

Antal, A. and Izraeli, Dafna N. (1992) 'An international comparison of women in management: women managers in their homelands and as expatriates', in E. Fagenson (ed.), *Women in Management*. Women and Work, Vol. 4. Newbury Park, California: Sage.

Barling, Julian (1990) *Employment, Stress and Family Functioning*. Chichester: Wiley.

Coltrane, S. (1989) 'Household labor and the routine production of gender', *Social Problems*, 36: 473–90.

Epstein C. (1971) 'Law partners and marital partners', *Human Relations*, 24: 549–64.

Fagenson, E. (ed.) (1992) *Women in Management*. Women and Work, Vol. 4. Newbury Park, California: Sage.

Feree, Myra M. (1987) 'The struggles of superwoman', in C.Bose, R. Feldberg and N. Sokoloff (eds), *Hidden Aspects of Women's Work*. New York: Praeger.

Gilbert, Lucia, A. (1985) *Men in Dual Career Families*. Hillsdale, New Jersey: Lawrence Erlbaum.

Goldsmith, Elizabeth B. (1989) *Work and Family: Theory, Research and Applications*. Newbury Park, California: Sage.

Greenhaus, Jeffrey H. (1989) 'The intersection of work and family roles: individual, interpersonal and organizational issues', in E.B. Goldsmith (ed.), *Work and Family: Theory, Research and Applications*. Newbury Park, California: Sage.

Gutek, Barbara, A., Stromberg, Ann H. and Larwood, Laurie (1988) *Women and Work: An Annual Review*, Vol. 3. Newbury Park, California: Sage.

Hearn, Jeff and Parkin, Wendy (1988) 'Women, men and leadership: a critical review of assumptions, practices and change in industrialized nations', in Nancy J. Adler and Dafna N. Izraeli (eds), *Women in Management Worldwide*. New York: M.E. Sharpe.

Hertz, Rosanna (1986) *More Equal than Others: Women and Men in Dual-Career Marriages*. Berkeley: University of California Press.

Hiller, Dana V. and Dyehouse, Janice (1987) 'A case for banishing "dual-career marriages" from the research literature', *Journal of Marriage and the Family*, 49: 787–95.

Hofstede, Geert (1980) *Culture's Consequences: International Differences in Work-Related Values*. London: Sage.

Izraeli, Dafna (1989) 'Burning out in medicine: a comparison of husbands and wives in dual-career couples', in E.B. Goldsmith (ed.), *Work and the Family: Theory, Research and Applications*. Newbury Park, CA: Sage.

Jowell, R., Witherspoon, S. and Brook, L. (eds) (1988) *British Social Attitudes: The Fifth Report*. Aldershot: Gower.

Keith, P.M. and Schafer, R.B. (1980) 'Role strain and depression in two job families', *Family Relations*, 29: 483–8.

Lapidus, Gail W. (1988) 'The interaction of women's work and and family roles in the USSR', in Barbara A. Gutek, A. H. Stromberg and Laurie Larwood (eds), *Women and Work: An Annual Review*, Vol. 3. Newbury Park, California: Sage.

Lein, Laura (1979) 'Male participation in home life: impact of social support and breadwinner responsibility on the allocation of tasks', *Family Coordinator*, 26: 489–95.

Lewis, Suzan and Cooper, Cary L. (1988) 'Stress in dual-earner families', in Barbara A. Gutek, Ann H. Stromberg and Laurie Larwood (eds), *Women and Work: An Annual Review*, Vol. 3. Newbury Park, California: Sage.

Lewis, Suzan (1992) 'Work and the family in the UK', in S. Zedeck (ed.), *Work, Families and Organizations*. San Francisco: Jossey-Bass.

Paloma, M.M. and Garland, T.N. (1971) 'The myth of the egalitarian family: familiar roles and the professionally employed wife', in A. Theodore (ed.), *The Professional Woman*. Cambridge, Mass: Schenkman.

Pleck, Joseph H. (1977) 'The work–family role system', *Social Problems*, 24: 417–27.

Rapoport, Rhona and Ropoport, Robert N. (1969) 'The dual career family: a variant pattern and social change', *Human Relations*, 22: 3–30.

Rapoport, Rhona and Rapoport, Robert N. (1971) *Dual Career Families*. London: Penguin.

Sekaran, Uma (1986) *Dual Career Families*. San Francisco: Jossey-Bass.

Tayeb, Monir (1988) *Organizations and National Cultures*. London: Sage.

Thomas, Veronica G. (1990) 'Problems of dual-career black couples: identification and implications for family interventions', *Journal of Multicultural Counselling and Development*, 18: 58–67.

Zedeck, Sheldon (ed.) (1992) *Work, Families and Organizations*. San Francisco: Jossey-Bass.

2
Culture, Policy, and Women in Dual-Earner Families in Israel

Dafna N. Izraeli

Women's strategies are always played out in the context of identifiable patriarchal bargains that act as implicit scripts that define, limit and inflect their market and domestic options. (Kandiyoti, 1988: 285)

Israeli society is of particular interest for the study of dual-earner couples because it is simultaneously an industrialized, urbanized society and a traditional one in terms of the structure of family life (Peres and Katz, 1981). It is a welfare state whose institutions were forged by a generation of pioneers committed to egalitarian, socialist ideals as well as a country in which the majority of citizens, particularly immigrants from Islamic countries and the Orthodox of all religions, adhere to ethnic/religious traditions in which the subordination of women is an integral component.

This chapter examines the factors that shape the ways in which dual-earner couples allocate time and effort to the domains of work and family in Israel. Since, to date, the most important cultural changes have occurred in women's roles, they are the major but not the sole focus. More specifically, this chapter maps out the institutional links between the family and work domains and demonstrates how, in both, social policy and cultural legacies shape women's options and reproduce gender inequalities. Another question explored in this chapter is why, despite the significant increase in women's education and labor force participation, gender inequalities have not resulted in widespread role strain, an important precondition for the development of a feminist movement (Klein, 1984).

The collectivistic legacy of the *yishuv* (pre-state Jewish community in Palestine), despite its commitment to socialist ideology, was not conducive to an open struggle for gender equality. The pioneering generation of pre-State Israel had a strong communitarian orientation that put prime value on personal commitment and involvement. The boundary between the public and private domains was blurred and in many respects private life was 'publicized' as individual purpose was harnessed to the welfare and the interests of the collective. An extreme example of this trend occurred in the kibbutz, where in the early years the privacy of family life was discouraged, and couples shared living quarters with additional kibbutz members. When the first children were born, childcare became a community issue. Women, however, remained responsible for doing the work. First-wave feminist organizations which emerged in response to women's exclusion from the main activities of state building in the first decade of this century, sought greater participation and partnership. They avoided an adversarial posture and spoke the language of equality of obligations rather than of entitlements and of individual rights (Bernstein, 1987; Izraeli, 1981). The legacy of this approach persists into the 1990s.

The theoretical premise of this chapter is that cultural legacies, public policy, and institutional arrangements influence women's options in the labor market and the family domain. The obligations and expectations surrounding domestic roles influence work roles. Women's opportunities in the workplace in turn affect how they play their family roles. Public policies shape women's opportunity structures and consequently their incentives to negotiate new definitions of their roles both at home and at work.

The major arguments in this chapter are, first, that Israeli society makes extensive demands on the family throughout the life cycle, assigning to women prime responsibility for meeting them. Secondly, public policies have enabled, even encouraged, women to combine family and work, but not to build careers. Inadvertently these policies contributed to the perpetuation of gender inequality in both domains. Thirdly, limited and unequal opportunities in the labor market and the high cost of pursuing the fast career track made the family option more attractive to women but also constrained them from successfully negotiating a more egalitarian division of labor within it. These are among the main factors that explain why Israeli women rarely earn high salaries or achieve positions of power. Fourthly, both the symbolic value attributed to motherhood and family life and the economic and legal protections public policy provides for women in family roles, mitigated the potential role strain resulting from gender inequalities in the labor market and even legitimized those inequalities.

The first section presents an overview of the spread of the dual-earner family resulting from the growth in married women's participation in the labor market. Section two focuses on the ways in which the cultural context constructs and amplifies women's family work. Section three analyzes public policies as both reflecting and constructing a particular vision of gender relations over the life cycle. Section four outlines women's employment strategies as primarily a response to the cultural and policy context. The final section attempts an overall evaluation of the family–work interface in Israeli society pointing to forces for continuity and change.

The spread of the dual-earner family in Israel

Between 1966 and 1989, the proportion of dual-earner families among married couples in Israel increased from 26 percent to 47 percent. Among couples in which wives were 25–54 years old, it rose from 27 to 55 percent. In 1989, married women constituted 69 percent of the total female labor force.[1] Participation rates vary with the number and age of children in the household (Kirschenbaum, 1988). However, having one or two children is hardly a deterrent to a mother's employment, especially among the more educated. Over 64 percent of all Jewish mothers with youngest child aged 2–4 are in the labor force (compared to 24 percent in 1968) and for such mothers with 13 and more years of education, the rate is 79 percent.

Labor force participation rates among married women also vary with ethnic/religious background and type of domicile. The greatest differences are between Jewish women from the predominantly Moslem countries of the Middle East and North Africa (locally known as Easterners) and those from the predominantly Christian countries of Europe and North America (Westerners); between Jewish women and non-Jewish (predominantly Arab) women; and between kibbutz and non-kibbutz (predominantly urban) women.

The Eastern–Western distinction is today more one of social class than of cultural origin (Hartman, 1980). The lower labor force participation rate among Eastern women (who constitute more than 50 percent of the Jewish population) is largely explainable by their lower educational achievement and occupational distribution. Eastern women, both foreign and Israeli born, are concentrated in personal service and clerical jobs needing less education and providing fewer opportunities for improved status and earnings (Bernstein, 1982). However, while the occupational status of Western women is on average significantly higher than that of Eastern women (Kraus, 1989), there is no difference in their average earnings (Semyonov and Kraus, 1983). The reasons are the lower earnings of all female-dominated occupations combined with minimum wage regulations and tax rebates for working mothers, which raise the income floor and reduce wage differentials among women.

The differences between Jewish women and Arab women, who constitute 17 percent of the population (Moslems 13.1 percent, Christians 2.3 percent and Druse and others 1.6 percent) are more substantial (Haberfeld and Izraeli, forthcoming). In 1988, only

15 percent of all non-Jewish women and 6 percent of all non-Jewish married women were in the labor force, compared to 45 percent and 49.9 respectively of Jewish women. The reasons for the low labor force participation of Arab women are traditional attitudes towards women's working outside the home, the lower level of education among Arab women and the higher birthrate (not among Christians). In addition, the Arab population is geographically segregated with limited employment opportunities for women in local markets (Semyonov and Tyree, 1981) and sanctions against women commuting to other markets. There are considerable differences, however, among the three major religious groups on all the indicators mentioned.

Among the kibbutz population, in contrast, 87 percent of the women were in the labor force, and among women aged 25–64, the proportion was over 97 percent. Since family income in the kibbutz is not linked to job or work hours and services are for the most part collectivized, the phenomenon of the dual-worker couple in the kibbutz is very different from that in the city or town (for a relevant review see Agassi, 1989; Palgi et al., 1983).

Eastern–Western distinctions will be made in the text where they are relevant. Dual-earner families among Arab and kibbutz populations will not be dealt with specifically in this chapter. Unless otherwise specified, all the data presented in this chapter refer to the total population of Israel, but the discussion below centers on Jewish families.

The cultural and institutional context of work and family roles

The communitarian ethos
Motherhood in Israel is more than a family role. It is a national role as well. Jewish women are expected to bear children not only to have a family of their own, but to increase the population, provide the future soldiers, reproduce the nation.

The legitimacy of any individual building a work career for him/herself is relatively recent. Prior to Statehood (1948) and even into the 1960s, when socialist ideology and collectivistic values were dominant in daily life, career (as different from 'calling') was a pejorative term. Building oneself a career or being a 'careerist' was synonymous with being selfish and exploitative, surpassed only by a *careeristit* (Hebrew female form). Men often had careers but did not admit to them. Few women had them, although a very large proportion contributed to the family income through their labor outside, inside or around the home. In other words, the individualistic ethos that fueled second-wave feminism in the United States resonated weakly with the collectivist norms prevalent in Israeli culture.

The centrality of the army as a training and elite recruitment institution and of army experience as the cultural clay from which heroes are molded reproduces women's secondary role in Israeli society. While compulsory military training is required of both (three years for men and two for women), only men fill combat roles, and with rare exceptions, only men fill the ranks of the most senior officers, do reserve duty (currently up to 45 days a year until the age of 49), and are mobilized in times of war. The fact that women are recruited to compulsory service enhances their sense of participation and involvement. Their limited participation, however, legitimizes their subordinate position within the military and by implication within society as a whole.

In Israeli ideology, men and women contribute to the security of the nation in different ways. Men do so in reserve duty over the adult life-time. Women's most significant roles in the service of the collective remain their contributions to family life. These contributions, however, are not similarly demanding. While the requirements of reserve duty are generally specific in terms of time, place, and tasks, those of women's family roles are not. They are also not symmetrically supported by the state. The law requires an employer to release a worker for military reserve duty for several weeks each year. It does not require an employer to respond similarly to the demands of family obligations, except for maternity leave – taken on average, three times over the life course. The state reimburses soldiers in full for lost income during reserve duty; women receive only 70 percent of their lost income during the 12 weeks' compulsory maternity leave. Exemplary service in the military makes the individual more attractive to employers, but exemplary motherhood does not. All the heroes in Israel are men. Women are the mothers and wives of heroes.

The centrality of family life

Israel is a family-centered society (Bar-Yosef et al., 1977; Peres and Katz, 1981, 1990). In 1988, over 95 percent of the women over 40 were married; the average number of children per family was 2.8; the divorce rate was only 16 percent (up from 9 percent in 1975), and only 1.3 percent of the births were by never married women. The choice between 'having children or having a career' is foreign to the Israeli cultural repertoire, where the assumption is that a woman will combine family and work, in that order of importance. Most people live in a family setting and relatively few live alone. Only 5 percent of the families are single-parent families. The Friday evening Sabbath meal as well as national holidays are usually celebrated within the family setting.

The great value placed on family life in general, and on having children in particular, has been attributed to the combined influence of a number of factors, including the Jewish religion; the traditional culture of immigrants from Moslem countries (Easterners); the desire of refugees of World War II to reconstruct the families lost in the war; the fear of losing a child (son) in battle or military skirmishes; the identification with collective goals associated with population growth such as 'national security' – defined in terms of a potentially large army – and the need to offset the growing Arab population. The anxiety aroused by continuous military unrest in Israel intensifies the need for security and support provided by intimate relationships and strengthens family ties (Bar-Yosef and Bachar, 1972; Peres and Katz, 1990).

Israelis value family roles for both men and women, but for women, being a mother is more highly valued than being employed. A 1983 survey examined perceptions among a representative sample of the adult Jewish population (excluding kibbutz) of the ideal woman. Eighty-two percent of both men and women listed 'having a home and well-cared-for children,' compared to 51 percent of the women and 39 percent of the men who listed 'being employed,' and 75 percent of both who listed a 'well groomed appearance' (Zemach and Peled, 1983: 61–2). When asked the same question about the ideal man, 67 percent of the women and 73 percent of the men listed 'having a home and well-cared-for children,' compared to 85 percent and 83 percent respectively who listed 'being employed.'

The division of labor in the family
Although the family is valued by both men and women, primary responsibility for caring for the family, in Israel, as elsewhere, is assigned to the woman. Whether women work outside the home or not, the amount of time husbands spend in housework and childcare does not differ significantly (Peres and Katz, 1984). Employed women, however, spend less time in these activities than full-time homemakers. Studies of women professionals found that the great majority have a traditional division of labor in the home, and that there is no relation between the amount of moral support women report receiving from their husbands and the division of labor (Mannheim and Schiffrin, 1984). In the author's study of Israeli managers, the women spent twice the time spent by men in family work. While psychologically the women were not less involved in their professional work than their male counterparts, on average they spent 15 percent less time in professional work. The correlation between work involvement and

actual hours spent in paid work was twice as strong for men as it was for women. In other words, while women were not less committed to their work, they were less likely to express that commitment by working longer hours on the job.

The large established women's organizations sponsor a neo-traditional version of the division of household labor, very much in keeping with the dominant ethos. It advocates increasing husbands' level of activity in household chores, but does not encompass a vision of partnership in its management. Representative of this approach is the slogan 'Be a Man, Give Her a Hand,' selected by Naamat, Israel's largest and most powerful women's organization, as the major theme for its 1985 'status of women month'. Through this attempt to redefine and emphasize 'manliness,' the husband is urged to take a greater share in family work but not in the responsibility. The message advocates enlightened paternalism rather than equality.

The Israeli rendition of the 'motherhood cult' does not require mothers to be sole child-carers. Family members and reliable nannies are legitimate substitutes for at least part of the day. Sending a two-year-old to a morning kindergarten is considered not only acceptable but even desirable for the development of the child's sociability and independence. The working woman who uses a full-day childcare facility (normally from 8 a.m. to 4 p.m.) is not subject to criticism, although this is not deemed to be an ideal arrangement. Approximately 50,000 children aged 6 months to 3 years (about 20 percent of the population) are in government-subsidized and controlled daycare centers, while the additional number in privately run centers is unknown.[2] The Financial Relations between Husband and Wife Law (1973) that provides that assets accumulated by a couple during the course of their marriage are the joint property of husband and wife, regardless of whether the wife was ever employed, symbolizes recognition of the economic contribution of the wife's housekeeping role.

Expanded family roles

The family's role as a consumer of goods and services and as carer for both the nation's soldiers and the elderly has expanded the demand for women's family work. The introduction of electrical home appliances, the commercialization of goods and services, as well as the decline in the birthrate (especially among Easterners) have eased women's burden. The family, however, has been assigned additional roles and some traditional ones have been expanded by circumstance, taxing its time and energy resources, especially those of women.

The family as consumer of goods and services   The number of tasks performed for the family outside the home, or those that link the family to services outside the home, have grown in recent years. They include a variety of time-consuming activities which in Israel are encapsulated in the term *sidurim* (literally, arrangements). Combined they constitute the boundary-spanning role that links the family to society and reflects as well as influences its standard of living.

When *sidurim* can be done outside 'normal' working hours, husbands are more likely to participate. Since the mid-1980s there has been a definite trend toward longer shopping hours, especially in the new urban shopping centers. In the major cities night shopping is possible in a number of supermarkets, and in Tel Aviv there are supermarkets open around the clock. Such structural changes permit greater flexibility in the division of household labor. For example, in a review of Israeli research on alternative work schedules, Bar-Haim and Shavit (1987) report that where employees work a five-day week (six was the norm until 1989), Friday is used primarily for shopping and family work and husbands participate in it. Husbands, however, are more likely than their wives to use the extra day for leisure activities.

The family as support for the nation's soldiers – the woman's crowded nest Compulsory military service involves an elaboration of the parenting role. In most countries with a nuclear family structure, when offspring leave home, usually after high school, the women's parental role is significantly reduced – a situation known as 'the empty nest.' In Israel, when a son or daughter is drafted (at 18), and even before then in the preparatory stage, parents are deeply involved both instrumentally and emotionally. Army policy views parents as partners in the production of the nation's soldiers and capitalizes on their involvement. It officially solicits the support of parents and encourages their participation in a series of *rites de passage* associated with their son's or daughter's army career. 'Parent of a soldier' is a cultural role that entails expectations of intensive emotional support as well as the provision of a variety of personal/domestic services (Bar-Yosef and Padan-Eisenstark, 1977).

While both parents share in the pride and worry, it is the mother who is usually the prime caretaker. Most soldiers come home every second weekend. The soldier's return home for the Sabbath is a cause considered worthy of the mother's increased investment in culinary and other pampering activities, expressions of her love and affection, and perhaps also a release for her guilt and anxiety. These are also expressed in packages containing home-made delicacies which are sent to the army base or brought along with the parents' regular Saturday visits, encouraged by the army. Soldiers frequently prefer to have their army clothes washed and ironed at home rather than take a chance on exchanging the dirty ones for a clean but less well-fitting set. A son's military service appears to elicit more mothering activities than does a daughter's service. If he is in a fighting unit, often the family's total life schedule during his three years of service is built around his military career.

This emotional and instrumental involvement of parents in their children's army life has become significantly more intensive in the last decade or so. One explanation for this development is the sense of guilt the contemporary generation of parents feels for not having been able to create a more peaceful society for their children. Another is that, in contrast to the previous generation who as immigrants had for the most part not served in the army, contemporary parents are more familiar with the hardships and dangers.

Although women now share the breadwinner role with their husbands, they do not directly share the military burden. After completing compulsory military service, as noted above, men, but not women, are called for reserve duty. Women internalize the message that whereas men guard the nation through military service, women watch over the nation's soldiers through their family work. In-depth interviews with women reveal women's double bind: they feel guilty that they have to send their men, especially sons, to the army and at the same time are proud of them when they volunteer for high-risk, high-prestige fighting units (Kriegel and Waintrater, 1985). Women expressed feelings of dependence on men for protection, of gratitude for their sacrifice, feelings of guilt that they do not share in the burden and also of relief that they are not required to do so. Such feelings probably contribute to the belief that the family division of labor is equitable and constrain a woman from negotiating a reallocation of domestic tasks among the members of her household as well as leading to increased domestic activity when a member of the family is in active military service. When her husband is on reserve duty, the wife usually carries the family load by herself. The normal balance of give-and-take is temporarily put out of kilter as the wife's instrumental and emotional work is intensified (Bar-Yosef and Padan-Eisenstark, 1977).

Children's release from the army does not necessarily empty the mother's nest. When the military service is over and the children marry, women more often than men are drafted into active grandparenting to help out, while the younger generation establishes its own work careers. For the younger generation of women who often combine higher education with having children and sometimes also employment, active grandparenting is invaluable for them to juggle their multiple roles.

The family as support for the elderly   The Israeli population is aging. In 1989, 9 percent of the population was over 65 years of age, compared to under 7 percent in 1969. Although only a small proportion of parents live with their married children, health policy regarding the care for the elderly and chronically ill inadvertently increases women's family burden. The available services are inadequate. In the attempt to provide more humanitarian care but also to reduce hospital budgets, government policy is to transfer, where possible, the care for the chronically ill and aged from the hospital to the home. A growing number of working women whose careers may still be on the upswing find themselves needing to respond to intensified demands for their time from aging parents. (See also Chabot, this volume.) The fact that Israel is geographically small and the population concentrated in three cities means that almost all parents live fairly close to at least one of their children, which makes them more accessible but also intensifies expectations of frequent visits. Caring for elderly and chronically ill parents is usually the daughter or daughter-in-law's responsibility, although among Easterners, sons play a more active care-giving role than among Westerners.

The legitimacy of the spillover of family into the workplace   Cultural norms compel employers to accept the legitimacy of the family's primacy in women's lives. The expectation of woman's responsibility for and commitment to her family, is embedded in the work culture. As will be shown, it is an institutionalized aspect of labor relations. Her identity as mother penetrates the workplace, and she may use it as a basis for making claims for time off and for other considerations. Employers may be displeased that a female worker has left early to care for a sick child and even decide not to promote her for doing so, but they are expected to understand that that was what she had to do.

The spillover of the motherhood role into the workplace, however, is a double-edged sword. On the one hand, it creates a more supportive environment and eases the psychological burden for women who have to manage work and family. On the other hand, it results in most women running on the unofficial 'mommy track'. As one headhunter for senior managerial talent recently explained to the Israeli Senior Women Managers' Forum:[3] 'Men are preferred for top positions. The potential employer presumes that if a woman has small children, she'll leave to take care of them. If she is single she is bitter and morose. If she is a divorcee or a widow, she's burdened with personal problems.' The burden is on her to prove not only her competence but also that although a mother, she is no less reliable and hard-working than her male counterpart. In this respect, the fact that only men are called for military reserve duty and may be absent from work for up to 45 days a year until the age of 49, works in women's favor.

Public policy and the dual-earner family

Israel is a welfare state and as such the assumption of female social and economic dependency and need for protection is central to its ideology. This ideology fueled social policy. The mass immigration following Statehood of Jews from Moslem countries (Easterners) where families have a patriarchal structure, and most women were functionally illiterate and did not work outside the home, heightened policy-makers' sensitivity to women's vulnerability and need for protection. Protective legislation characterizes what Raday (1991) calls the 'first phase' (1954–64) of legislation affecting women, when the Knesset adopted 'all the protections for women workers recommended by the International Labor Organization during those years.' Public policy supported women's presence in the labor force as permanent workers and referred to them primarily as 'working mothers' (*imahot ovdot*), emphasizing the priority for women of the family over the work roles.

Social policy reflects the national concern for the integrity and welfare of the family but, until very recently, it also sponsored a traditional view of the family according to which women are the primary caretakers of home and children. Employment policy in relation to women, however, has been primarily pragmatic, geared to serving national interests. For example, during the 1950s and early 1960s, when a policy priority was to keep immigrant families from leaving the development towns in favor of urban centers, considerable investment was made to create jobs for men. The argument was that for these immigrants, where the man is considered head of the household, it was essential to preserve his status as its major breadwinner. Only secondary attention was given to jobs for women even if such jobs increased the family standard of living. Yet the absorbing society looked favorably on the entry of such immigrant women into the labor force and regarded it 'as a first sign of successful adaptation to Israeli society' (Honig and Shamai, 1978: 405).

For women entering the labor force, social policies were introduced to protect them in both the biological and social dimensions of their lives.

The biological dimension

The Women's Employment Law (1954) forbids the employment of a woman overtime or in night work from the fifth month of her pregnancy. It grants her the right to be absent from work for up to 40 hours if employed full time and 20 hours if half time for health reasons related to her pregnancy, at the employer's expense. She may take extensive health leave covered by her sick leave rights and national health insurance. An employer may not fire a pregnant women without authorization by the Minister of Work and Welfare, provided she has been employed for six months prior to pregnancy, even if he or she was unaware that she was pregnant when s/he hired her. While the mother is breast-feeding, she is entitled to be absent for up to an hour a day at the employer's expense, provided she is employed for at least six hours a day.

The Women's Employment Law (1954) provides 12 weeks' maternity leave (possibly 14 in the case of twins) during which a woman receives 75 percent of her salary (excluding certain fringe benefits) paid by the National Insurance Institute. During this period, it is a criminal offence to make a woman work or fire her. While maternity leave was clearly designed to permit recovery from birth, the fact that a mother of a stillborn baby may reduce the period to three weeks suggests that the intention was also to assure the mother (but not the father) the right to care for her infant during the early weeks. When the laws were initially passed, the benefits were comparatively generous, but they now compare unfavourably with those in many European countries (Antal and Izraeli, 1992).

The family/work dimension

Laws forbidding women's night work and requiring them to retire at 60 (compared to 65 for men) combined a concern both for women's physical well-being and for their family roles. The Prime Minister's Commission on the Status of Women (1978), however, recognized that protective legislation, once considered an important achievement for women, now appeared to be depriving women of economic opportunities and served as a disincentive for employers to hire women for more lucrative jobs. It took almost a decade of lobbying by women's organizations and the Prime Minister's advisor on the status of women to get the Knesset to shift to a more reserved protectionist stance. In 1986 the Knesset amended the Women's Employment Law (1954) and removed prohibitions on employers to hire women for night work (a prohibition more honored in the exception) but preserved women's right to refuse to work at night for family reasons. In 1987 it passed the Equal Pension Age Law equalizing pension age for men and women at 65 while preserving women's right to earlier retirement where the collective labor agreement provides for it. The nature of these changes highlights the pragmatic, rather than principled, ethos of Israeli policy toward women. The women who sponsored these modified protectionist policies argued that since women's opportunities were still not equal, individual women were entitled to retain the privilege of choosing whether to be protected or not.

Collective labor agreements in the public and labor-owned (Histadrut – Israel Federation of Labor) sectors, where the majority of the female labor force is employed, include special benefits for working mothers. Mothers with one child under 8 years or two children under 12 for women in state employment (under 14 in Histadrut employment) were permitted to work one hour less a day, at employers' expense. This option is not available to fathers. In the 1989 collective agreement that covered the conditions for the change from a six-day 45-hour work week to a five-day 42½ hour work week, the time allowance for mothers was reduced from an hour to 25 minutes a day. The women's lobby protested and argued that while the new arrangement shortened the work week, it lengthened the work-day from eight to eight and a half hours, making the one-hour mothers' allowance even more essential, especially since the childcare services had not yet made parallel changes in their schedules. The Treasury counter-argued that it was not equitable to give the mother accumulated advantages of a shorter week along with all workers *as well as* an additional hour a day. This position was undoubtedly influenced by the mounting rate of unemployment in the 1980s, which provided an incentive to discourage the trend of women's increasing labor force participation. As a compromise interim measure, mothers of young children were granted the hour allowance (instead of only 25 minutes) in return for a 6 percent salary cut. In addition, each employee was entitled to negotiate flexible working hours with her/his superior.

In 1988, the Equal Opportunity in Employment Law, which expanded the terms of reference of an earlier 1981 version of the law, made discrimination on the basis of a person's sex, marital status, and parental status a criminal offence. (It also defined sexual harassment as discrimination.) The anti-discrimination clauses covered recruitment to work, conditions of employment, promotion, training, and severance. Rights previously granted to mothers only were now granted to either parent. These include the right of up to 12 months' unpaid leave after the 12-week mandatory maternity leave (granted also in the case of an adopted child), the right to resign with severance pay for the purpose of caring for a new baby (also for adopted children) and where granted by collective agreement, the right to use sick leave to care for a child. No change was made regarding either the three-month mandatory maternity leave or the shortened work-day provided by collective labor agreements, the latter purportedly because of the technical difficulty of preventing both parents from simultaneously exploiting the privilege.

Fiscal policies

Income tax policy as formulated after the 1975 tax reform was intended to encourage married women to enter the labor force. For example, the husband and wife's income are assessed separately and not combined for income tax purposes. The wife's employment, therefore, does not push the couple into a higher income tax bracket. There are exceptions, such as when couples work together in a family business, or a professional partnership where the husband's and wife's combined income is treated as a single salary for tax calculation. This law discourages couples from entering into partnership, although in some cases, there are ways to circumvent the tax problem. Doing so, however, requires a special effort.

While intended to encourage married women to enter the labor force, the tax reform did not provide potentially high-income women with an incentive to make the large investments in alternative childcare and domestic services required for advancing to high-status positions. Income tax policy, until 1990, provided the working mother with one tax credit point for each child (in addition to child allowances) and an additional automatic quarter tax credit point for travel. Each credit point raises the minimum amount at which she begins to pay tax. Consequently, because of the wife's tax discounts, the after-tax net income is greater for a dual-earner family than for a single-earner family with the same gross income. The credit point system was intended to offset family expenses incurred in a mother's going to work. The amount of the credit point, however, is modest and not directly related to the actual expenses incurred. Women whose gross earnings are just above the minimum taxable income benefit most from the system, and pay no taxes at all. In 1990, however, the tax credits for the second and fourth child were eliminated. Characteristic of the pragmatic (rather than programmatic) approach of the government to women's employment and indicative of the failure of the women's organizations to mobilize around the issue, this cut was a response to the Treasury's need to reduce budget expenses.

Childcare and school schedules

Government's pragmatic approach to women's employment is also reflected in its policies related to childcare and the length of the school-day. In the 1970s, to encourage young mothers to enter the labor force, the Ministry of Work and Welfare expanded day-care facilities for preschoolers. It took over responsibility for the infrastructure of childcare services from the voluntary women's organizations that administer and supervise the service and accelerated construction of new centers. The move was prompted by the need to increase the labor force, especially of industrial workers. The expansion of the military forces after the Six Days War (1967), the development of defense and other industries and the growth in community services, especially health and education, created labor shortages. The previous policy of filling available places in government-subsidized childcare services almost exclusively with children of welfare families was redefined, and priority was shifted to the children of working mothers, especially full-time industrial workers. Payment for services was graduated according to mother's income only, on the assumption that the family's decision regarding women's work was based on calculations of the cost of alternative services relative to wife's potential earnings. If the services cost more than the amount a woman would earn, she would be unlikely to go to work. The payment policy was intended to provide an incentive for the family to contribute the woman's labor to the state. Priority was given to full-time workers in economic branches experiencing a shortage of female labor. Currently, childcare services operate 9–10 hours a day and accept children from the age of 6 months to about three years, after which 3- and 4-year-olds may attend kindergarten that is compulsory for 5-year-olds, provided space permits.

The 1980s ushered in a period of relative economic stagnation and rising unemployment. There was no incentive to encourage more women to enter the labor force. Consequently, construction budgets for childcare services were cut sharply. In 1985, payment for day-care was linked to the per capita family income, thus removing the special incentive for women, but at the same time emphasizing the fathers' as well as the mothers' responsibilities for child support. It also benefits working mothers employed in weak sectors of the economy. While those with few children and higher incomes pay the full cost of the service, full-time working mothers with low incomes and many children are heavily subsidized.

The special character of public policy that curtails women's ability to pursue careers is best reflected in the scheduling of the schoolday. While there are extensive, although not sufficient, day-long (8–4) services for the 6-month baby to the almost 3-year-old, children from 3 to 7 or 8 attend school for only four hours a day. Those from 8 to 11 years attend for five hours. Those in high school have schedules that vary daily in length but average six hours a day. When a woman has a 4–5-year-old who returns home at noon, there is little advantage in placing her infant in a day-long service.

During the 1980s, plans for expanding the 'extended school-day' programs devised in the mid-1970s to assist working mothers were shelved. Where they had been implemented, they were in most cases discontinued. Under the heavy hand of budget cuts in educational and other public social services, teacher hours were cut and 'non-essential' school hours eliminated. Lunchtime programs were closed for lack of money. Family eating patterns, with the main meal taken at midday, intensify the pressure on women to be home at midday. Where there are children of different ages, the midday meal may well be served in succession with the arrival home of each in turn. (In addition, in 1989, the average worker had approximately 86 non-working days a year, and the average pupil 150 non-school-days a year.)

In March 1990, the Knesset passed 'The Long School Day Law,' which lengthened the school-day to eight hours. The long school-day was to be implemented initially in the development towns (where the great majority of population are Easterners) with the intention to extend it eventually to the rest of the country, but no time commitment has been specified.

The long school-day has been on the political platform of women's organizations for decades. The government does not object in principle – to the contrary – but claims it cannot afford to implement such a program. The situation at present, however, is in keeping with its implicit policy regarding working mothers, which is to encourage or discourage them from seeking employment as the state needs more or fewer workers.

Women's employment strategies

Women's labor market strategies reflect their options. A dominant – and perhaps *the* dominant – career consideration is the possibility a job offers for combining family and work. A local witticism queries: what are the two best things about a teaching job? The answer is – July and August. Studies of work values among the adult population (Elizur, n.d.; Gafni, 1981; Shapira and Etzioni-Halevy, 1973) consistently find that women specify 'working hours' or 'working close to home' as a more important job characteristic than do men. In the author's studies of physician couples and men and women managers, overall satisfaction with one's job was associated with satisfaction with the ability the jobs afford for integrating family and work life for women, but not for men. Under pressure to juggle family and work roles, women gravitate to part-time jobs and to jobs that are synchronized with the children's school schedules, such as teaching, or that have flexible working hours, such as nursing.

Part-time jobs
The part-time job is the single most popular solution for working mothers. Forty-five percent of employed married women (compared to 14 percent among men) hold part-time jobs – defined as less than 35 hours a week (Central Bureau of Statistics, 1989).[4] The most common

reason given for working part time for women is family responsibilities; for men it is their being on pension. The more children a woman has, the more likely she is to work part time or not at all (Kirschenbaum, 1988). The growth in the proportion of educated married women in the labor force during the past two decades increased the proportion of women in part-time employment, since educated women are more likely than others to work part time. The proportion of part-time workers among women employed in the professions and semi-professions is greater than those employed in clerical or industrial jobs.

The increase in part-time work among married women in the labor force is partly due to the greater availability of part-time jobs (Central Bureau of Statistics, 1986: 94). Comparing age cohorts, we find that the proportion of women employed in full-time jobs at each stage in the life cycle was significantly greater a decade ago than it is today. Public policy supports the part-time option. Unlike other countries, in Israel women are not penalized, at least in the short run, for taking part-time jobs. Part-time work (minimum 4 hours a day) entitles the worker to a proportionate share of almost all the rights and benefits paid to a full-time worker, including security of tenure, national insurance, and various fringe benefits.

For the mother with school-age children, selecting a part-time job is often economically expedient. She is spared the high cost of additional childcare services to bridge the time gap between the end of the school-day and that of her own job. Her gross earnings are likely to fall below taxable income. Approximately 58 percent of married employed women with children do not pay income tax (Gabai, 1990).

Female niche
A second strategy is to select occupational niches with shorter and clearly defined work hours. For example, convenient and congenial working hours are among the major attractions of the civil service, where in 1989 over 60 percent of those employed were women. For similar reasons female professionals are far more likely to be employed in the public than in the private sectors of the economy. In 1987 women constituted 71 percent of the pharmacists and 57 percent of the lawyers employed in the civil service (Civil Service, 1987: 177) compared to approximately 55 percent, and 25 percent respectively, in the labor force as a whole.

Delayed entry and the late upbeat
Two other coping strategies are to delay entry into the labor force or to keep work investment 'simmering on a low fire' while the children are small and to increase time investment in the workplace when they grow older.

Table 2.1 *Life cycle changes by marital status and rate of employment activity (percentages)*

Employment status	Survey year of cohort							
	1967		1972		1977		1982	
	Married	Single	Married	Single	Married	Single	Married	Single
Full-time	23.1	25.0	24.5	70.7	23.2	62.3	29.4	50.5
Part-time	13.4	12.5	17.9	14.2	27.7	22.3	26.5	24.1
Previous	3.1	10.8	1.1	0.6	2.1	0.2	0.3	5.8
Not in labour force	55.9	48.9	50.0	12.4	38.9	10.9	31.9	3.2
Total	33.5	66.5	77.7	22.3	85.4	14.6	87.8	12.2

Source: Kirschenbaum (1988)

Table 2.1 presents data on labor force participation over a 15-year period (1967–1982) for one cohort of women who were 18–24 in 1967. They indicate that consistently over the life cycle the proportion of married women not in the labour force decreases while the proportion of women in part-time employment increases until the cohort reaches the 33–39 age bracket. At that stage, the proportion of married women working full time increases from over 23 percent to over 29 percent. Thus, while there is an increase in the proportion of women taking full-time employment after the children enter school, the 'slow-burn late-up-beat' is a less prevalent strategy than is 'delayed entry' into the labor force.

Opportunities forgone
Caught in the 'greedy institution' of the family (Coser and Coser, 1974), women have tended to juggle family and work by forgoing job opportunities or avoiding demanding occupational roles, especially those with inflexible job structures. In my own study of 860 Israeli managers, I found that 48 percent of the women and 35 percent of the men indicated that they had on some occasion refused an opportunity for promotion or had held back their career advancement. The reasons for doing so, however, differed by sex: 77 percent of the women and 21 percent of the men gave 'fear of causing harm to children' as a reason, while 'lack of interest in the job' was a reason given by 47 percent of the men and 19 percent of the women. It should be noted that for a variety of reasons, including the small size of the country, relocation is generally not an issue. One exception is in the army, where certain careers require frequent relocations often from one end of the country to the other, and even going abroad.

The small proportion of women among managers (14.7 percent in 1988) is in part explainable by the fact that management has none of the characteristics which facilitate a woman juggling her multiple roles (Izraeli, 1988). It is resistant to part-time work – only 24 percent of women managers work part time. While managers generally have more discretion to determine their work schedules than do lower-level participants, their workload is also less predictable and more likely to expand beyond official work hours. In addition to its functional value, working overtime has important symbolic value as an expression of one's commitment to the organization. In this sense the managerial role intrudes more sharply into the domestic time sphere than do other occupational roles. Only 50 percent of ever-married female administrators and managers have children at home under age 14, compared to 67 percent of academic and professional workers and 74 percent of other professional and technical workers. (Managers on average are also older than those employed in other occupations.)

Women pay a price for their 'preference' for working close to home. Semyonov and Lewin-Epstein (1991) found that 48 percent of the income gap between commuters and non-commuters among women is due to the advantageous market conditions associated with commuting, and that the relative loss to non-commuting women is greater than that to non-commuting men.

Opportunity loss is usually less immediately obvious since it is the long-term consequences of women's career strategies that seriously damage their competitive positions. For example, women constitute only 15 percent of the tenured faculty in Israeli universities. All universities grant tenure-track personnel a sabbatical in the seventh year with full pay and incentives to spend the year outside the country. A study of the decision to go on sabbatical leave in academia among dual-career couples (Doenias, 1988) found that men gave more weight to factors related to their own careers than to the careers of their wives. Women, in contrast, gave greater weight to considerations related to their spouse's career and were more influenced than the men by how they perceived their spouse's reactions to their careers, and less to factors related to their own careers. Women were less likely than men to go abroad on a sabbatical and those who went were more likely to go for a shorter time. If we consider that the sabbatical offers a unique opportunity for the academic to establish and strengthen informal networks critical in a myriad ways for career advancement, Doenias' findings contribute another dimension to our understanding of why the proportion of women narrows so radically as we move up the academic ladder (Toren, 1987).

Delayed domesticity
Common to all the above tactics is that they are designed to accommodate work to family life. In each, achievement in the world of

work is subordinated to the demands of home and children either present or anticipated. There are recent indications, however, that the relative salience of family and work in women's lives is changing. A growing number of young women, especially among the more educated, are accommodating their family plans to their career aspirations. They are delaying marriage, having fewer children (Bakki, 1986) and planning their families more rationally (Peres and Katz, 1984: 29). In 1988, a woman 20–24 years old had a 22 percent greater probability of being never married than in 1968, and a woman 25–29 years old a 68 percent probability.

Cohabitation, especially during college years (following army service) has become more prevalent. While there is no Israeli research on the subject, impressionistic and anecdotal evidence suggests that the relationship is premised on a more egalitarian division of labor than that existing among their parents. To what extent egalitarian patterns established during cohabitation are preserved after marriage and especially after the birth of the first child will probably be influenced by how women perceive their labor market options.

More women are making long-term investments in higher education, accumulating human capital, and adopting a career perspective to their work. Women constitute approximately 50 percent of the students in the lower years of almost all traditionally male professional schools such as law and medicine. Engineering, and to a lesser extent architecture, where the proportion is considerably lower, are exceptions.

These trends suggest that a shift may be taking place in the relative salience of family and work in women's lives and in the norms regarding the division of labor in the home.

The price of gender inequality

The gender gap in earnings, the small proportion of women in senior positions, and their virtual absence from centers of power in every domain of society, are the most visible indicators of the price women pay for gender inequality in family life and work opportunities. In 1988 women's hourly income was approximately 71 percent of that of men. Women are equally discriminated against in the core, the public and the peripheral sectors of the economy (Lewin-Epstein and Stier, 1987). The gender difference in income is not explained by women's inferior skills or abilities. Controlling for human capital and comparing men and women with similar levels of education, seniority, training and the like, does not reduce the earnings gap (Efroni, 1980; Semyonov and Kraus, 1983; Moore, 1987). Lewin-Epstein and Stier (1987: 118) reported that almost two-thirds of the gender gap in their study based on a 1975 income survey of employed Jewish workers resulted from the application of different rewarding criteria for men and women. Researchers attribute the gap primarily to discrimination. A company-level analysis of promotions reached the same conclusion (Shenhav and Haberfeld, 1988). Women with the same human capital resources as men got fewer promotion opportunities.

The gender gap in earnings was greater in 1988 than it had been a decade earlier when women, on average, earned 78 percent per hourly income of men (Efroni, 1989). Efroni (1989) explains the deepening of the gender gap with regard to the civil service by the greater weight of fringe benefits in gross earnings in 1988 compared to 1978. In an effort to increase the control of local-level managers over subordinates, they were granted greater discretion in the allocation of certain fringe benefits. While basic hourly pay levels are determined by collective labor agreements between employers and unions and are applied on a universal basis, fringe benefits are more often negotiated between the employer and the individual employee.

At this level, gender discrimination is more pronounced. For example, men's jobs are more likely than women's to be defined as 'entitled to car expenses.' Employers perceive men as the major wage earners and believe they are entitled to earn more than women. Men are more convinced of their entitlements to fringe benefits, put more pressure on employers to grant them such benefits and are more skilful in negotiating preferential terms for themselves. Consequently, the current trend toward individual employment contracts for more senior positions augurs bad tidings for women.

Attributions, equity and prospects for change in the dual-earner family

How a society, and its oppressed groups, attribute responsibility for apparent inequalities is pertinent to understanding their response to them. Israelis are generally aware that men and women are treated differently in the labor market. Women's inferior position, however, is perceived to be the consequence of their family responsibilities. A recent public opinion survey conducted among a representative sample of the adult Jewish population – excluding kibbutz (Dahaf, 1990) – presented four possible reasons for gender discrimination with the following results: 76 percent of the respondents attributed it to the belief that women are absent more often from work; 73 percent that they are able to devote less time and effort to work; 65 percent to the fact that employers are generally men; and only 40 percent to the belief that women are less competent. Employer discrimination, therefore, is implicitly legitimized as a rational response to and inevitable consequence of the reality of women's family responsibilities. Since women are assumed to accept their family responsibilities willingly, they ironically become responsible for their own discrimination.

Furthermore, while most Israelis believe that women should be fairly rewarded for their work, they do not believe women are entitled to the same rewarding jobs as men. Zemach and Peled (1983), found that close to 90 percent of both genders believe that men and women performing the same work should receive the same pay, but just over 50 percent believe that men should be given preference over women in recruitment to jobs and in promotion, while women should be given preference in working conditions. Thus employer discrimination is legitimized on normative grounds as well.

Research suggests that women perceive blocked opportunities and gender differences in rewards as an individual (Moore, 1987) rather than as a structural problem, that is, as a personal rather than a political issue. For example, women are rewarded at lower rates of return for their human capital than men (Semyonov and Kraus, 1983), but do not see this situation as unjust. 'Instead they react to the question of fairness as if their shortages in work-related inputs are solely responsible for – and therefore justify – their income disadvantage' (Yuchtman-Yaar et al., 1984). This response is explained by women's tendency to compare their earnings to those of other women and to avoid comparing themselves to men. This is true even for women in male-dominated occupations, who report even lower degrees of deprivation than do women in female-dominated occupations (Moore, 1987). Intra-gender comparisons lead to a 'scaling down' of their standards of fairness.

Why do women in male-dominated occupations fail to compare their earnings with those of men in the same occupations? Such comparisons, by increasing their consciousness of discrimination, would heighten their sense of relative deprivation and stimulate a more adversarial response. Why have no more than a dozen women filed claims of gender discrimination since the 1950s when anti-discrimination legislation was first introduced? A full analysis of these issues requires further research but a few hypotheses are relevant for understanding the potential forces for change. Individual women are reluctant to press charges of discrimination lest they be labelled trouble-makers, or lose their jobs, or be harassed (Kamir, 1990: 6). At the macro-level there are no institutional supports for adversarial action. Women's organizations in Israel have traditionally avoided an adversarial position with regard to men (Izraeli, 1981) and have resisted sponsoring claims of discrimination. With only rare exceptions, the trade unions have not supported women's claims and in most cases brought to court have even sided with the employer. The Equal Opportunity in Employment Law (1988) did not include affirmative action in its definition of equality nor did it provide for enforcement agencies to implement its principles in the courts. The tendency of the courts in general and the labor courts in particular has generally been, to accept protective stereotypes of women's role even where these limit her ability to compete equally in the labor market. (Raday, 1991)

The belief in the justice of their deprivation, in the existence of equal opportunity for 'competent and motivated' women in Israel, in the innately natural and voluntary character of women's family roles, combined with the lack of institutional supports for making claims, inhibit the development of women's consciousness, an important precondition for social change.

In the absence of external pressures for change, women's inferiority in the family and in the market is being reinforced. Women's limited market opportunities are a major disincentive for changing the traditional division of labor in the home. When their potential earnings are significantly smaller than those of their husbands, neither is motivated to find alternative arrangements. In the author's study of physicians, among couples where the wife contributed equal or more than the husband to the total family income (Izraeli and Silman, 1989) husbands spent more time in family work, were more likely to be the ones to stay home with a sick child, attributed greater relative importance to their wives' work and had more egalitarian gender attitudes. It may be argued that these supports contributed to women's higher earnings. It is equally likely that the wife's anticipated earnings were significant in eliciting such non-traditional behavior from her husband.

The large number of immigrants currently arriving from the Soviet Union is not likely to enhance gender equality, although it will increase the proportion of dual-earner families. Studies of Soviet immigrants indicate that women remain responsible for the home and family and that although they experience a drop in occupational status upon immigration, they are not dissatisfied and even choose to work fewer hours than they had in Russia (Ben Barak, 1988; Hartman and Hartman, 1980; Kats, 1982).

Historically, over the last hundred years three environmental conditions proved particularly favorable to women's status in society: a generally liberal ethos, a shortage of educated workers and economic growth, in addition to women's own political clout (Antal and Izraeli, 1992). None of these conditions exists in Israel at this time. In fact the trends are in the opposite direction. There are strong winds of anti-liberalism fanned by the military threat to national survival and by growing influence of the right wing and religious political parties. The state, furthermore, is not threatened with a skills shortage. The largest cohorts ever (the post-1967 war baby boom generation) are currently completing compulsory military service. The mass immigration from the Soviet Union includes a large proportion of highly skilled technological brain-power. In addition, economic growth has been virtually stagnant during the last decade, and in 1989 unemployment was higher than it had been since the mid-1960s. The mass immigration from the Soviet Union will make the situation, at least in the short run, more acute. Within the context of a society that is highly fragmented politically and preoccupied with physical survival, women's political clout at the beginning of the 1990s was at a low ebb. They held fewer than 6 percent of the seats in the Knesset – the lowest number in Israel's history. It is thus unlikely that in the near future equal opportunity for women in dual-earner families will receive much, if any, priority on the public agenda.

Notes

An earlier version of this chapter was published in Arie Globerson, Amira Galin and Eliezer Rosenstein (eds), *Human Resources and Industrial Relations in Israel*. Tel Aviv University, Ramot, 1990 (in Hebrew). The prevalent theoretical assumption in Israel, even among women academics who do research in gender, is that women have many more opportunities than they actually exploit, that the choices they make are in line with their own preferences and the outcomes are satisfying to them. I have come to cast doubt on the extent of the truly voluntary nature of women's 'choices' and the validity of 'satisfaction' as a measure of an egalitarian society. My perception is that women are in large measure coerced, sometimes more subtly, sometimes less, into making the choices they do by the structure of opportunity and by the psychological pressures to perform to script.

I have discussed the ideas in this chapter with many colleagues over the years and have learnt much from them and their work. I am especially grateful for comments made on earlier drafts by Yael Atzmon, Debbie Bernstein, Rhoda Blumberg, Linda Efroni, Hana Herzog, Helen Hootsmans, Ruth Katz, Sue Lewis, Yochanan Peres, Michael Shalev, and Naomi Shefer and on later drafts by Rose Coser, Judy Lorber, Rosanna Hertz, Theda Skocpol, and Eva Etzioni-Halevy.

1. Unless otherwise indicated, all 1988 and 1989 data are from the *Statistical Abstract of Israel*, 1989 and 1990, published by the Central Bureau of Statistics, Jerusalem.

2. Personal communication, Yvette Saadon, Director of the Women's Bureau, Ministry of Work and Welfare.

3. Meeting held spring 1990; author recorded the statement.

4. Of all women who generally worked less than 35 hours a week, almost 20 percent said their jobs were considered full time.

References

Agassi, Buber, Judith (1989) 'Theories of gender equality: lessons from the kibbutz', *Gender and Society*, 3: 160–86.

Antal, A. and Izraeli, Dafna N. (1992) 'An international comparison of women in management: women managers in their homelands and as expatriates', in E. Fagenson (ed.), *Women in Management*. Women and Work, Vol. 4. Newbury Park, California: Sage.

Bakki, Roberto (1986) 'The demographic crisis of the Jewish people', *Ha'aretz* (Hebrew daily), 1 June.

Bar-Haim, Aviad and Shavit, Zeev (1987) *Alternative Work Schedules: A Literature Review and a Research Proposal*. Jerusalem Research Institute and the Open University (unpublished, Hebrew).

Bar-Yosef, Rivka and Bachar, A. (1972) *The Psychological and Social Factors Affecting Fertility*. Research report. Jerusalem: Hebrew University.

Bar-Yosef, Rivka and Padan-Eisenstark, Dorit (1977) 'Role system under stress: sex roles in war', *Social Problems*, 20: 135–45.

Bar-Yosef, Rivka, Bloom, Anne and Levy, Tzvia (1977) *Role-Ideology of Young Israeli Women*. Jerusalem: Work and Welfare Research Institute, Hebrew University.

Ben Barak, Shalvia (1988) 'Attitudes toward work and home of Soviet immigrant women', Paper presented at the annual meeting of the Israel Sociological Association, Haifa University, February.

Bernstein, Deborah (1982) 'Economic growth and the female labor force: the case of Israel', *The Sociological Review*, 31: 263–92.

Bernstein, Deborah (1987) *The Struggle for Equality: Urban Women Workers in Prestate Israeli Society*. New York: Praeger.

Central Bureau of Statistics (CBS) (1985) *Households, Marriages, Couples, Fertility*. Reprint from the Supplement to the *Monthly Bulletin of Statistics* 9.

Central Bureau of Statistics (CBS) (1986) *Part-Time Employed, 1979–84*. Supplement to the *Monthly Bulletin of Statistics*, 35 (4): 90–125.

Central Bureau of Statistics (CBS) (1989) *Labour Force Surveys 1987*. Special Series no. 848. Jerusalem.

Civil Service (1987) *Annual Report* 37. Jerusalem: Ministry of Finance.

Coser, Louis and Coser, Rose Laub (1974) 'The housewife and her greedy family', in L. Coser (ed.), *Greedy Institutions*, pp. 89–100. New York: Free Press.

Dahaf, Research Institute (1990) *Equal Opportunity for Women at Work: Existent or Non-existent?* Public Opinion Survey Report, Tel Aviv (July).

Doenias, Iris (1988) 'The decision to go on sabbatical in academia among dual-career couples', MSc thesis, Faculty of Management, Tel Aviv University (in Hebrew).

Efroni, Linda (1980) 'Promotion and wages in Israel', PhD dissertation, Hebrew University, Jerusalem (in Hebrew).

Efroni, Linda (1989) *Women in Government Service: A Comparison 1979–1988*. Research report. Jerusalem: Civil Service, Training and Education Service (in Hebrew).

Elizur Dov (n.d.) 'Sex differences in work values: a structural analysis', Dept. of Economics, Bar-Ilan University.

Gabai, Yoram (1990) 'Working mothers and women in the labor force,' Conference on Women Money and Power sponsored by the American Jewish Committee and the Israel Women's Network, 1 February, Tel Aviv (in Hebrew).

Gafni, Yael (1981) 'The readiness of women and men in Israel to accept top management positions', MA thesis, Dept. of Political Science, Bar-Ilan University (in Hebrew).

Haberfeld, Yitzhak, and Izraeli, Dafna N. (forthcoming) 'Gender inequality within majority and minority groups in Israel', in Elizabeth Almquist, Dudley Posen and Kathryn Ward (eds), *Gender Inequality in Minority Groups in Fifteen Countries*. New York: SUNY University Press.

Hartman, Moshe (1980) 'The role of ethnicity in married women's economic activity in Israel', *Ethnicity*, 7: 225–55.

Hartman, Moshe and Hartman, Harriet (1980) 'The effect of immigration on women's roles in various countries', *International Journal of Sociology and Social Policy*, 3: 86–103.

Honig M. and Shamai, Nira (1978) 'Israel', in S.B. Kamerman and A.S. Kahn (eds), *Family Policy, Government and Families in Fourteen Countries*, pp. 400–27. New York: Columbia University Press.

Izraeli, Dafna N. (1981) 'The Zionist women's movement in Palestine: 1911–1927', *Signs*, 7: 87–114.

Izraeli, Dafna N. (1988) 'Women's movement into management', in Nancy Adler and Dafna N. Izraeli (eds), *Women in Management Worldwide*. New York: M.E. Sharpe.

Izraeli, Dafna N. and Silman, Naomi (1989) 'She earns more, she earns less, she earns the same: a profile of dual-career couples', paper presented at the GASAT Conference. Technion-Israel Institute of Technology, Haifa, Israel, September.

Kamir, Orit (1990) ' "I don't want to be a troublemaker": finding a precedent', *Networking for Women* (Jerusalem), 4(1): 6.

Kandiyoti, Deniz (1988) 'Bargaining with patriarchy', *Gender and Society*, 2: 274–90.

Kats, Rachel (1982) 'The immigrant woman: double cost or relative improvement?', *International Migration Review*, 16: 661–77.

Kirschenbaum, Alan (1988) 'Life cycle changes and female labor force participation', unpublished paper, Faculty of Industrial Engineering and Management, Technion – Israel Institute of Technology.

Klein, Ethel (1984) *Gender Politics*. Cambridge, Mass: Harvard University Press.

Kraus, Vered (1989) 'Ethnicity, gender and the process of status attainment in Israel', *Research in Inequality and Social Conflict*, 1: 93–217.

Kriegel, Danielle and Waintrater, Ragine (1985) *This Night Too Golda Will Not Sleep: Israeli Women and the Wars*. Paris: Jean Claude Latice (in French).

Lewin-Epstein, Noah and Stier, Haya (1987) 'Labor market structure, gender and socioeconomic inequality in Israel', *Israel Social Science Research: A Multidisciplinary Journal*, 5: 107–20.

Mannheim, Bilha and Schiffrin, Meira (1984) 'Family structure, job characteristics, rewards and strains as related to work-role centrality of employed and self-employed professional women with children', *Journal of Occupational Behaviour*, 5: 83–101.

Moore, Dahlia (1987) 'Relative deprivation in the labor market', *Israel Social Science Research: A Multidisciplinary Journal* 5: 121–37.

Palgi, Michal, Blasi, Joseph Raphael, Rosner, Menachem and Safir, Marilyn (eds) (1983) *Sexual Equality: The Israeli Kibbutz Tests the Theories*. Norwood, Pa: Norwood Editions.

Peres, Yochanan and Katz, Ruth (1981) 'Stability and centrality: the nuclear family in modern Israel', *Social Forces*, 59: 687–704.

Peres, Yochanan and Katz, Ruth (1984) *The Employed Mother and Her Family*. Research Report. Jerusalem: Ministry of Labor and Welfare (in Hebrew).

Peres, Yochanan and Katz, Ruth (1990) 'The family in Israel: change and continuity', in Lea Shamgar Handelman and Rivka Bar-Yosef (eds), *Families in Israel*. Jerusalem: Academon (in Hebrew).

Raday, Frances (1991) 'Women, work and the law', in Barbara Svirski and Marilyn Safir (eds), *Calling the Equality Bluff*. New York and Oxford: Pergamon Press.

Semyonov, Moshe and Kraus, Vered (1983) 'Gender, ethnicity and income inequality: the Israeli experience', *International Journal of Comparative Sociology*, 24 (3–4): 258–72.

Semyonov, Moshe and Lewin-Epstein, Noah (1991) 'Local labor markets, commuting and gender inequality', *Social Science Quarterly*, 32.

Semyonov, Moshe and Tyree, Andrea (1981) 'Community segregation and the costs of ethnic subordination', *Social Forces*, 59: 649–86.

Shapira, Rina and Etzioni-Halevy, Eva (1973) *Who is the Israeli Student?* Tel Aviv: Am Oved (in Hebrew).

Shenhav, Yehouda. A. and Haberfeld, Yitchak (1988) 'Scientists in organizations: discrimination processes in an internal labor market', *The Sociological Quarterly*, 29: 451–62.

Toren, Nina (1987) 'Israeli women in academe', *Israel Social Science Research: A Multidisciplinary Journal*, 5: 138–46.

Yuchtman-Yaar, Ephraim, Moore, Dahlia and Fishelson, Gideon (1984) 'To be deprived and complacent: fairness judgments of earnings among Israeli women', Working paper 17–84, Forder Institute for Economic Research, Faculty of Social Sciences, Tel-Aviv University.

Zemach, Tamar and Peled, Ziona (1983) *The Status of Women in the Eyes of the Public*. Research report submitted to the advisor to the Prime Minister on the status of women (in Hebrew). Jerusalem.

3
Middle-Class Dual-Earner Families and their Support Systems in Urban India

Uma Sekaran

India is a land of paradoxes. It is the ninth most industrialized country in the world (Brata, 1985), occupies the third position in the world in terms of scientific and technical expertise – following the USA and USSR (Bharol, 1989), and yet, it is poor. Indian women are perceived as having very little power, yet India (like Sri Lanka) was ahead of many developed countries in having a woman prime minister, who made a significant difference to the shaping of the nation. The literacy rate in India is low, but the number of educated urban women pursuing careers is steadily increasing.

The number of dual-earner (including dual-career) families is growing, especially in the metropolitan and urban cities of India. Nevertheless Indian society does not appear to be experiencing turmoil in the transition from single-earner to dual-earner families to the same extent as some other developed countries. This chapter discusses the impact of the family support structure, as well as environmental, work and non-work factors mitigating the strains of this transition among middle-class dual-earner couples in urban sectors in India.

The chapter focuses on dual-earner families among the middle class. While only a small minority of the total population, they are a vanguard of change, of special significance to women's status in Indian society. The vast majority of working women are uneducated cultivators and agro-laborers residing in villages (Chakravarthy, 1985). Most of them are unpaid laborers working on the family farm. Sixty-three percent of all educated women who have at least a high school diploma are non-employed. Of the 37 percent educated women who are employed, 15 percent are clerks, 5 percent teachers, 7 percent nurses, and 10 percent are other professionals (Kameswaran, 1985). Most of the educated women live in the metropolitan and urban cities. Although dependable statistics are not available, it is safe to presume that there are more dual-career families in the metropolitan cities of Bombay, Calcutta, Delhi and Madras, and in some of the urban cities such as Bangalore and Hyderabad, than in the other parts of the country.

Indian urban employed women can be categorized into three social strata, upper, middle, and lower class. Women in the upper stratum, such as wives of army officers and cabinet ministers, are not, as a rule, gainfully employed outside the home. They generally participate in voluntary activities during their spare time. Others, such as wives of wealthy merchants and lawyers, might run their own independent 'boutiques' or 'shops', if they prefer not to work for others. Educated married women in middle-class urban families usually take gainful full-time employment outside of the home in service industries and government organizations, and sometimes in private companies. Women from the lower stratum who have had no access to education are usually employed as maids in other people's homes. Caste membership also influences type of employment. For instance, the uneducated women from the 'Shudra' caste usually work as maids, while those from the 'Brahmin' caste who need employment usually work as full-time or part-time cooks for others.

This chapter discusses the quality of life experienced by urban, middle-class, educated working couples with particular focus on the impact of support systems. First, however, factors conducive to the growth of dual-earner families are discussed.

Factors conducive to the growth of dual-earner families

Until the early 1950s, few educated women worked outside the home. A number of social, economic and demographic developments as well as governmental interventions contributed to the increase of dual-earner families in India in the last three or four decades. Primary among these is economic necessity. Today two incomes are essential for the vast majority of the middle class wishing to maintain a comfortable standard of living. This is the case irrespective of whether they live in urban, semi-urban or, to some extent, even rural areas. Other factors include nationalization of several sectors of the economy, which created job opportunities for women, organizational policies, and the Indian family values and structure. These are now discussed in greater detail.

New job opportunities

Most service industries such as banks and insurance companies were nationalized during the 1960s. Nationalized industries, such as the railways, have more readily accepted qualified women in entry-level and junior officer positions than private sector industries. The nationalized service industries thus created opportunities for career women, who have since risen to middle management, and in some cases, to senior executive positions. Private sector organizations also recruit capable women educated in the various management institutes in India. These organizations provide women with good on-the-job training, with promotions to higher-level positions even as the women rear a family of one, two or even three children.

Indian women receive the same salaries as men in the same jobs and do not quit work to raise a family. Maternity leave policies and other support systems described in this chapter enable the modern Indian woman to pursue a career and family simultaneously, rather than parenthood following employment or employment following parenthood (Sekaran and Hall, 1989).

Maternity leave policies
Legislation provides for three months' maternity leave following the birth of each baby, a maximum of three times during a woman's work career. This is on full pay, and paid by employers, as there is no national insurance scheme. Most women take the full leave, unless they hold very high-level positions and have full-time servants, in which case they occasionally choose to return earlier. An employed woman can, for all practical purposes, be on leave for as long as a year when she combines her maternity leave, vacation time (which can be accumulated up to three months), and sick leave. Sick leave cannot officially be taken for childcare. However, medical certificates stating that the mother needs more rest before returning to work are easily procured. Sick leave can be accumulated up to six months on half-pay, and beyond with no pay. Leave without pay does not count towards length of service. So, in most cases, the child gets full-time maternal care for the first year of its life. The important point is that the woman can come back to her job without fear of losing her position or jeopardizing her chances of further advancement. Promotional opportunities for women, especially in the public sector organizations (where seniority is one of the criteria for eligibility for promotion), have not been adversely affected, simply because women have been away from work for a year following the birth of children. Thus, governmental policies and organizational practices in India facilitate women in simultaneously pursuing their careers and family life without experiencing undue psychological tensions and physical stress.

Demographics and changing expectations
In all except two of the states and territories of India the number of males exceeds that of females – 933 women per 1,000 men (see *Statistical Outline of India*, 1988).

In a country where arranged marriages are still common, this gender composition relieves the pressure on parents to find husbands for their daughters at a young age. In urban areas more women are being encouraged to pursue higher education, and the age at which women marry is increasing. For instance, in the 1940s girls in South India were married off between the ages of 14 and 16, whereas in the early 1950s the norm for marriageable age rose to 21 and currently parents do not feel uncomfortable having unmarried daughters who are 24 years and older, either studying or working, and living at home. Furthermore, even in conservative South India, women are beginning to find their own marital partners at the workplace or at social gatherings rather than having their parents arrange their marriage. These changes have led to the emergence of 'instant' dual-earner families, where upon marriage women already have jobs or careers. Men prefer to marry women who have high-paying jobs or careers. It enables them to begin married life with a higher standard of living than would otherwise be the case. Men's attitudes further encourage women to plan for long-term work involvement without the lurking fear of remaining an 'old maid' or having to stop working after marriage. This is in contrast to the time when men objected to wives' employment and women worked mainly as an interim arrangement until they got married (Khanna and Verghese, 1975), or in even starker contrast to the late 1940s, when it was not acceptable for women to work outside the home.

Family structure and values
In India family members and relatives have a strong sense of their duties, responsibilities and obligations towards each other, irrespective of their physical proximity. The relationship among family members is characterised by intimacy, mutuality of interest, and pride in the strong bonds among the family members who reach out to each other spontaneously (Conklin, 1974; Ross, 1961). Whether working couples live under the same roof with their parents/parents-in-law or not, they are assisted with childcare and other emergency help. Cultural norms encourage even distant relatives, friends and neighbors to help one another. Also, it is not unusual to see women leaving their children in the care of neighbors whom they trust, day after day, and walk in and out of their homes with extreme informality. Concerns regarding reliable day care or 'who will take care of the children when I am gone on business travel?' do not surface for most Indian working women.

Although some young couples live separately from their parents after marriage, it is quite common for married couples to live with the husband's parents if they live in the same city. It is also socially acceptable for working spouses living in one area to leave their young children for several years with the parents or parents-in-law living in a different area or city. These children thus grow up under grandparental guidance and nurturance.

Family involvement in childcare is helpful since other childcare facilities are rare, although there are schools for children aged three and above. Recently however, some organizations, such as the Defence Electronics Laboratory in Hyderabad, are starting crèches.

Hired help

Hired help is also available although it is now becoming more expensive. Women who have had no formal education but who are keen on supplementing their family income, work as maids in several homes, cleaning utensils, washing clothes, sweeping the house, and doing sundry other duties such as running errands and grinding rice, for extra tips. As mentioned earlier, uneducated Brahmin women also render services as cooks. Hired domestic help provides significant assistance to middle-class working women. However, the growth in demand for domestic workers by employed women, the increasing cost of such help, and the difficulty in relying upon maids to appear before the couple leave for work in the morning, make this source of support more problematic than it was a decade ago.

Why do married Indian women pursue careers?

Currently, the vast majority of educated married women living in the cities simultaneously pursue a career and a family life. A few consider their careers as their primary goal in life. In Tamil Nadu, for example, (a state in Southern India) about 25 percent of the doctors are women, and so are 68 percent of the prize-winners in educational systems (Kameswaran, 1985). There is also an increasing number of women who are state ministers, legislative council and assembly members, and members of various boards. What motivates these women to pursue careers?

Women pursue careers for numerous reasons, important among which is the fact that this provides them with economic and personal independence and also offers them a higher standard of living (Khanna and Verghese, 1975). Responses to an interview survey of 100 career women I conducted in Madras and Bombay in 1983 identify additional reasons. Firstly, a career bestows higher status on the women in the eyes of their relatives. This in turn, provides them with some bargaining chips with their in-laws with regard to limiting their involvement in household chores and having greater say in decision making; secondly, the knowledge that they are pursuing serious careers rather than trivial clerical jobs provides them with enormous satisfaction. Many career women also feel that once they have proved themselves as effective performers, they gain the respect of the others in the system – both men and women.

Nevertheless, there are several problematic issues pertaining to the organizational context. Though pay and promotional policies are not believed to be discriminatory, women are still treated paternalistically in many organizations. For instance, in interviews I conducted in 1981 with bank executives, many of the men indicated that it was not appropriate to entrust to women the job of carrying huge amounts of cash for bank deposit at the end of the day, because they might be assaulted, despite the usual police protection given to such depositors. Many older men were reluctant to let women interact with the public at night-time, especially if they were by themselves. Many men also thought it inappropriate to send women on out of town overnight travel assignments, or to transfer them to other cities where they would have to be away from their family. While the stresses on family life might be reduced to some extent by such 'protectionism', it may also be detrimental to the professional development of women, especially if the women themselves desire to be involved in these activities. However, this is beginning to change to some extent with more women being promoted to higher-level positions. Women are transferred to other cities to get a well-rounded training for taking on higher responsibilities and they are given travel assignments.

Some background information on Indian dual-earner families

Indian dual-earner couples, in general, do not report feeling highly stressed, even though the Indian women still take on responsibility for household management and child rearing. Generally, men do not participate in household work at all, and do not assist with childcare (Ramu, 1987). However, the availability of hired help and the assistance given by extended family members mitigate the burden of the Indian employed woman. The wife, although generally outwardly conforming to the subdued and compliant behavior prescribed by the culture, nonetheless exerts considerable influence on household decision making, such as how money is spent, which schools children attend and what activities they engage in. The wife's demonstration of power and the acceptance of her influence by the husband in dual-earner families is now more openly acknowledged (Ramu, 1987).

Indian dual-earner couples, however, are generally not concerned over the issue of exercising their autonomy in decision-making. Conjugal dyadic identity often gets submerged in the family structure, which encompasses parents, brothers and sisters and their respective families (Khatri, 1975). The fact that the total family is the anchor point for couples in the establishment of their rights and responsibilities (the younger one is in the family, the less power one has) overcomes the individualistic tendencies which are usually the basis for quarrels over rights and privileges between marital partners elsewhere. Thus, in their relationship with the 'family', couples have a special mutual understanding and accommodating relationship between themselves, which helps them to take on collaborative rather than confrontational stances and attitudes in the nuclear family decision-making context. So the common perception that the wife sacrifices her wishes to the superior role of the husband in decision making may often be inaccurate in the context of Indian dual-earner families.

The husband's non-participation in household work is not a source of irritation or anger for the Indian working wife. Ramu (1987) in his study of the household work done by Indian husbands, found that wives often reported the belief that their husbands were incompetent and inept at housework and that no amount of coaching would improve matters. This may be interpreted as the typical governing ideology which sustains women in traditional societies. Be that as it may, such beliefs assuage any anger and resentment felt by Indian women over the unequal division of labor. They resolve the problem of work overload in other ways. The strategies of working women include engaging full-time or part-time help, negotiating with their in-laws not to expect them to perform household tasks in addition to pursuing their careers, and cutting down on social obligations.

Certain organizational and cultural factors help the Indian working wife to feel less stressed than many of her western counterparts. Professional advancement at the workplace is not nearly as competitive in India as, for instance, in the US. Promotions in Indian organizations – especially in the government sector – are based primarily, though not solely, on seniority, thus reducing much potential stress. Furthermore, the larger social unit in which couples are so enmeshed provides important sources of emotional satisfaction for them in addition to those derived at the workplace.

Conjugal relations are said to become more and more egalitarian as the couple grow older (Srinivas, 1978), and this certainly would help the advancement of women to high-level positions without evoking feelings of jealousy or rivalry between the partners. Since greater responsibility is usually given based on seniority, it is not unusual for men and women to be promoted to higher-level managerial positions after the age of 45 or 50, a very propitious time for the Indian couples to advance in their careers without evoking ill-feelings between them. Shukla (1987) in her study of dual-career couples confirms that these older couples have egalitarian relationships and that the wives exercise substantial power in household matters. Egalitarian behaviors are manifested in terms of expressing feelings more openly, taking initiatives in and making commitments on behalf of the family. For instance, a woman may decide that she will help an ailing relative by sending a substantial amount of money in an emergency, without consulting her husband, just as the husband would do without consulting the wife. Previously the wife would not have had the inclination or courage to commit herself without consulting her husband. One should also remember that families at this stage are stepping into the extended family status with their sons and daughters married and having families of their own. The older couple then take on the role of 'heads of the family' as grandparents, which also bestows on them power and higher status.

Quality of life

Some indications of the quality of life experienced by Indian dual-earner women and men are provided by my study, reported below, of the impact of certain work and non-work variables on career satisfaction, life satisfaction and mental health.

Work-related factors examined by a questionnaire survey were: *career salience* or the importance of the career to one's life; the *income* earned; and *discretionary time* or the amount of time that one spends/has to spend beyond regular work hours on work-related matters. Unduly long periods of time spent on work at the expense of family interactions are likely to lower the experienced quality of life. Among the non-work factors were *enabling* or the extent of support (both physical and moral) that the working spouses extend to each other; *multiple role stress* or the stresses experienced by the couple because of the different roles they play as spouse, parent, child, neighbor, friend and so on; and one's *self-esteem* or how good one feels about oneself. All of these factors have been shown to influence the quality of life factors in studies of American dual-earner families (Sekaran, 1983, 1985, 1986). These work and non-work factors were also measured in the Indian setting.

The sample comprised 123 dual-earner couples working in various organizations including banks, insurance companies, transportation systems, and other service and business settings in the metropolitan city of Bombay. Bombay is the California of India – a trend-setter for various practices that individuals in other parts of the country follow sooner or later. Members from two-earner families, whose spouses were also willing to respond to a questionnaire in their own homes, were enlisted as the sample. Thus, this was a voluntary group of respondents. Respondents were instructed to answer the questions independently without consulting their partners or others at home.

The completed questionnaires were collected from the primary contact persons within ten days of distribution.

The mean age of the husbands was 39 and that of the wives was 34. On average, the couples had been married for 11 years and no one in the sample had been divorced. The husbands had worked an average of 14 years in their current organization and the wives an average of 11 years. The vast majority of respondents had worked only for that organization. This is not unusual in India, where there are limited new job openings and the competition for them is fierce. The average number of children in the family was two, the number ranging from none to six. Of the 123 families in the sample, in 65 both spouses pursued managerial or executive careers, and in the remainder one or both spouses had 9-to-5 jobs such as clerks and typists.

Information on demographic variables such as age, number of children, job level and income was collected through direct single questions. Details of measures used for the other variables are provided in the Appendix. For further details of these measures see Touliatos (1989).

T-tests were used to test for gender difference in mental health, and multiple regression analyses were used to examine the relationships between the independent and dependent variables, to explore the antecedents of mental health and to examine whether there was any spillover from job satisfaction to life satisfaction and vice versa for women and men. Additionally, more sophisticated regression analyses were performed by dummy coding gender and career orientation to detect any gender or career orientation differences in the paths to the mental health of the dual-earner family members.

The means, standard deviations and correlations for the variables of interest to this study are shown in Table 3.1 for the entire sample. Results of *t*-tests to detect any significant gender differences are shown in Table 3.2.

As can be seen, there were no significant mean differences between husbands and wives in career satisfaction, life satisfaction and mental health – the three quality of life factors. Men were significantly higher in age, and income, and husbands spent three times as much discretionary time on career-related work. Husbands had higher self-esteem while wives experienced greater stress, especially among career-involved couples.

Separate multiple regression analyses for husbands and wives revealed that mental health was determined largely by life satisfaction. There were no linkages between job satisfaction and life satisfaction and further analysis revealed this to be the case regardless of gender or career orientation. It appears that there is no spillover in satisfaction between employment and non-work domains, although career salience

Table 3.1 *Means, standard deviations, and correlations (n = 246)*

Variables	Age	Children	Income	Discretionary time	Career salience	Self-esteem	Enabling	Multiple role stress	Life satisfaction	Job satisfaction	Mental health
Age	36.72 (7.74)										
Children	.38***	2									
Income	.28***	.01									
Discretionary time	.01	-.04	.24***								
Career salience	.21***	.11	-.06	.02	5.12 (1.1)						
Self-esteem	.24***	.12*	.26***	.09	.23***	5.51 (0.81)					
Enabling	.19**	-.06	.06	-.05	.21***	.28***	3.49 (0.58)				
Multiple role stress	-.21***	-.04	-.01	-.06	-.04	-.16**	-.16**	2.59 (0.66)			
Life satisfaction	.18**	.14*	-.07	-.10	.43***	.32***	.39***	-.30***	3.49 (0.52)		
Job satisfaction	-.02	.06	-.20***	-.08	.09	-.09	-.06	.09	-.06	44.74 (25.21)	
Mental health	.18**	.19***	-.07	-.10	.23***	.21***	.17**	-.12	.51***	.01	3.74 (0.27)

Figures on diagonal represent mean (standard deviation).
* $p < .05$; ** $p < .01$; *** $p < .001$

Table 3.2 *Results of t-tests to detect gender differences*

	Husbands (n = 123)		Wives (n = 123)			
Variable	Mean	Std dev.	Mean	Std dev.	t value	p <
Age	39.24	7.58	34.20	7.08	5.39	.0001
Income	3.87	1.23	2.94	1.24	5.87	.0001
Discretionary time	7.52	12.42	2.62	4.36	3.98	.0001
Career salience	5.11	1.03	5.13	1.17	-0.14	ns
Self-esteem	5.64	0.82	5.38	0.78	2.61	.01
Enabling	3.48	0.61	3.51	0.55	-0.41	ns
Multiple role stress	2.50	0.62	2.67	0.70	-2.07	.04
Career satisfaction	45.61	26.32	43.88	24.14	0.54	ns
Life satisfaction	3.48	0.52	3.51	0.52	-0.51	ns
Mental health	3.45	0.26	3.43	0.28	0.64	ns

ns = not significant

affects life satisfaction and high amounts of discretionary time spent on work-related activities adversely impact on women's life satisfaction.

There was no gender difference in mental health, and the paths to the mental health of both husbands and wives were influenced directly by the satisfactions experienced only in the non-work domain of their lives. This is in contrast to findings from a study of US dual-earner families, where the mental health of wives was found to be significantly lower than that of the husbands, and the paths to the mental health of husbands and wives were different (Sekaran, 1985). The mental health of the husbands in the US study was influenced by both job satisfaction and life satisfaction, whereas that of the wives was influenced only by life satisfaction.

For details of results of the multiple regressions, see Table 3.4 in the appendix. A visual depiction of path analyses is shown in Figures 3.1 and 3.2.

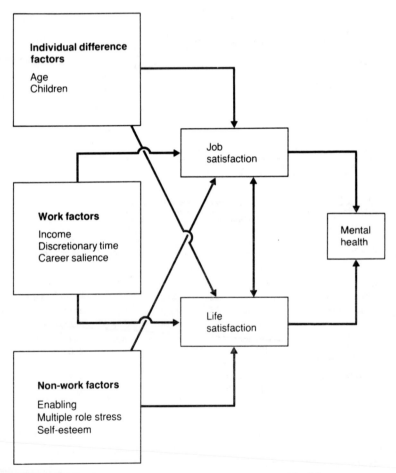

Figure 3.1   *Conceptual model tracing the paths to mental health*

A possible reason why work satisfaction does not affect life satisfaction and why mental health is influenced only by life satisfaction for both spouses is that most Indians do not expect their work life to provide mental satisfaction and happiness. Jobs are difficult to come by in India. Many people are forced to join an organization or pursue a particular type of work that they do not really like. The tight employment situation also limits inter-organizational mobility. Work and life satisfactions are quite separate.

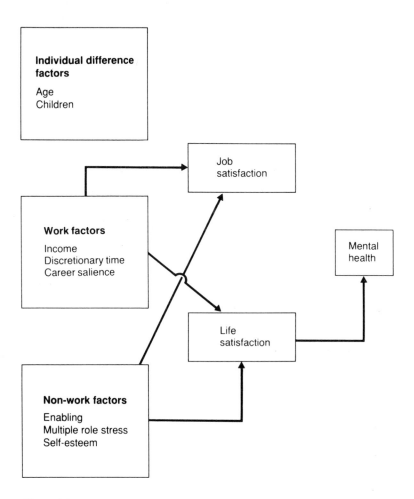

Figure 3.2 *Actual paths to mental health*

A futuristic perspective

Indian lifestyles are changing slowly but visibly. Some of the shifts, such as later age at marriages, higher education for women, and more women participating in careers, have already been noted. The following predictions, though speculative, reflect emerging trends and the expected diffusion of ideas from other countries.

There are some women in India who even today argue for greater equality at the workplace. It is quite possible that a few decades from now, working women may organize to fight for greater acceptance at work, a position likely to meet with male resistance.

As parents live longer lives, attending to the elderly may impose stresses and strains on dual-earner families and the quality of life they experience. Indian culture expects couples to care for the elderly in their time of need, usually while living in the same house. At present there are a few 'homes for the aged' but these are not accepted as a viable alternative for the care of the elderly. The very idea arouses feelings of guilt and discomfort among couples as well as resentment and anger among the elderly toward their children, who are culturally obliged to support them (see also Chabot, this volume).

The upcoming generation of educated women will also find more competition at the workplace as greater numbers of capable women and men enter the job market. There is growing evidence that performance criteria and evidence of potential are going to be treated as just as important as seniority for career advancement (Cherian, 1987). Unemployment in India is high and increased competition could encourage ambitious women to postpone marriage in order to devote themselves to realizing their career aspirations. Though single-career women are almost insignificant in number at the moment in India, in the future more may opt for the 'unmarried live-in partners' lifestyle.

As educational opportunities open up for more men and women, there could be a shortage of household help in the future. Wives might then expect their husbands to share in domestic responsibilities. A possible problematic issue that might arise if hired help becomes difficult to find is more tension generated within the extended family as career women refuse to get involved in household work. Career wives who live with their mothers-in-law are already negotiating for less housework. Of the 100 women I interviewed in the early 1980s, a third reported informing their mothers-in-law of their unwillingness to share in the household chores and their expectation that their children would have to be cared for mainly by the relatives. One woman reported telling her husband's mother that since she worked hard in the office to earn the salary she brought home, which afforded them all a better standard of living, she could not expend her energy in household tasks. She indicated that she had encouraged her mother-in-law to engage a full-time servant so that nobody would have to work too hard. She had made her expectations clear. She had to be 'served' coffee when she got home tired after working all day in the office. Given the authority structure in India and the possible dearth of help in the future, such open expressions of unwillingness to participate in household work may well result in discord in the household.

Indian dual-earner couples have hitherto solved intricate problematic issues that have confronted them in ways in keeping with their cultural values, and have maintained a reasonably high quality of life. It will be interesting to see if they continue to do so, since these families are likely to serve as role models for the lifestyles of future dual-earner families in India.

Note

Dr Meera Komaraju's useful comments on the first draft of this chapter and the comments of the editors are gratefully acknowledged.

Appendix

Table 3.3   *Details of measures used in the study*

Variables	No. of items	Cronbach's alpha	Source of measure
Mental health	22	.81	Kornhauser (1965)
Life satisfaction	12	.81	Kornhauser (1965)
Job satisfaction	72	.82	Smith, Kendall and Hulin (1969)
Career salience	7	.77	Sekaran (1982)
Discretionary time	2[a]	—	—
Enabling	8	.79	Sekaran (1986)
Multiple role stress	20	.82	Sekaran (1986)
Self-esteem	9	.70	Rosenberg (1965)

[a] These two items asked for the average number of hours beyond regular work hours that were spent per week on job-related matters (a) at home or elsewhere; and (b) at the workplace.

Appendix continues overleaf

Table 3.4   *Results of repression analyses showing path coefficients and associated probabilities for husbands and wives*

Variables	Husbands (*n* = 123)		Wives (*n* = 123)	
	Path coefficient (PC)	*p* for PC	Path coefficient (PC)	*p* for PC
For job satisfaction				
Age	.02	ns	−.13	ns
Children	.06	ns	.11	ns
Income	−.17	.03	.01	ns
Discretionary time	−.04	ns	−.25	.008
Career salience	.12	ns	.38	.0004
Multiple role stress	.06	ns	.06	ns
Enabling	−.07	ns	.13	ns
Self-esteem	.06	ns	.20	.04
Life satisfaction	−.07	ns	−.09	ns
For life satisfaction				
Age	−.04	ns	−.02	ns
Children	.09	ns	.13	ns
Income	−.06	ns	−.16	ns
Discretionary time	−.11	ns	−.29	.0003
Career salience	.36	.00001	.33	.0003
Multiple role stress	−.22	.0001	−.15	ns
Enabling	.23	.0001	.26	.002
Self-esteem	.17	.004	.15	ns
Job satisfaction	−.84	ns	−.06	ns
For mental health				
Age	.08	ns	.05	ns
Children	.08	ns	.08	ns
Income	−.08	ns	.03	ns
Discretionary time	−.03	ns	−.06	ns
Career salience	−.01	ns	.14	ns
Multiple role stress	.04	ns	.04	ns
Enabling	−.05	ns	−.19	.04
Self-esteem	.09	ns	.21	.03
Job satisfaction	.01	ns	−.05	ns
Life satisfaction	.48	.00001	.42	.0003

ns = not significant

References

Bharol, C.R. (1989) 'Problem of R&D manpower in India', *R&D Management*, 19(4): 335–41.

Brata, S. (1985) *Labyrinths in the Lotus Land.* New York: William Morrow.

Chakravarthy, S. (1985) 'Women and economic development: its multi-facet effects', *Proceedings of the National Seminar on Education and Employment for Women in India*, Mother Teresa Women's University, Kodi, India.

Cherian, D. (1987) 'Tough or timid?', *Business India*, 9–22 March: 39.

Conklin, G.H. (1974) 'The extended family as an independent factor in social change: a case from India', *Journal of Marriage and the Family*, 36 (November): 798–804.

Kameswaran, L. (1985) 'Emerging patterns in the field of medical education and careers for women in South India', *Proceedings of the National Seminar on Education and Employment for Women in India*, Mother Teresa Women's University, Kodi, India.

Khanna, G. and Verghese, M.A. (1975) *Indian Women Today*. New Delhi: Vikas Publishing.

Khatri, A.A. (1975) 'The adaptive extended family in India today', *Journal of Marriage and the Family*, 37 (August): 633–42.

Kornhauser, A.W. (1965) *Mental Health of the Industrial Worker: A Detroit Study*. New York: Wiley.

Ramu, G.N. (1987) 'Indian husbands: their role perceptions and performance in single- and dual-earner families', *Journal of Marriage and the Family*, 49 (November): 903–15.

Rosenberg, M. (1965) *Society and the Adolescent Self-Image*. Princeton, N.J.: Princeton University Press.

Ross, A.D. (1961) *The Hindu Family in its Urban Setting*. Oxford: Oxford University Press.

Sekaran, U. (1982) 'An investigation of the career salience of men and women in dual-career families', *Journal of Vocational Behaviour*, 20: 111–19.

Sekaran, U. (1983) 'Factors influencing the quality of life in dual-career families', *Journal of Occupational Psychology*, 56: 161–74.

Sekaran, U. (1985) 'The paths to mental health: an exploratory study of husbands and wives in dual-career families', *Journal of Occupational Psychology*, 58: 129–37.

Sekaran, U. (1986) *Dual-Career Families: Contemporary Organizational and Counselling Issues*. San Francisco: Jossey-Bass.

Sekaran, U. and Hall, D.T. (1989) 'Asynchronism in dual-career and family linkages', in M.B. Arthur, D.T. Hall and B.S. Lawrence (eds), *Handbook of Career Theory*. Cambridge: Cambridge University Press, pp. 159–80.

Shukla, A. (1987) 'Decision making in single- and dual-career families in India', *Journal of Marriage and the Family*, 49 (August): 621–9.

Smith, P.C., Kendall L.M. and Hulin, C.L. (1969) *The Measurement of Satisfaction in Work and Retirement*. Chicago: Rand McNally.

Srinivas, M.N. (1978) *The Changing Position of Indian Women*. New Delhi: Oxford University Press.

Statistical Outline of India (1988) Tata Services, Department of Economics and Statistics, Bombay.

Touliatos, J. (1989) *Handbook of Family Measurement Techniques*. Newbury Park, California: Sage.

4
Dual-Earner Families in Singapore: Issues and Challenges

Edith C. Yuen and Vivien Lim

Women's participation in the Singapore economy has received considerable attention from social scientists, women's organizations and government policy-makers. They have produced a significant literature focusing on this theme, ranging from student reports and theses to reports by government organizations and task forces commissioned to look into ways of encouraging more women to take up paid employment (Pang, 1975; Wong, 1975, 1980; Lim, 1982; Chia, 1987; Yu-Foo, 1985; Teo, 1985). The influx of married women into the labor force in recent years has shifted interest to the problems faced by dual-earner families in general, and by women in dual-earner families in particular.

This chapter reviews a number of issues associated with dual-earner families in the Singapore context: marriage and birth rates, division of household labor and childcare. Government policies aimed at addressing problems relating to dual-earner families will also be discussed. The review is made against the background of the government's attempts to encourage women, especially married women, to enter and remain in the workforce and at the same time to reverse the declining birth rate by encouraging the better-educated women to marry and have children.

Traditional influences on the role of women in Singapore

The role of women in Singapore has been shaped by the immigrant history of its population. There are three main ethnic communities in Singapore – the Chinese (76 percent), Malay (15.2 percent) and Indian (6.5 percent). Together they account for 97.7 percent of the population (*Population Report*, 1988). Central to the religious and cultural traditions of these three ethnic communities was the belief that women are inherently weak, incapable of fending for themselves and dependent on men (Wong, 1975). The cultural emphasis on continuity of the male lineage, especially in the Chinese and Indian communities, reinforced the premium placed on the male members in society and resulted in the subjugation of the womenfolk. Women were discouraged from participating in economic activities outside the home. Malay women were relatively better off than their Chinese and Indian counterparts in that they were treated more generously according to traditional custom. The Malay woman had complete ownership rights over her own property (the property she brought into the marriage as well as that which she earned during the marriage) and on her husband's death, was entitled to one-fourth of his property unless there were children, in which case she would be entitled to inherit one-eighth of his property (Wong, 1975).[1] Like the Chinese and Indians, however, the Malays generally believe that the woman's position is subordinate to that of the man.

As a British colony, Singapore attained internal self-government in 1959 and independence in 1963 under the People's Action Party, which has been in power ever since. The government faced many problems in the mid-1960s: acute unemployment with declining entrepôt trade, a high rate of population growth (3.3 percent annually) and an underdeveloped manufacturing sector. The government embarked on a program of industrialization as a solution to these problems. At the same time it introduced a family planning program reinforced by disincentives to discourage large families. These included no maternity leave after the second child; income tax relief only up to the third child; higher accouchement fees for the fourth and subsequent children; and lower priority for admission to high-quality primary schools for the third and subsequent children (*Census of Population*, 1980). By the second half of the 1970s, with the successful implementation of the industrialization and family planning programs, the government faced the prospect of a tight labor market. Women were consequently encouraged to join the workforce, and from the early 1980s, to marry and have more children. In relation to the government's policy towards women and the family, two distinct phases can be identified. The first phase from the mid-1960s to the late 1970s was anti-natalist but the majority of women were homemakers. The second phase, from the early 1980s, was clearly pro-natalist while women were encouraged to participate in the labor force.

As the result of two and a half decades of economic, social and cultural change, the Singapore woman of today has come a long way since the time when she was considered her father's property before marriage, her husband's property after marriage and her son's property after her husband's death. The profound changes in the position of women in Singapore during this era did not evolve gradually. They were rather the result of deliberate government planning and the by-product of government policies in the single-minded pursuit of rapid economic growth and development.

Several factors facilitated women's increased presence in the labor market. Chief among these is the increase in the literacy rate and the educational attainment of the female population in Singapore resulting from a policy which now ensures equality of educational access for males and females. The government's successful industrialization program created a demand for labor. Improved education led to women's greater employability and gave them access to more rewarding jobs, thus increasing the attractiveness of paid employment outside the home. Labor laws were also amended to give women the right to equal treatment at work. The anti-natalist policy of the late 1960s and 1970s had led to a reduction in family size, making it more viable for women to take up paid employment outside the home. With industrialization and modernization, it has also become much more acceptable for women to work outside the home (according to the 1983 *National Survey on Married Women*, only 2.5 percent of married women stopped working because of objections from family members, mainly husbands and in-laws). Finally, the rise in the standard of living makes it 'necessary' for the women in the family to work in order to afford the many 'luxuries' which have become part and parcel of 'modern living'. Overall, the success in getting women into the workforce can be attributed partly to the exposure of the population to western ideas and partly to the carefully co-ordinated efforts of the government in different policy areas.

Patterns and characteristics of women's participation in the workforce

General patterns
Between 1973 and 1989, the number of employed women rose from 233,938 to 503,235 and their proportion of the labor force increased from 29.25 percent to 39.4 percent. The female labor force has a high proportion of young workers. Forty-nine percent are below 29 years old and 65 percent below 34 years (*Yearbook of Labor Statistics*, 1989). Female earnings are lower than male earnings. Comparing men and women with the same educational background (without controlling for experience or industry), Thomas (1986) found that women with less than secondary education earned only 66 percent of the men's pay and women with secondary education earned 72 percent. The gender gap for women is the greatest among those with university education – they earn only 60 percent of men's pay. For the occupational distribution of women in Singapore see Table 4.1.

Female labor force participation rate
The increase in the female labor force participation rates was not uniform across all ethnic groups. Whereas in 1980 female participation

Table 4.1   *Occupational distribution of women in Singapore, 1988*

Occupation	Total (men & women) (no.)	Women in occupation (%)	Distribution of labor force Female (%)	Male (%)
Professional, technical and related workers	152,409	39.00	12.23	12.01
Administrative, managerial and executive workers	97,668	24.44	4.88	9.58
Clerical and related workers	192,606	71.17	28.02	7.20
Sales	146,137	31.54	9.42	12.99
Services	162,925	54.64	18.19	9.59
Production, transport and related workers	454,955	29.17	27.12	41.83
Others (including not classifiable)	52,982	1.50	0.14	8.80
Total	1,259,682		100	100

Source: based on statistics from the *Yearbook of Labour Statistics* (1988)

rates were about the same for all ethnic groups (see Figure 4.1), in 1988 clear differences emerged (*Labour Force Survey*, 1988). The increase was greatest for Indian women (from 43 percent in 1980 to 51.7 percent in 1988), followed by the Chinese (from 44.6 percent in 1980 to 47.3 percent in 1988). The overall participation rate of Malay women, however, declined in that period from 45 percent to 43.4 percent despite increased participation rates for Malay women aged 35 and older. The decline was due mainly to delayed entry of younger women into the workforce as the result of prolonged education. Comparing the female labor force participation rate of the three different racial groups in 1980 and 1988, while the labor force participation rates of Indian and Chinese women declined more gradually in 1988 after peaking at the 20–24 age group, the pattern remained unchanged for the Malays. Malay women continue to leave the workforce after marriage in anticipation of a family or after child-bearing, a practice which like some other aspects of the Malay culture, remains relatively unchanged with industrialization and modernization.

As expected, the female labor force participation rate also varies with marital status. The participation rate of the married, divorced or widowed is half that of their never-married counterparts in almost every age group. Of 26,000 persons who left the workforce between June 1987 and June 1988, 68.6 percent were women (*Labour Force Survey*, 1987, 1988). Most cited family commitments after marriage as the main reason for leaving the labor force.

The participation rate of the women who are or have been married in

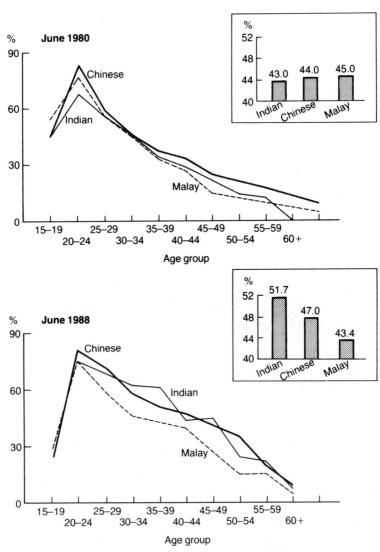

Figure 4.1   *Female labour force participation rate, by age and race,*
1980 and 1988 (Report on Labour Force Survey, 1988)

Singapore peaks at the age group 20–24 after which it declines, due to
marriage and child-rearing responsibilities (see Figure 4.2). The curve
does not show signs of picking up after that. The female labor force
participation curve of women in Singapore thus deviates from the
bi-modal or double-peak pattern found in most developed countries.

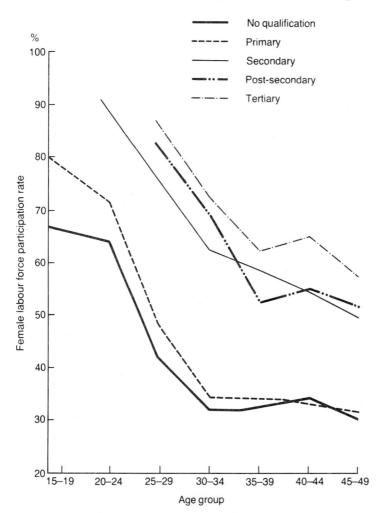

Figure 4.2 *Female labour force participation rate, by educational attainment, 1982 (Report on Labour Force Survey, 1988)*

There are three explanations for the absence of the bi-modal pattern: First, women's occupational opportunities are constrained by their need to work fewer hours. Secondly, Singaporean mothers are often involved in the education of their school-age children. The formal education system places great emphasis on examination results and is keenly competitive, making parental, especially maternal, involvement in children's education a common phenomenon. Thirdly, early retirement age (55 years for both men and women) coupled with the lack of opportunities for adult education are factors which may have discouraged married women from re-entering the workforce in their late thirties/early forties. In relation to the last explanation, it is interesting to note that the labor force participation rate of higher-educated women does not rebound at age 40–44 (see Figure 4.2).

With the large number of women leaving the workforce upon marriage and childbirth, government attention has shifted to policies to retain married women in the workforce and encouraging those who left to re-enter at a later stage. It is clear that neither issue can be addressed without due regard to the special issues and problems pertaining to dual-earner families.

Dual-earner families in Singapore

The following section focuses on three issues – life priorities of educated women, childcare, and the division of household labor. To a certain extent, the choice of the issues to be discussed was constrained by the availability of local data.

Life priorities of educated women

Higher educational attainment and better job opportunities have led to a shift in the life priorities of the better-educated women in Singapore who increasingly regard both marriage and career as important. The mean age at first marriage among brides increased over the years from 24.4 in 1978 to 26 in 1988 as a growing proportion of women postponed marriage, a trend especially evident among educated women. In 1988, 61 percent of university-educated women in the 25–29 age group and 38 percent in the 30–34 group remained single (*Population Report*, 1988). There is also an increasing tendency for more of them not to marry at all, either by choice or due to the difficulty educated women face in finding a suitable marriage partner.

Table 4.2 shows the percentage of resident females who remained single by age group and educational qualification in 1988. The proportion of never-married women among those with higher education in the 30–34 and 35–39 age groups reached almost 38 percent and 22 percent respectively in 1988, compared to 35 percent and 19 percent in 1987.

While the national fertility rate in Singapore fell below the 2-child family level to an average of 1.5 per family in 1985, the decrease was greatest among educated women. As shown in Table 4.3, the gross reproduction rates for women with upper secondary education and above are significantly lower than those with less education.

This trend has alarmed policy-makers who are concerned about a declining birth rate among educated women, believing that better-educated mothers are more likely to produce more intelligent children.

Table 4.2 *Percentage single among resident females, by age group, ethnic group and educational qualification, 1988*

Single[a]	20–24	25–29	30–34	35–39	40–44
Total (no.)	101,054	53,719	25,535	13,061	5,504
Total (%)	82.3	41.0	19.8	12.0	7.1
Chinese	86.4	43.9	20.8	12.6	7.3
Malays	68.2	27.8	12.9	9.3	5.8
Indians	74.8	39.0	21.3	10.7	4.2
No qualification	70.9	27.6	12.7	6.0	4.1
Primary	65.8	28.7	14.4	9.8	6.2
Secondary	85.1	45.1	24.4	17.6	13.1
Post-secondary	95.7	56.7	29.0	20.5	14.9
Tertiary	95.6	60.9	37.5	21.5	11.9

[a] The term single refers to those who have never married.

Source: Population Report (1988)

Table 4.3 *Mean number of children born alive to women who are or have been married, by ethnic group and highest qualification*

Highest qualification	Total	Chinese	Malays	Indians
Total	3.4	3.3	3.8	3.3
No qualification	4.4	4.3	4.9	4.5
Primary	2.3	2.3	2.4	2.7
Secondary and upper secondary	1.6	1.6	1.4	1.8
Tertiary	1.6	1.5	0.7	1.8

Source: *Census of Population* (1980)

In the words of the Prime Minister, if these trends are allowed to continue, 'Singapore will be a society with a lower level of performance' and 'the nature of our society will be altered' (*Straits Times*, 18 August 1986). In response to this trend, government ministers have made constant reminders in ministerial speeches targeted at the better-educated women to reconsider their priorities. At the same time, the virtues of married life and motherhood are extolled.

Childcare

In this section, we review childcare arrangements used by dual-earner families for pre-school children, noting differences across socio-economic strata.[2] The overall quality of local childcare arrangements is considered. This is followed by a discussion of the social perceptions of parental responsibility in relation to child development.

There are a number of distinctive characteristics of childcare practices among dual-earner families in Singapore. These include: the predominant reliance on relatives, especially grandparents for the provision of childcare; the use of foster care (day care as well as day-and-night care); the engagement of domestic maids and the limited use of child care/child development centres.

Relatives   Over 60 percent of the working mothers rely on their relatives for the care of the pre-school children (*National Survey on Working Mothers*, 1986). Grandparents are by far the most common caretakers, providing care to 50.8 percent of the first-born children of working mothers and 44.3 percent of second children. The heavy reliance on relatives, especially grandparents, can be explained by the fact that as many as 38.5 percent of the sample (n = 1,610) in this survey lived in extended families. Furthermore, with 86 percent of the population living in high-rise public housing estates (*Housing Development Board*, 1988), and with kin often residing in the same or neighboring estates, it is convenient to arrange childcare with non-working relatives.

Among the different childcare alternatives, surveys show care by relatives to be 'most preferred' by working couples, being the cheapest mode of childcare and considered by working mothers as highly reliable and convenient (Tee, 1988; *National Survey*, 1986). The use of relatives as providers of care for pre-school children is especially prevalent among younger age groups (*National Survey*, 1986). While dual-earner couples receive help in childcare from their parents, they in turn, when the time comes, have the responsibility of caring for their elderly parents. (See also Chabot, this volume.)

Foster care   There are two major forms of foster care: the child is either cared for by a 'foster mother' during the day and taken home by the parents after work or is under foster care for the week and taken home for the weekend. In the 1986 National Survey, roughly 18 percent of the working mothers reported using the foster care alternative. This was a decrease from the 25.8 percent reported in the 1984 *National Survey on Married Women*. While part of the difference may be due to sampling error, the decline may be due to a number of reasons. As alternative forms of childcare have become more available, the popularity of foster care has declined, especially among more educated mothers. Furthermore, with more women participating in the workforce, suitable foster mothers have become more difficult to find.

Foster care is used more often for very young children. Thirty-four percent of working mothers in a national survey reported using this type of arrangement for children below the age of 1 year. In the case of a first child, 83 percent of the parents who opted for this kind of arrangement confined it to day care. In the case of a second child, however, as many as 30 percent of the parents using foster care opted for day-and-night care, taking the child home only on weekends (*National Survey on Working Mothers*, 1986). The use of foster day-and-night care for very young children can be traced back to the traditional Chinese practice (among the well-to-do) of employing wet-nurses to breastfeed and care for infants.

The availability of foster care and its acceptability by the 'less westernized' sector of the society provide an important alternative for working couples who might otherwise find it difficult to cope with the dual demands of career and family. This may explain the more extensive use of day-and-night care in the case of a second child.

Domestic servants   While part-time local domestic helpers are commonly engaged for housework by the relatively well-off, live-in domestic servants for childcare cum housework services are provided mainly by women from the less developed neighbouring countries. In 1986, roughly 12 percent of working mothers engaged domestic maids (*National Survey*, 1986). As the employment of domestic maids is costlier than other forms of childcare, it is more commonly used among the more affluent, who also tend to be more educated. In 1983, as many as 45 percent of university graduates engaged maids (*Public Forum*, 1983) and the popularity of this alternative among those who can afford it has since increased.

As a childcare alternative, the use of domestic maids is rated the least satisfactory for a number of reasons: servants do not stay long; servants are from a different culture and may have language problems; they provide only custodial care and lack childcare experience (*National Survey*, 1986). Despite these drawbacks, the employment of domestic servants remains popular among the higher-income earners as, in addition to childcare, servants also help with housework.

Childcare centers   With care by the immediate family, by relatives, foster mothers and servants together accounting for almost 96 percent of the childcare arrangements made by working mothers, the use of childcare centers in Singapore is limited to only 4 percent (*National Survey*, 1986). The limited use of childcare centers may be attributed to the following factors.

Local childcare centers generally do not cater for children below the age of one. Once parents make satisfactory childcare arrangements, they are unlikely later to switch to other alternatives. Furthermore, the quality of the care in these centers to date has not been high, and children are considered more likely to catch infectious diseases than under home-based individual care.

In recent years, government bodies have encouraged the use of childcare centers in an effort to reduce dependence on foreign domestic servants and the social problems associated with foreign workers. Recent surveys suggest that childcare centers are gaining greater acceptance among educated working mothers, especially for children between the ages of 3 and 5. Parents rated childcare centers significantly higher in potential for child development: the development of better communication and socialization skills; the acquisition of greater independence and discipline (Tee, 1988); greater opportunity for learning, playing and interacting with peers (*Public Forum*, 1983) and formal classroom learning to prepare the child for school (*National Survey*, 1986). As the formal education system becomes increasingly competitive, the perceived advantages of childcare centers in skill and attitude development have become increasingly important in childcare decisions.

Childcare and parental responsibility

In Singapore the demands of childcare extend beyond the pre-school years. A system of qualifying examinations at the primary educational level and perceived parental responsibility for supervising their children's schoolwork extend the period of heavy parental involvement in their children to the age of 12. In the 1984 *National Survey on Married Women*, 85.9 percent of the respondents agreed that a woman who was not a breadwinner should sacrifice her career for 8–10 years so as to bring up her children properly, and 78.4 percent felt it essential for a working mother to stop working for 8–10 years in order to supervise her children's schoolwork. Two-thirds of the respondents reported checking their children's schoolwork regularly. Those who did not were mainly those who felt academically unable to do so. According to the same report, fewer mothers worked when their children were in the schooling age (31.5 percent) than in the pre-school period (39.3 percent), although this cannot be solely attributed to childcare. (Other reasons can be poor health as the women get older, and the need to care for aged parents and in-laws.)

Although the responsibility for childcare, especially physical care, still rests with the mother, Singaporean fathers participate actively in the development of their children. In *Public Forum* (1983), it was noted that more Singapore fathers were involved in childcare than before. In Tee's study, 47.2 percent of the fathers surveyed spent more than 3–4 hours daily with their children and an additional 19.4 percent spent five or more hours. In addition, 89.3 percent of the men and an even more surprising 91.6 percent of women reported that 'both spouses share equally in child care responsibility' (Tee, 1988).

While Tee's figures may have been inflated by sampling error due partly to small sample size and partly to the socio-economic background of the sample, other studies also report high paternal involvement in childcare. Chua (1990), found that fathers spent an average of 19.36 hours weekly with their children (compared with 31 hours spent by mothers). In the 1986 *National Survey on Working Mothers* it was found that 67.1 percent of fathers had moderate or high scores for engaging in activities with their children. Even among couples at the lower end of the socio-economic scale, most fathers were actively involved in the discipline and control of children (84 percent), taking children on outings (82 percent), care of children during illness (73 percent), taking children to the doctor or clinic (64 percent) and tutoring and supervising children's studies (48 percent) (Singapore Council of Women's Associations, 1989).[3] Women do, however, take more days off work to care for a sick child than do men. They are also more likely than men to feel guilty about 'neglecting' their children and to refuse a job promotion or transfer if it means less family time (Tee, 1988).

As for mothers' involvement in childcare, the 1986 survey showed that the amount of time the mother spent with children varies with her educational level. Among tertiary-educated mothers, 62 percent (and 58.3 percent of their husbands) scored high on 'engaging in activities with their children'. At the other end, only 18 percent of women with 'primary and below' education (and 14.5 percent of their husbands) scored high on this item.

Division of household labor

There is considerable gender inequality in the division of household labor. Men's participation in housework is significantly less than in childcare. In Singapore, yard work, car repairs and to a large extent general repairs, traditionally men's work in the west, are either not required, or performed by service agents. Only minor repairs and paying bills remain in the 'masculine' chore list. Women's employment does not produce an appreciable increase in the number of hours their husbands spend in housework. Chua (1990) found that, compared to 44 percent of husbands of non-working women who shared (or were involved) in marketing/shopping for food, cooking and household repairs, only 46 percent of husbands of working women shared these tasks. As for dishwashing and house cleaning, only 7 percent of dual-earner men shared this work. On the whole, working mothers spent 65 percent more time than their husbands on household chores.

On the average, working mothers spend over 15 hours a week on housework (Chua, 1990). However, the variance in hours spent on housework in Chua's study was considerable (s.d. = 11.4). The factor which best explains the variance is whether or not a family has the financial resources to engage a domestic servant. As educated women tend to earn more than other women and are also more likely to marry men who earn more, it is not surprising that the educational level of working mothers is negatively related to the amount of time spent on housework (*National Survey*, 1986). In the 1986 survey only 28.6 percent of the tertiary-educated mothers as compared to 71 percent of those with primary education or below and 59 percent of those with secondary education reported that they spent much time on housework.

In general, working mothers in Singapore seem to cope well with a support system comprising relatives, domestic servants, spouse and foster mothers. In response to a question on whether they 'felt nervous or under stress in the past three months', only 15.3 percent of the mothers (and 39.3 percent of the fathers) answered in the affirmative (Tee, 1988). The less educated lower-class employed mothers, however, spend more time on household work as they have less access to paid domestic help and their husbands share less in this area, although younger men are more likely to share in household work than older ones (Singapore Council of Women's Associations, 1989).

Policy responses to the problems of dual-earner families

Since the early 1980s, public policy has been geared to the seemingly contradictory policies of encouraging married women to re-enter and remain in the labor force and of increasing the population by encouraging more educated women to marry. This section discusses the policies introduced, in particular the maternity leave scheme, revised tax policy, the government's role in providing and regulating childcare facilities and the provision of part-time employment for working mothers.

Maternity and sick leave

The policy interventions introduced to enable more mothers to work outside the home address women's reproductive and nurturing functions. The law requires a mandatory eight weeks' maternity leave for married women with full pay for the first and second child. The cost is to be borne by employers. In the case of third and subsequent children, mothers are not eligible for paid maternity leave but are entitled to a $20,000 tax rebate in lieu of maternity leave – a policy which will be further discussed under 'tax incentives'.

In addition, since 1987, mothers (but not fathers) employed in the civil service have the option of unpaid leave of up to four years to look after their young children provided the leave is taken within the first four years after the birth of the child; this is subject to employer approval based on exigencies of service.[4] Working mothers in the civil service are also entitled to a full-pay unrecorded leave of five days for each child under six years old, up to a maximum of fifteen days per year, to attend to a sick child. Application of this leave, which has to be supported by a medical certificate, is not offset against the normal annual and sick leave to which the female employee is entitled (*Straits Times*, 7 March 1987). This scheme was adapted from a similar policy currently in practice in Germany. However, both the unpaid leave and leave to attend to sick children are confined to the public service (which in 1989 included 5 percent of the workforce in the civil service and a further 2 percent in the public education sector). In the private sector these benefits are not mandated by law and are seldom practiced.

Part-time employment

Part-time employment is not a new work arrangement in Singapore. In 1981, the Ministry of Labor introduced a Part-Time Employment Assistance Scheme which provided informational assistance to married women in their search for part-time jobs. The part-time job arrangement is not confined to women in lower levels of work. As part of the government's efforts to retain married women in the workforce, the arrangement was extended in 1987 to female employees in the civil service, regardless of their level of appointment. Under this scheme, mothers employed in the public sector can request to work part-time (with the options of working for half, two-thirds or three-quarters of the full-time working hours), for one year at a time, up to a maximum of three years, and enjoy the same benefits as full-time workers on a pro rata basis (*Straits Times*, 4 March 1989). The option is not available to working fathers. According to the 1988 report, the majority (74 percent) of the women who opted for part-time employment did so because of housework or childcare demands (*Labor Force Survey*, 1988).

In the private sector, although the part-time work arrangement is not mandated by law and its practice so far has been limited, there are signs that because of the tight labor market and the need to invest in training, employers are becoming more open to part-time employment for female workers. The trend is to consider each applicant by case depending on the needs of the organization and the performance of the employee.

Childcare

Although at present relatives provide an important source of childcare, the trend toward nuclear families is likely to result in parents having to assume greater responsibility for the care and upbringing of their children. In the long term, government intervention in providing formal childcare arrangements is crucial. The government's decision to be involved in this area is reflected in the passing of the Childcare Center Bill in January 1987, which provides for minimum standards in staffing and facilities at privately operated childcare centers. In 1990, there were about 113 childcare centers with 6,900 places. This is an improvement on the 33 centers which provided only about 2,000 places for children in 1982 (*Straits Times*, 5 March 1989). Most of these centers are government supported (with the exception of the childcare centers at workplaces) and regulated. The latest estimate shows that about 300 childcare centers with 20,000 places will be needed if Singapore wants to achieve a 50 percent female labour force participation rate by 1995 (*Straits Times*, 5 March 1989). Another attempt to entice more married women into the workforce is to convert the current half-day school sessions (both primary and secondary) to full-day sessions, a policy which was announced in September 1990 and is due for full implementation by the year 2000.

Tax incentives
Since the early 1980s, Singapore's income tax policy has been pro-natalist, and is especially aimed at persuading the better-educated, higher-income career women to have more children while at the same time dissuading them from leaving the workforce. A working mother who has attained at least five O-level passes or equivalent in one sitting may claim relief from her total taxable income, the amount of which is linked to the number of children she has as follows:

First child   – 5 percent of the mother's earned income;
Second child – 10 percent of the mother's earned income;
Third child   – 15 percent of the mother's earned income.
(The maximum relief for each child is limited to $10,000.)

In 1989 an additional tax incentive was introduced, which provides a $20,000 tax rebate each for the third and fourth child for the mother (and if the mother is not employed, for the father), regardless of the actual tax paid. The rebate is intended to be in lieu of paid maternity leave for third and fourth children. This tax incentive represents a direct reversal of the income tax policy of the anti-natalist era of the 1970s which neither allowed paid maternity leave nor tax deductions for the third and subsequent children born on or after 1 August 1973. While the earlier tax policy was intended as a deterrent to those who considered having large families, tax incentives introduced since 1982 were aimed at encouraging working women to have more children.

In 1989, a further tax holiday aimed at correcting the delayed child-bearing patterns of married women in Singapore was declared in a ministerial budget statement (*Straits Times*, 22 December 1989). As a result, women with post-secondary and tertiary education were encouraged to have their second child earlier through another package of procreation incentives. This includes additional tax rebates of:

$5,000 for families who have their second child before the mother reaches 31;
$10,000 before the mother reaches 30;
$15,000 before the mother reaches 29;
$20,000 before the mother reaches 28.

The rebates can be set against either or both of the parents' income tax liabilities within seven years (*Straits Times*, 22 December 1989).

Another variation of the tax incentive to encourage married women to continue working is income tax relief for foreign maids. While the government tried to slow down the overall demand for foreign workers by raising the foreign-maid levy from $170 per month in 1987 to $250 in 1990, married working women are allowed to deduct twice the annual levy for one foreign maid from their total taxable income. The main beneficiaries of this incentive are of course career women drawing high salaries, as their income tax rates tend to be high.

Tax policies in Singapore have come a long way since the days when the man was regarded as the family's only breadwinner. Women are now recognized for their earning power and the revisions in the tax policies in recent years are a step towards encouraging more married women to combine work with family responsibilities.

Conclusion

Looking back at the changes in the position and roles of women in the family and society in Singapore, two distinct features can be identified: the pace of change and the role of government interventions in effecting such changes. Changes relating to family size, the age of child-bearing, and the participation of the more educated women in the labor force were deliberately planned, implemented with extensive public education through the mass media, and reinforced by incentives and/or disincentives. So far, this change in strategy has proved to be very effective due to the nation's small size, and the existence of a strong government which has been in power since the founding of the nation-state two and a half decades ago.

Other peculiarities of the situation in Singapore include the emphasis on education, heavy parental involvement in children's education, restricted living space, which brings about closer interaction among family members, the existence of an extended family network, and the availability of domestic maids and foster care. Generally speaking, working mothers in Singapore have more support than their counterparts in the west. However, they also face more pressure, having to closely supervise their children's progress in the education system.

One of the disadvantages associated with changes being effected primarily through policies and the use of incentives or disincentives is that attitudinal changes often lag behind. For example, men's attitude towards sharing in housework remains largely unchanged. Ingenious though many of the policies are, there are behaviours and attitudes which can neither be mandated nor enforced through incentives and disincentives.

Notes

1. At present, Malays in Singapore come under Muslim inheritance law unless a person deliberately opts for civil inheritance law in his/her will. The rest of the population comes under the Wills Act and, in the absence of a will, the Intestate Succession Act, which allocates half of the property to the surviving spouse and the other half to the children of the deceased.

2. Four recent studies as well as a couple of earlier surveys provide the basis of the reconstruction of the Singapore scenario: Chua (1990); Singapore Council of Women's Associations (1989); *Married Women in Public Housing* (1989); Tee (1988); *National Survey on Working Mothers* (1986); *National Survey on Married Women* (1984); *Public Forum* (1983). Of these studies, the *National Survey on Working Mothers* (1986), the *National Survey on Married Women* (1984) and *Public Forum* (1983) involved a random sample, while Singapore Council of Women's Associations (1989) concentrated on the lower socio-economic strata (n = 810) and the studies by Tee (1988) (n = 36 males and 70 females) and Chua (1990) (n = 270) involved subjects from higher occupational and income groups. Most of the studies referred to define childcare as the care of children under the age of six.

3. One reason for the large amount of time parents spend with their children is living space. The great majority of the families live in flats which, by western standards, are relatively small. As a result, family members spend their evenings together, often in the same room.

4. 'Exigencies of service' means that while in principle approval will be given, leave can only be taken when a replacement is available or when the replacement is adequately trained to take over the job. On return, the employee will be given her original job although the tasks involved may be different.

References

Census of Population (1980) Singapore: Department of Statistics, Singapore Government.
Chia, Siow Yue (1987) 'Women in the Singapore economy', in *Women's Economic*

Participation in Asia and the Pacific, Bangkok: Economic and Social Commission for Asia and the Pacific.

Chua, Mun Yuen (1990) 'An investigation of a home/job goal model of working wives' convenience consumption patterns', academic exercise, Faculty of Business Administration, National University of Singapore.

Housing Development Board Annual Report (1988) Housing Development Board, Singapore Government.

[*Report on*] *Labour Force Survey* (1987, 1988) Ministry of Social Affairs, Singapore Government.

Lim, Linda (1982) 'Women in the Singapore economy', Occasional paper no. 5, Singapore Economic Research Centre, National University of Singapore. Singapore: Chopmen Publishers.

[*Report on*] *Married Women in Public Housing* (1989). Singapore Government.

[*Report on*] *National Survey on Married Women, their Role in the Family and Society* (1984) Ministry of Social Affairs, Singapore Government.

[*Report on*] *National Survey on Working Mothers* (1986) Research Section, Ministry of Community Development, Singapore Government.

Pang, Eng Fong (1975) 'Labour force growth, utilization and determinants in Singapore', unpublished monograph, Singapore Economic Research Center, National University of Singapore.

Population Report (1988) Ministry of Health, Singapore Government.

Public Forum on Married Women in the Workforce (1983) Ministry of Social Affairs, Singapore Government.

Singapore Council of Women's Organizations (1989) *Report on Survey of Married Women in Public Housing*. Singapore.

Survey on Married Women: Their Roles in the Family and Society (1983) Ministry of Social Affairs, Singapore Government.

Tee, Diane Wan Ping (1988) 'Executive guilt: a Singapore experience', academic exercise, School of Management, National University of Singapore.

Teo, Nancy (1985) 'Working women: their needs and contributions to society', *May Day Annual*: 79–81.

Thomas, Margaret (1986) 'Sex and salaries: the vital statistics', *Woman Now*, October: 32–5.

Wong, Aline (1975) *Women in Modern Singapore*. Singapore: University Education Press.

Wong, Aline (1980) *Economic Development and Women's Place: Women in Singapore*. London: Charge International Reports.

Yearbook of Labour Statistics (1989) Ministry of Labour, Singapore Government.

Yu-Foo, Yee Shoon (1985) 'Problems of working women and their needs', *Family Digest*, 1 (1): 46–9.

5
Sweden's Sex-Role Scheme and Commitment to Gender Equality

Karin Sandqvist

Sweden's ideological commitment to gender equality and its progressive social policy have attracted considerable research interest
(Adams and Winston, 1980; Andersson, 1989; Cochran, 1977; Cochran
and Gunnarsson, 1985; Dowd, 1989; Haas, 1981, 1982, 1987a, 1987b;
Intons-Peterson, 1988; Lamb and Levine, 1983; Moen, 1989; Popenoe,
1987). Most studies have examined the effects of these policies on
maternal and child welfare. Far less attention has been paid to the role
of the husband/father and the changing cultural concepts of manhood
and masculinity, which are important for an analysis of dual-earner
families. This chapter focuses on dual-earner families in Sweden,
emphasizing the role of manhood and the interplay of structure and
ideology in shaping gender roles. We begin with an analysis of the
emergence of an explicit ideological and policy commitment to gender
equality, and present some facts and figures concerning dual-earner
families in Sweden. Conflicting evidence is then reviewed on the
question of whether gender roles are disappearing in Sweden, in this
context. Possible reasons for the continuity of gender differences in
tasks and occupations, despite less pronounced differences in
personality in Sweden than elsewhere, are explored.

Development of the 'equality in the family' paradigm

'A wave of concern with sexism, sex discrimination, and the unequal
opportunities available to men and women swept the country in the
1960s with an intensity exceeding that manifest elsewhere in the world'
(Lamb and Levine, 1983). Why did this concern arise at the time it did?
There were a number of interrelated factors. The ruling Social
Democratic Party had from its formation in 1889 adopted 'equality' as
one of its tenets, including both class equality and gender equality,
although until 1960 class equality had been its prime concern. In
keeping with its Marxist ideological roots, the Party viewed the
achievement of equality and emancipation for women as depending on
their participation in paid employment. Rapid economic growth in the

early 1960s created a shortage of human resources, which forced industrial leaders to exploit the potential of women. The newly employed women, however, could not rely on hire of domestic help to replace them in the home. The successful struggle for class equality had made the bourgeois life-style, based on maids for domestic work, both ideologically unacceptable and economically unfeasible. Women writers and journalists brought women's dilemma to public attention and succeeded in placing it on the public agenda: if women were to work outside the home just as men do, who then would do the family work? And their answer was – fathers, just like mothers. In addition, good childcare services must be made available outside the home. In keeping with its overriding concern with equality, the dominant Social Democratic Party accepted this solution and incorporated these ideals into its political program.

It is important to note the simultaneous commitment to both class and gender equality underlying the Swedish realization that men's roles must also be changed. Rosanna Hertz (1986) has pointed out that in the United States women in high-level executive positions rely on a class of less privileged women for childcare and other family work. This dilemma was obvious to the Swedes in the 1960s, and the achievement of gender equality at the expense of retaining the class system was neither an acceptable nor a feasible solution.

Although well-educated women with leftist ideology were the most active in this debate, the new 'equal-roles family paradigm' appealed to values of fairness and equality widely shared by the Swedes. Generally, men are more conservative regarding gender role ideology than women. Nevertheless, in a national poll of men's attitudes in 1981 (Trost and Hultåker, 1983), a convincing majority of 70 percent wanted to change men's and women's roles, 'to make the roles similar'. Twenty-five percent held the conservative view that no change was needed. Very few selected the remaining alternatives of making 'women's roles more like men's' or vice versa. Consistent with these attitudes, the majority held that while it was better for young children to be cared for at home, it did not matter whether the caring parent was the father or the mother.

The new family paradigm prompted two important legal changes concerning family finances, both in effect by the mid-1970s. First, the separate assessment of husbands' and wives' incomes for tax purposes replaced the earlier system of joint assessment. The effect of this in a progressive tax system is that the lower income is taxed less. Consider the example of a husband who earns 100,000 Skr, his wife 50,000. Under joint taxation, the income is calculated to be 150,000 which, in a progressive tax system, results in the family entering a higher tax bracket. When we consider that child care costs are not tax deductible, the net gain for the family of the wife's paid work becomes negligible. In contrast, with individual taxation, the low income of 50,000 Skr is reduced very little by taxes, and the wife's work produces real income for the family. If childcare costs are avoided, for example by the mother working evenings or weekends when the father is at home, even a low income of 20,000 or even 5,000 will make a considerable difference in the family economy. On the other hand, if the father increases his earnings from 100,000 to 120,000 by working overtime, the extra 20,000 will result in a higher tax rate for him, and will not be as profitable for the family. Tax allowances for dependants and tax-deductible childcare costs have hardly been used in Sweden, which instead has relied on cash child allowances and subsidized childcare to supplement family earnings. (The tax system is, however, due to change somewhat in 1991 when it will become less progressive and therefore less punitive of income increases for the already well paid, a change prompted entirely by national economics.) A second change was that 'parental' insurance replaced the six-month paid 'maternity' leave following childbirth, and the benefit was extended to a whole year. Parents are able to divide the allotted time between them as they wish. Mothers use over 90 percent of the allotted days. Nevertheless, viewing the program from the perspective of families, 44 percent of married fathers take at least some parental leave, usually a month or two in the latter half of the leave period (Dunér and Halmeenmäki, 1990). The parental insurance scheme also covers leave to care for sick children under 12. Mothers and fathers use this privilege almost to the same extent (Sandqvist, 1987b).

Cohabitation among young couples without marriage became increasingly widespread in the 1960s. Almost all couples currently start out living together before marriage, and the arrival of children is only sometimes a reason for changing marital status (Hoem and Hoem, 1988). Most Swedes express no strong feelings either for or against marriage, see little difference between being legally married and cohabitation, and consider the very fact of living together as a reason to share the domestic economy and be responsible for one another, especially if there are children involved (Trost and Lewin, 1978; Hoem and Hoem, 1988). For simplicity, I will use the terms 'married' and 'divorce' as including the paperless marriages and their dissolution.

The equal-roles family paradigm maintains that both husband and wife should be equally responsible for earning money, both should have equal opportunities to pursue a career, and both should be equally responsible for household work and childcare. Since equal opportunities in paid employment requires availability for full-time work, childcare outside the home is necessary for the model to function. However, ever since the 1960s women engaged in the public discourse have been aware that full-time work for both parents puts excessive strain on the family. The ideal of making a reduced work-day (from eight to six hours) the norm for all employees, and especially for parents, is currently widely held. In 1979, parents of children under the age of 8 received the legal right to reduce their working day to six hours, with a corresponding reduction in pay, but otherwise retaining equal work rights and benefits. Practice however lags behind ideology and it is primarily women who reduce their time in paid work. The male-dominated Trade Union Confederation (LO), recently opted for a sixth week of vacation in its program (five weeks of vacation is now the legal minimum), instead of opting for a shorter work-day or even work-week. The six-hour day was treated as an ideal to be realized by an unspecified future date. The conservative and liberal political parties are less committed than the Social Democrats to basic changes in the family structure and the benefits of raising children 'collectively'. However, it is indicative of the ideological climate that 'mothers' or 'housewives' are rarely mentioned; instead the gender-neutral term 'parents' is used, even by opposition parties.

The success of the equal-roles family paradigm can be measured by changes in three areas: mothers' employment, the growth of childcare services, and the increase in fathers' involvement in family work. These are discussed below. Later sections of this chapter consider the complex interrelationships between the equal-roles family paradigm and gender roles in Sweden.

Mothers' and fathers' employment

The increase in mothers' employment (which is almost equivalent to an increase in dual-earner families), was motivated less by ideology than by family economy for many families. Two incomes are necessary to remain above the poverty line (Official Statistics of Sweden, 1982) for almost all Swedish families. Although a minority of individual families may be unhappy about the mother working outside the home (Forecasting information, 1984: 4) policy makers regard the dual-earner family as the 'norm'. For example, economic aid is not given to families with a full-time housewife, unless childcare is impossible to arrange.

Figure 5.1 illustrates the increase in employment of married mothers with children under the age of 7 since 1970. Even though the childcare problems and costs for this group often reduce the benefits of paid work, almost 80 percent are employed. This figure includes 17 percent on paid parental leave. For mothers of older children, the employment rate is even higher.

The increase in female labor force participation has occurred mainly

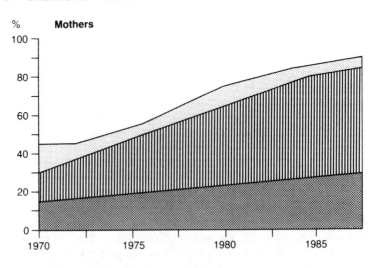

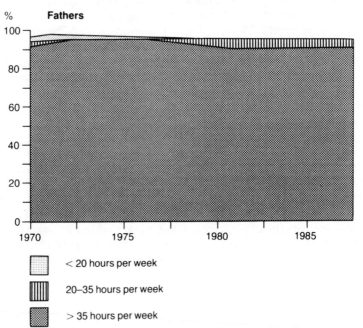

Figure 5.1   *Employment of married mothers and fathers with children under 7 (based on unpublished data, Statistics Sweden)*

for mothers of young children employed between 20 and 35 hours per week, often called 'long part-time' in Sweden. Long part-time work carries the same fringe benefits and job security provisions as full-time work. In some economic sectors, parents are able to choose the extent of their reduction in work-time quite easily and increase their work involvement when their children become less dependent, a benefit used far more often by women than by men. Long part-time is roughly equivalent to a six-hour day – the ideal level of work involvement according to the 'equal-roles' family paradigm.

Although working-class women generally experience greater economic need to find employment, educated women are more likely to be employed, and also to work longer hours (Forecasting information, 1983: 4; Sandqvist, 1987a). This may be partly due to the especially strong commitment to the equal-roles paradigm among the middle class and to the fact that educated women view their work as more interesting than the less educated (Forecasting information, 1984: 4). Economic factors are also important however, especially for women aspiring to a middle-class lifestyle, with their own house (rather than an apartment). In addition, the cost of working full time is low, as educated mothers working office hours tend to use day-care centers for childcare and the charges for this remain the same regardless of actual care time. In contrast, less educated mothers often work evenings and weekends and thus avoid childcare costs, but find it difficult to extend their hours to full time.

The labor force participation rates for fathers of children under the age of 7 has not changed in the last twenty years, with about 95 percent of fathers working full-time over the whole period. The number of househusbands is negligible. However, studies using more sensitive measures of work involvement indicate some reduction in work involvement by fathers of young children, even those officially working full time. For instance Sandqvist (1987a) found an average difference of two working hours per week between fathers with preschoolers and those with children over 6; Lundén-Jacoby and Näsman (1989) found fathers who changed jobs to be able to spend more time with their children; and Haas (1987b) reported that fathers who had taken parental leave worked slightly shorter hours after going back to work than other fathers, all of which might be an indication of future change.

Childcare

According to the most recent childcare survey (Statistics Sweden, 1990), 49 percent of the under 7-year-olds are regularly cared for by centers and day-care mothers organized by the municipality (see Figure 5.2). Centers dominate in urban settings. Parents pay the municipality, not the center or the day-care mother, and the system is heavily subsidized by local and national government. The demand for

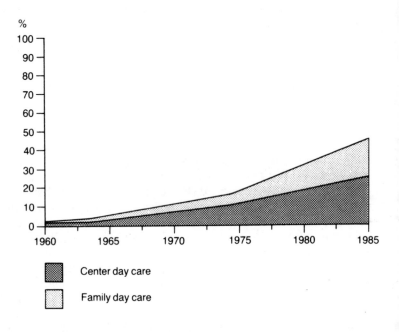

Figure 5.2   *Percentage of fathers at least 'helping out' in municipal day care in Sweden (Statistics Sweden, 1990)*

these services has constantly been greater than the supply, despite their very rapid expansion.

The discrepancy between the 80 percent figure for dual-earner families and the lower 40 percent figure for children cared for in municipal care is due to several factors. (1) 'Day-care mothers' look after their own children while employed. This is one way for mothers to combine earning money with staying at home. Most day-care mothers are employed by the municipality (county), and are therefore eligible for social security, vacations and parental benefits and considered 'employed'. According to the *Child Care Survey* (Statistics Sweden, 1990), 4 percent of children under 7 were cared for by their own mother who was employed as a day-care mother. (2) Seventeen percent of the mothers classified as 'employed' in Figure 5.1 are actually on parental leave following childbirth (Statistics Sweden, 1987). (3) Some parents arrange their work schedules so that each works different hours or on different days. This arrangement means that the father regularly cares for the child while the mother works part time. It also means night or weekend work for one of the parents, an arrangement that prohibits long business trips for either parent. (4) Six percent of children are regularly cared for by 'privately paid day care', which usually means a privately paid day-care mother. (5) Only 2–3 percent of children under 7 receive 'unpaid non-parental care', which usually means a grandmother, or two neighbouring mothers who take turns in part-time paid work and looking after the children.

Publicly organized childcare is the only viable solution for dual-earner families, where both parents have full-time employment. Thus, professional and middle-class families are overrepresented in center care. Centers are usually open from 6.30 a.m. to 6.00 p.m., Monday to Friday. Consequently fathers with career wives can technically continue playing their traditional role, not taking increased responsibility for their children. In practice, however, such a situation is rare, and dual-career couples typically share the tasks of bringing and fetching children to and from the center. In addition, they stagger their work-hours to keep their children's day at the center as short as possible (Lundén-Jacoby and Näsman, 1989).

Fathers and family work

An overview of research in different countries (Western Europe and the USA), shows a surprisingly stable pattern of father participation in different housework tasks. Participation is greatest in shopping, particularly non-food shopping, and dish-washing, less in housecleaning, even less in cooking, and least in laundry and particularly ironing. Fathers who iron are rare gems (Sandqvist, 1987a). Figure 5.3 shows the increase in Swedish fathers' participation in washing dishes and cooking between 1957 and 1981. This information is based on three different surveys conducted in 1957, 1975 and 1981, using slightly different methods. Unfortunately, no recent figures are available. A new survey is scheduled for 1991. Clearly, however, Swedish fathers have become more involved in family work, whether we consider fathers in general, or fathers with wives in full-time employment who (not surprisingly) have a higher level of involvement than other men. However, just as clearly, in 1981 most of the housekeeping work was still performed by mothers. If the number of fathers doing at least half of the work in 1977 and 1981 had been shown in the tables, the percentages participating in each task would have been considerably lower.

In addition to this quantitative research there are several recent, independent, qualitative studies all showing modern fathers to be greatly involved in family work and taking much more responsibility for the care of their young children than men in earlier studies (Åström, 1990; Lundén-Jacoby and Näsman, 1989; William-Olsson, 1990). A trend towards more father involvement in family work has

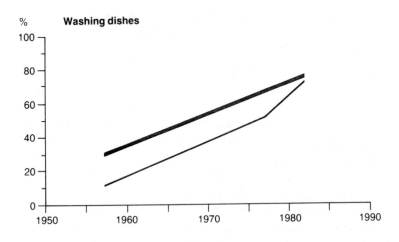

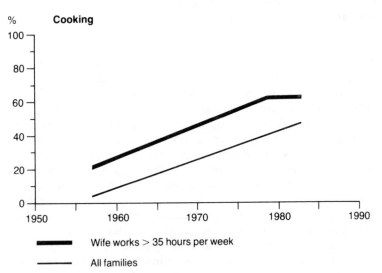

Figure 5.3   *Fathers' participation in selected household tasks (based on Boalt, 1961; Official Statistics of Sweden, 1981; Statistics Sweden, 1982: 2)*

also been documented elsewhere, for example in Denmark and the USA (Andersen, 1988; Pleck, 1985), especially younger American fathers, although to a less extent than in Sweden (Sandqvist, 1987a).

Are gender roles disappearing in Sweden?

Several studies suggest that gender roles are less clearly differentiated in Sweden than elsewhere.

Hofstede (1980) conducted a study of employees in 40 subsidiaries of a single multinational corporation around the world. Although conducted in the context of business management, it provides a rare opportunity to view the Swedes in a cross-cultural comparative context. Four dimensions of cultural differences emerged from the study. The most relevant for this discussion is 'masculinity', on which Sweden scored the lowest of the 40 countries (other Scandinavian countries also scored low). Only responses by men were used for cross-cultural comparisons in this dimension, so Swedish men can be said to be relatively more 'feminine' than men in other countries. An examination of the contents of the 'masculinity' items reveals that the Swedish men were relatively indifferent to certain rewards from work, such as earnings, recognition, advancement and challenge while valuing good relations with the manager and cooperation. While one might object to the gender stereotyping of the characteristics, Hofstede concludes that gender roles are disappearing in Sweden (and neighboring countries), especially since a sub-sample of Swedish women were equally or more 'masculine' than the Swedish men.

Block (1973) studied conceptions of gender roles in six countries: the USA, England, Sweden, Denmark, Finland and Norway. Using descriptions of ideal self with a Q-sort technique, she found that the self-descriptions of Swedish (and Danish) male and female youths were less sex-differentiated than those of youths from other countries. In this study, 'agency' (assertiveness or dominance) and 'communion' (relatedness or affiliation) were the dimensions underlying the masculine/feminine distinction. For Sweden, only one agentic trait, 'practical/shrewd', and one communal trait, 'generous', differentiated between the sexes in the expected directions. For the USA, there were many more: six agentic and two communal traits differentiated between the sexes.

Intons-Peterson (1988) carried out parallel studies of gender concepts of young people in Sweden and in the USA, in 1983. Against the backdrop of the gender equality ideology prevalent in Sweden since the 1960s, her research inquired whether Swedes perceive the two sexes as more similar than do Americans and whether the concept of gender differs in the two countries. Based on data collected from 11–14 and 18-year-olds in both countries (a total of 950 subjects), her general answer to both questions was 'yes, somewhat'.

In both countries, the male role was more valued than the female role but this was less pronounced in Sweden. The Swedish girls felt markedly better about their gender than did the American girls, which was evident when writing stories on the theme of suddenly becoming a person of the opposite sex. Swedish men and boys showed less interest in developing self-esteem than Americans, while valuing 'feminine' attributes, such as cooperation, more. From this study, Swedish men and women appear quite similar in their value orientations.

Gender roles are as strong in Sweden as in other places

Now we shall consider evidence to the contrary, namely, that gender roles are just as sharply differentiated in Sweden as in the USA. Intons-Peterson (1988: 169) found a major country difference in future plans regarding occupational choices among her 18-year-old subjects. In Sweden, the ideal occupations were highly gender segregated with women interested in service occupations, such as flight attendant, hospital work and children's caretaker, and men in business-oriented occupations, such as technician, computer operator, engineer, and owning their own business. The choice of ideal occupations by American youths was less gender differentiated, with both females and males listing doctor, dentist, attorney and chief executive officer of their own business among their top choices.

A study by the author (Sandqvist, 1987a) showed that housework is

Table 5.1   *Division of labor in household tasks in Sweden and USA*

	Mean score	
Task	Sweden ($n = 75$)	USA ($n = 73$)
Car maintenance	4.7	4.6
Household repairs	4.5	4.4
Gardening	3.3	3.1
Managing family budget	3.3	3.0
Shopping and errands	2.6	2.5
Window washing	2.1	2.6
Washing dishes	2.3	2.0
Cooking	2.0	1.7
Picking up after people	1.9	1.9
Sweeping and dusting	1.9	1.6
Scrubbing floors	1.4	1.6
Washing clothes	1.4	1.5
Ironing	1.2	1.4
Mending	1.2	1.4

Combined fathers' and mothers' responses.

Scale: 1 = only mother does task; 3 = equal share; 5 = only father does task

Source: adapted from Sandqvist (1987a)

similarly gender segregated. Table 5.1 provides a comparison of the division of labor between Swedish and American couples matched for social class, urbanity and age of child. However, a greater proportion of Swedish than of American mothers were employed. From the table, we observe first that most household tasks are performed predominantly by either fathers or mothers; and secondly that the division of labour for each task across countries was similar, with a Pearson correlation of 0.98 for the 14 task scores between the two samples.

At the extremes, car maintenance and household repairs on the male side, and ironing and laundry on the female side, there is no indication of a less sex-typed division of labor in Sweden than in the USA. Thus, although Swedish fathers' involvement in housework has increased in recent decades, as in other countries, task-division is still as sex-typed as in American families. In terms of types of careers and occupations, there is also little evidence of change.

Masculinity and femininity – personality or learned skills?

Studies that show less differentiation between the sexes in Sweden than in other countries tend to treat 'masculinity' and 'femininity' as personality traits or value orientations. Studies that show equal differentiation tend to focus on differences in terms of task performance or occupations.

Researchers studying personality differences often assume that the observed relative absence of such gender differences is a modern phenomenon resulting from Sweden's conscious gender equality ideology. However, there is no direct evidence that such change has occurred. Rather, it can be argued that the lack of differentiation in the realm of personality is deeply rooted in Sweden's cultural tradition. The Swedish distinction between 'masculinity' and 'femininity' lies more in the realm of task domains, interests and areas of expertise, than in the realm of values and personality structure.

Because both personality traits and task assignments often differ between male and female, they are frequently combined in gender concepts. There is often an implicit assumption that caretaking tasks and caring, altruistic personality traits or values necessarily 'go together'.

Certainly there are good reasons for task assignments and personality traits to harmonize in cultural definitions of gender roles, but there is still a certain degree of freedom for variation. A finding from comparative research on fathers will illustrate this point. Observations of parent–child interactions have revealed Swedish fathers not to engage in the exciting, gross motor play, for example hoisting children in the air, which is very typical of American fathers

(Lamb et al., 1983). Such daring excitement could well be a fatherly expression of what has been termed a 'give 'em hell' personality dimension of manliness, which is strong in American culture (David and Brannon, 1976), but rare in Sweden. Thus, although both American and Swedish fathers are quite competent in the 'feminine' task of caring for infants, their performance of the task is differently colored by personality.

Similarly, a quite direct piece of evidence that Swedes tend to see sex roles as a matter of learned tasks and domains of expertise rather than as inborn personality types or sets of rights and duties emerges from a Swedish study based on responses to change-of-sex stories. The difficulty of suddenly becoming a person of the 'other' sex was attributed to having spent many years in learning the skills of a 'first' sex (Intons-Peterson, 1988).

Gender role behavior is an important ingredient in parental roles. The family system of western industrialized culture expects fathers to be 'instrumental' (or 'demanding') and mothers to be 'expressive' (or 'nurturant') in relation to their children (Parsons and Bales, 1985). However, in a Swedish study conducted in the 1950s (Kälvesten and Meldahl, 1974) only 54 percent of mothers and as many as 37 percent of fathers were judged to have an 'expressive' or 'nurturant' role. In other words, some mothers were more 'instrumental' than the fathers in the family. In this study, the classification of parental roles was based on the emotional relationship with the boy (no girls were studied), not on the performance of household tasks. Although the difference between the male and female parents was clearly in the expected direction, the study shows an extensive overlap in fathers' and mothers' relationship to their children even before the 1960s (when the modern equality family paradigm emerged).

Valuing women and femininity

In Sweden women tend to be regarded as persons who have special and valuable contributions to make to society rather than trivialized as sexual playmates for men. Although some Swedes may deny that there are specialized roles for either sex and claim that women can do men's work, and vice versa, it is taken for granted that 'women's work' is serious business and necessary for society.

Intons-Peterson (1988) noted 'contradictory' findings when she studied gender concepts of Swedish youths, especially in respect to the young women's attitudes. On the one hand, the Swedish young women viewed their lives as women in a more favorable light than their American counterparts; on the other hand, they were less ambitious in their occupational choices. However, in the context of the Swedish cultural definition of sex roles, the findings are not contradictory. For the young women desiring to become a 'childcare worker' or 'hospital nurse' these labels do not stand for demeaning 'service occupations', but for becoming a valued expert in caring for others. This is reflected in women's wages. Although these are lower, on average, than men's, the gender gap is much narrower in Sweden than elsewhere (Illich, 1982; Ståhlberg, 1991).

A stronger valuation of 'feminine' attributes such as 'gentle', 'cooperative' and 'helpful' as important attributes on the part of both sexes has been found in Sweden, compared to the USA (Intons-Peterson, 1988).

Older sources also convey a picture of girls being brought up to be useful rather than pretty and entertaining. The children's author Astrid Lindgren, born in 1907, describes how her mother, a farmer's wife, never reprimanded her daughter for tearing or dirtying her clothes when playing, but definitely taught all her children strict work habits (Lindgren, 1975). Her father had a very kind and warm personality, although he was still a well-respected and competent man who was good at leading the work of farm-hands.

Of course, there are many sources stressing the importance of women's work in agricultural settings (Cowan, 1983; Ehrenreich and English, 1979; Gaunt, 1983; Illich, 1982), but in Sweden not even the bourgeoisie seems to have allowed women much vanity. An analysis of child-rearing advice in the prestigious women's magazine *Idun* at the turn of the century reveals the values and concerns of the educated class (Gleichmann, 1989). Writers often deplored the habit of keeping girls indoors; girls as well as boys need to build up physical strength. Self-control and self-restraint were considered very important for both sexes. For girls, it was important to guard against their tendency to become vain and frivolous instead of good and pure. Indeed, women telling of their childhood in this milieu very often remember having been told they were not pretty, but that this did not matter because 'inner beauty' (i.e. moral qualities) was more important (Åström, 1987).

Boys were viewed as energetic and vital; their most serious fault was domineering tendencies (Swedish: *härskarfasoner*). Here mothers had to walk a thin line between bringing up a tyrant and injuring male pride. The recommended solution was a rather close mother–son relationship: mothers should encourage manly responsibility by confiding in their sons and asking about their views, but not accept displays of selfishness or dominance (Gleichmann, 1989).

Although there were large differences between life in the middle class and the agrarian community, we can note parallels in the concepts of femininity and masculinity in the early literature. Girls were not regarded as particularly frail. Morality and practical skills were emphasized more than looks and frivolous pleasures. Male authority was recognized, but openly dominant behavior was frowned upon by middle-class mothers, and mild men suffered no disrespect in the rural community.

The Swedish mentality

The personality of Swedish men and women can be approached from yet another angle: from the viewpoint of 'national character' or 'mentality' (Daun, 1989). Although Hofstede (1980) found Swedish men to be relatively unconcerned with earnings and advancement as rewards from work, and to value good relations with people at work, this should not be taken to mean that Swedes are sociable and easygoing. In fact, available evidence shows the opposite, and Swedes have often been described as shy, unsociable and gloomy (Daun, 1989).

There are many explanations as to why Hofstede's questionnaires found Swedish male employees not to be strongly motivated by 'male' work rewards such as earnings, recognition, advancement and challenge. First, work and responsible competence are very important in Swedish culture, so much so that many Swedes would feel they should do their job even in the absence of external rewards. 'The puritan Lutheran world view is restrictive. Pleasure is allowed but mainly in forms of short breaks or ways of regaining strength needed for work. "Too much" pleasure gives rise to guilt feelings' (Daun, 1989: 263).

Secondly, the social structure of Sweden has not favoured a 'get-ahead spirit'. 'Wordly and spiritual authorities have asked for moderation and retiring manners: remember your smallness!' (Daun, 1989: 265). Thus, the Swedish work ethic demands excellence at work, but not outdoing other workers. Competition and individualism are not stressed. Hofstede's study also found Swedes to score lower on 'individualism' (vs. 'collectivism') than Americans. Since competitiveness and individualism are so often equated with 'masculinity', Swedish men appear less 'masculine' in this respect.

One reason why Swedish men value good relations with the manager and co-workers (a characteristic scored as 'feminine') is probably related to the very strong Swedish trait of conflict avoidance. 'Swedes tend to strongly favor agreement and consensus' (Daun, 1989: 257). Of course, conflict avoidance is not easily combined with aggressiveness, another personality trait that many cultures define as 'masculine'.

Another typical trait of the Swedish national character is an emphasis on reason and control of feelings. Here, Swedish ideals come close to the masculinity dimension which has been termed 'Sturdy

Oak', also characterized by 'toughness, confidence and self-reliance (David and Brannon, 1976: 12). 'Stands up under pressure' is a trait which Swedish young men considered important (Intons-Peterson, 1988). The emphasis on rationality, control, endurance and personal independence in the Swedish value system means that these personality traits are not restricted to men, but also characterize Swedish women.

So there are many aspects of the Swedish value system related to the 'ideal personality' which combine to allow Swedish men to deviate from some definitions of 'masculinity', and Swedish women to deviate from some definitions of 'femininity'. In terms of personality, Swedish traditional culture tends to define an 'ideal person' rather than an 'ideal man' and 'ideal woman'.

In terms of tasks and domains of competence and expertise, the situation is more ambiguous. In their conscious ideals, modern Swedes encourage both men and women to learn the tasks traditionally performed by the opposite sex. For example, girls and boys both have to learn sewing and woodwork in school. At a more basic and subconscious level, traditional concepts of 'masculinity' and 'femininity' still exert a powerful influence. When teenagers select their subject of study and reflect on their future careers (which may be more deeply related to identity and ideology than are daily, practical tasks in the home), we find a conventional pattern emerging. Girls study humanities and boys study technology, women work with people and men work with objects (Statistics Sweden, 1987).

Traditional values and modern equality

Looking back over history, we find a recurrent theme of hard-working women in Sweden. Structural changes since the 1960s, such as municipal childcare and progressive taxation, have supported mothers' paid work. These changes were motivated by ideology (reinforced by a labor shortage at the time). The issue I have raised here is whether this ideology is new or traditional.

The fact that women's work is now performed in formal work settings is perhaps less a break with tradition than a continuation of a deep-rooted appreciation of women's work adapted to modern forms. It can even be argued that day-care centers also continue an old tradition of more privileged women using other women to care for their children while they engage in more status-enhancing pursuits.

Yet there are other aspects of the modern Swedish family structure and family life which are less easily reconciled with old patterns. Particularly significant is modern fathers' strong interest in having an intimate relationship with their children.

Thus, within the family, there is evidence for a movement towards equal roles in parental behavior. This is consistent with the 'equal-roles paradigm' and with Sweden's ideological and policy commitment to gender equality. Within the workplace there is less evidence of equal roles, because men and women do different work. There is, however, some evidence that equal value is attached to these different roles.

References

Adams, C.T. and Winston, K.T. (1980) *Mothers at Work. Public Policies in the United States, Sweden, & China.* New York: Longman.

Andersen, D. (1988) *Danskernes Dagligdag 1987* [The Danes' Daily Life in 1987]. Bind 1. Socialforskningsinstituttet. Rapport 88:4 Copenhagen.

Andersson, B.-E. (1989) 'Effects of public day-care: a longitudinal study', *Child Development*, 60: 857–66.

Åström, L. (1987) *I kvinnoled* [In Women's Line]. Stockholm: Liber.

Åström, L. (1990) 'Fäder och söner' [Fathers and sons], in K. Sandqvist (ed.), *Fäders Familjeliv* [Fathers' Family Life]. Stockholm: Stockholm Institute of Education. pp. 10–15.

Block, J.H. (1973) 'Conceptions of sex roles: some cross-cultural and longitudinal perspectives', *American Psychologist*, 28: 512–26.

Boalt, C. (1961) '1000 husmödrar om hemarbetet'. [1000 housewives on household work]. *Konsumentinstitutet meddelar*. Stockholm: Konsumentinstitutet.

Cochran, M. (1977) 'A comparison of group day-care and family child-rearing patterns in Sweden', *Child Development*, 48: 702–7.

Cochran, M. and Gunnarsson, L. (1985) 'A follow-up study of group day-care and family-based child rearing patterns', *Journal of Marriage and the Family*, 47: 297–309.

Cowan, R.S. (1983) *More Work for Mother. The Ironies of Household Technology from the Open Hearth to the Microwave.* New York: Basic Books.

Daun, Å (1989) *Svensk Mentalitet. Ett jämförande perspektiv* [Swedish Mentality. A Comparative Perspective]. Stockholm, Rabén & Sjögren.

David, D. and Brannon, R. (1976) *The Forty-nine Percent Majority: The Male Sex Role.* Reading, MA: Addison-Wesley.

Dowd, N.E. (1989) 'Envisioning work and family: a critical perspective on international models', *Harvard Journal on Legislation*, 26: 311–48.

Dunér, B. and Halmeenmäki, V. (1990) 'Uttag av föräldrapenning under barnets första levnadsår' [Usage of parental leave during the child's first year], *Riksförsäkringsverket informerar*, Statistikinformation Is, 1: 16.

Ehrenreich, B. and English, D. (1979) *For Her Own Good. 150 Years of Experts' Advice to Women.* London: Pluto.

Forecasting information (1983: 4) *Work and Children. Employment Patterns among Women in the Childbearing Ages.* Stockholm: Statistics Sweden.

Forecasting information (1984: 4) *Children – But How Many? Interviews with Women about Children, Family and Work.* Stockholm: Statistics Sweden.

Gaunt, D. (1983) *Familjeliv i Norden* [Family Life in Scandinavia]. Malmö: Gidlunds.

Gleichmann, L. (1989) *Böra barn lyda? Uppfostringsråd i Idun Praktisk Veckotidning för Qvinnan och Hemmet 1888–1926* [Should Children Obey? Child-rearing Advice in *Idun. Practical Weekly Magazine for Woman and Home*, 1888–1926]. Uppsala: Stockholm Institute of Education, Department of Educational Research.

Haas, L. (1981) 'Domestic role sharing in Sweden', *Journal of Marriage and the Family*, 43: 957–67.

Haas, L. (1982) 'Parental sharing of child care tasks in Sweden', *Journal of Family Issues*, 3 (3): 389–412.

Haas, L. (1987a) *Fathers' Participation in Parental Leave* (Social change in Sweden, no. 37). Stockholm: Swedish Information Service.

Haas, L. (1987b) 'The effects of fathers' participation in parental leave on sexual equality in the family', in *Nordic Intimate Couples – Love, Children and Work*. Stockholm: JÄMFO.

Hertz, R. (1986) *More Equal than Others. Women and Men in Dual-Career Marriages.* Berkeley: University of California Press.

Hoem, B. and Hoem, J. (1988) 'The Swedish family: aspects of contemporary development', *Journal of Family Issues*, 9(3): 397–424.

Hofstede, Geert (1980) *Culture's Consequences: International Differences in Work-related Values.* London: Sage.

Illich, I. (1982) *Gender.* New York: Pantheon Books.

Intons-Peterson, M.J. (1988) *Gender Concepts of Swedish and American Youth.* Hillsdale, NJ: Lawrence Erlbaum.

Kälvesten, A.L. and Meldahl, G. (1974) *217 Stockholmsfamiljer* [217 Stockholm Families]. Stockholm: Tiden.

Lamb, M.E. and Levine, J. A. (1983) 'The Swedish parental insurance policy: an experiment in social engineering', in M.E. Lamb and A. Sagi (eds), *Fatherhood and Family Policy.* Hillsdale, NJ: Lawrence Erlbaum.

Lamb, M.E., Frodi, A.M., Hwang, C.P. and Frodi, M. (1983) 'Effects of paternal involvement on infant preferences on fathers and mothers', *Child Development*, 54: 450–9.

Lindgren, A. (1975) *Samuel August från Sevedstorp och Hanna i Hult* [Samuel August from Sevedstorp and Hanna in Hult]. Stockholm: Rabén och Sjögren.

Lundén-Jacoby, A. and Näsman, E. (1989) *Mamma, pappa, jobb. Föräldrar och barn om arbetets villkor* [Mummy, Daddy, Job. Parents and children on the Impact of Work]. Stockholm: Arbetslivcentrum.

Moen, P. (1989) *Working Parents. Transformations in Gender Roles and Public Policies in Sweden.* Madison: University of Wisconsin Press.

Official Statistics of Sweden (1981) *On Children's Living Conditions.* Living Conditions Report 1981: 21.

Official Statistics of Sweden (1982) *Perspectives of Swedish Welfare in 1982.* Living Conditions Report 1982: 33.

Parsons, T. and Bales, R.F. (1955) *Family Socialization and Interaction Process.* Glencoe: Ill: The Free Press.

Pleck, J. (1985) *Working Wives/Working Husbands.* Beverly Hills: Sage.

Popenoe, D. (1987) 'Beyond the nuclear family: a statistical portrait of the changing family in Sweden', *Journal of Marriage and the Family*, 49: 173–83.

Sandqvist, K. (1987a) *Fathers and Family Work in Two Cultures. Antecedents and Concomitants of Fathers' Participation in Child Care and Household Work.* Stockholm: Almqvist & Wiksell International.

Sandqvist, K. (1987b) 'Swedish family policy and attempts to change paternal roles', in C. Lewis and M. O'Brien (eds), *Reassessing Fatherhood: New Observations on Fathers and the Modern Family*, pp. 144–60. London: Sage.

Ståhlberg, A.C. (1991) 'Kvinnor och statistik om socialförsäkringar' [Women and statistics about social insurance], in *Mannen som Norm i Statistiken?* (Man as the Norm in Statistics?). Stockholm: Delegationen för Jämställdhetsforskning (Delegation for Equality Research). Report 20.

98 Dual-Earner Families

Statistics Sweden (1982) *Tabellbilaga till kvinnor och barn* [Table Appendix] 1982:2. Stockholm: Statistics Sweden.

Statistics Sweden (1987) *På tal om kvinnor och män: Lathund om jämställdhet* [Speaking of Women and Men: numbers about Gender Equality]. Stockholm: Statistics Sweden.

Statistics Sweden (1990) *Child Care Survey 1990*. Stockholm: Statistics Sweden.

Trost, J. and Hultåker, Ö. (1983) 'Undersökning av mäns asikter om hem, arbete och ekonomi' [A study of men's views on home, work and economy], in L. Jalmert (ed.), *Om svenska mån. Fostran, ideal och vardagsliv*. Stockholm: Arbetsmarknadsdepartementet.

Trost, J. and Lewin, B. (1978) *Att sambo och att gifta sig* [To Cohabit and to Marry]. Stockholm: Justitiedepartementet.

William-Olsson, I. (1990) 'Frånskilda fäder' [Divorced fathers], in K. Sandqvist (ed.), *Fäders Familjeliv* [Fathers' Family Life]. Stockholm: Stockholm Institute of Education. pp. 37–42.

6
Dual-Earner Families in Hungary: Past, Present and Future Perspectives

Christine Clason

In communist Hungary full-time employment was both a right and an obligation for every adult. The role of the male as main breadwinner became virtually extinct and household work and childcare at home were considerably reduced. These changes transformed the dual-earner couple pattern all at once into the ideological norm and the basis for societal organization, thereby creating an enforced experiment in social change (Berend and Ránki, 1985; Clason, 1977; Szalai, 1989).

The change in Hungary from a feudal, still largely agricultural country into an industrialized agricultural state was accomplished under a double-pronged repression – of Russia over Hungary and of communists over others – causing thorough disruption of both the family and the total societal structure (Szalai, 1989). The state enforced a complete change in the division of labor and demanded equality for men and women. In analyzing the communist experiment in Hungary I will consider whether the far-reaching forced changes succeeded in fostering permanent structural changes in line with the aspired objectives, or whether they hampered natural change, causing people to cling to old norms and values.[1]

In order to understand the impact of the communist experiment in Hungary on gender roles it is first necessary to examine the historical context. This chapter presents a short outline of the developments in Hungary between 1944 and 1989, that is from the time of its transformation into a communist-Russian satellite to the regaining of political independence and the rejection of communism. The development of the dual-earner family in Hungary is discussed in this context.

Pre-communist Hungary

The organization of Hungarian society before the Russian occupation in 1944 was based on the patriarchal family and its kinship relations. It was an accepted norm that wives took an active part in wage-earning for the family when it was economically necessary for them to do so. The husband, however, always remained the ruling head of the family.

'Career' was seen primarily in terms of a validation of an ascribed high status, based on one's lineage and birth. Careers involved the attainment of increasingly more prominent positions in the public domain. The higher positions in public life were not open to women.

The end of the war in 1945 found the country looted, impoverished, in a state of extreme social and political turmoil and occupied by foreign troops. From 1945 to 1948 Hungary became a one-party communist state.

From the recasting into a communist-Stalinist society to the suppression of the 1956 revolution (1948–57)

At the beginning of communist rule steps were taken to create a 'People's Republic'. A number of these steps are of direct relevance to the dual-earner family (Ferge, 1979; Kolosi, 1989; Kulcsar, 1984; Szalai, 1989). All those belonging to the so-called 'capitalist class' or considered to be 'intellectuals' along with their relatives, including children, were no longer considered full citizens ('comrades') with the same rights and duties as others. This meant deprivation, and in many cases deportation, imprisonment, hard labor or even death. To be considered of working-class origin was a prerequisite for acceptance in society. Combined with party membership, it provided probable access to opportunities. All forms of private property and independent entrepreneurship were eliminated. Employment became state employment, also known as 'the socialist sector'.[2] The new wage system was based on four principles. First, the individual was the basic unit of the wage system and of its complementary rights, such as the old-age pension and medical insurance. Secondly, wages were kept at a low level and largely undifferentiated. Thirdly, all individuals employed by the state were entitled to additional payment in kind such as housing, a place for one's children in the nursery, kindergarten and vacation camps, meals in the canteen, holidays in the vacation resorts of the firm, and sports facilities. Fourthly, differentiation among workers was achieved by the differential quality of working conditions and benefits. For example the vacation resorts of a governmental ministry had better locations and more facilities than those of a teacher's organization, party members had better-quality facilities than non-party members and officials in higher positions had better facilities than those in lower positions.

The transition to the communist-Stalinist order was abrupt. All previously acquired rights of pensioners, widows and others were annulled. A system of childcare facilities and household services was developed to replace the services rendered by the private household. The economy was restructured towards the main goal of rapid industrialization with an emphasis on heavy industry. All industry and services were organized in mammoth centralized structures controlled by the party.[3] A system was developed to secure complete control of assignment to education and jobs. The number of people allocated to each form and level of education and occupation was determined according to gender, social origin, region and party membership. This system also determined where an individual would be employed, in what capacity and with what opportunities for the future. An attempt was made to achieve full equality for men and women through the employment of women on the same terms as men.

In addition to the explicitly stated ideological goals of creating a socialist society, the modernization of society, equality between the sexes and the struggle against poverty, the new rulers also had more implicit goals, which they pursued with even more fervor. The main goal of this hidden 'Marxist-Leninist' agenda was to control the population, to indoctrinate people in the new teachings and to ensure that they lived according to these dictates (Gadourek, 1953). It was therefore important to leave people as little time as possible to spend at home or with their family, relatives and friends. Full, and full-time, employment of married women, combined with long working hours, were intended to limit the influence of the family. The caring of children in state facilities and schools was also meant to reduce the influence of parents. Activities were organized through the place of employment and through schools, to ensure continuous supervision and control of adults and children alike.

Despite this hidden agenda the new rulers remained ensnared by many of the old values internalized during childhood. Inconsistency between the new goals and old values, as well as limited resources, gave rise to a number of different problems. Whereas women were forced to do the same manual work in heavy industries as men and to take over work traditionally considered men's work in agriculture and services, men did not enter traditional women's domains. On the one hand biological differences between the sexes were disregarded to the extreme. For instance, few provisions were made for pregnancy and childbirth. On the other hand women were pensioned five years earlier than men. The apparent premise was that these retired women would assist their children in the household and help care for grandchildren. As state childcare facilities and household services were inadequate, families had to provide additional care. This remained the responsibility of women. In practice this restricted women's occupational opportunities, although full-time employment remained obligatory.

The reluctant transition (1957–68)

In 1948 Hungarians had accepted the situation with resignation. In 1956 the population arose in general revolt, rejecting Russian rule and defending their freedom in a full-fledged war with the Russian Army. The first years following this crushed revolution were years of great repression, terror and despair. Apathy set in.

The oppression became gradually more tolerable when Party Secretary Kádar formally issued his famous order 'Whoever is not against us, is with us' (Kolosi, 1989). Prior to this, repression had been based on the doctrine that everyone not explicitly in favour of the regime, as well as every individual belonging to the 'capitalist class' or to the 'intellectuals', was suspect and not protected by regular law. With Kádar's words this became: whoever is not explicitly against us, we will leave alone. This was a precedent in the communist world.

To prevent further revolt it was also considered necessary to improve the standard of living of the population. To this end some degree of social and economic decentralization was allowed. The reforms were very modest and half-hearted but culminated in 1968 in what at that time seemed a revolutionary new program: the 'New Economic Mechanism' (Berend and Ránki, 1985).[4] The reforms offered women new opportunities to find employment near to home. New social legislation on family and employment was also introduced (Ferge, 1979; Szalai, 1989). A declining demand for workers in certain sectors, which threatened the realization of the basic Marxist principle of full employment, combined with a low birthrate and frequent abortions, the high costs of state childcare and household services to foster the introduction of this new legislation (Berend and Ránki, 1985; Ferge, 1986). The measures aimed to raise the birthrate and make motherhood and employment more compatible. The legislation, which was extremely progressive for its time, included the prohibition of work potentially endangering women's reproductive capacities, both health and job protection during pregnancy and paid maternity leave set at 20 weeks. It provided for a variety of material supports such as better housing for parents, diapers and clothes for the new infant, a guaranteed number of paid and unpaid extra days' leave per month while children were young and additional leave to care for sick children. Two other measures were quite unique: the right of the wife to a new job of comparable nature and level if her husband had to relocate (*A Dolgozó Nö*, 1964), and the childcare grant introduced in 1967 (Ferge, 1979). This grant guaranteed a mother the right to stay at home until her child reached the age of 4, with the maintenance of her job and a fixed minimal income. Hungary was the pioneer country in paying women to stay at home to care for children, with a guaranteed job on their return, but the income was so small that it was not a realistic option for most families at its introduction. All these rights were for women only. While easing women's burden they reduced opportunities for women in the labor market.[5] Segregation of jobs on the basis of gender increased. The content of a woman's job became secondary to the possibilities it afforded her to combine household work and caring with employment. Public provision of care for the elderly was sparse and of poor quality and so eldercare too became the responsibility of female relatives. The dual-earner family remained the norm, but gender roles were accentuated.

Increasingly, higher occupational positions became attainable through achievement and competence rather than on the basis of political reliability alone (Berend and Ránki, 1985; Ferge, 1979). There was thus the potential for couples to pursue a dual-career lifestyle. The career of the husband retained priority, however, and his prospects for success remained much greater.

Experimentation within Marxist-Leninist boundaries (1968–89)

Although the general standard of living gradually improved after 1968, goods and services remained scarce (Kolosi, 1989). Practically from the beginning of communist rule, individuals began bartering and earning extra money by privately using the resources, such as power, products, raw materials, tools and machines, to which their jobs provided access. These practices, which became increasingly widespread, were gradually accepted as the 'second economy' (Andorka et al., 1990; Horváth and Sziráczki, 1989; Sas, 1984, Spéder, 1990) and were ultimately fully legalized. The second economy encompassed the total society. To be excluded from bartering in the second economy meant dire poverty. Since 1982 it has been possible to work a full day as a state employee, and then continue at *the same place using the same machinery and material and often doing the same work* as a partner in an official, semi-private firm. The extra work is not overtime work.[6] The small, official, semi-private company was set up legally with a number of colleagues and with full consent and help of the employer and the state. That 'firm' negotiated the work to be done, the period of delivery, the money and other conditions with its own 'employer' (Gábor, 1989). The outcome was an official contract. The productivity of these 'firms' was much higher and the quality of the work much better than that achieved by the 'mother' company during the regular working hours.

The labor market situation of the 'first economy' continuously deteriorated. A formal shortage of labor existed, but at the same time there was a large degree of underemployment. Women were gradually allowed to take part-time state employment, or to provide paid childcare for others or take on other paid work at home while at home receiving the formal childcare grant. In this way redundant workers of the first economy were transferred to the second economy (Andorka et al., 1990; Horváth and Sziráczki, 1989). There were no real incentives to work when 'at work', that is, in one's first-economy job. People reserved their energies for their second or even third job, or for work at home. Producing goods and services in their own household and/or agricultural plot became more profitable for women, as more and increasingly better materials and tools became available (Ferge, 1979, 1986).[7] A woman's first and her second jobs were primarily chosen for the opportunities they afforded to remain at home or close to home. Men thus had more opportunities in choosing their jobs in the first as well as in the second economy.

While the dual-earner family pattern remained dominant throughout this period (Andorka et al., 1990; Hungarian Central Statistical Office, 1990), its content changed drastically. The childcare grant, described earlier, turned out to be a successful labor market device, particularly after it officially allowed women to become active in the second economy. In 1985 another form of childcare leave, the childcare allowance, was introduced, guaranteeing women 75 percent of their last salary and job security for two years after childbirth. This measure was attractive for highly educated women with more interesting jobs, who would not use the childcare grant. In 1988 one of every ten women employed was on childcare leave (Andorka et al., 1990). Although both kinds of leave are now open to fathers as well as mothers, only 0.1 percent of all parents taking any form of childcare leave in 1988 were men. Maternal rights have been changed to parental rights, but men and women seem to disregard this as irrelevant. Children and household are considered women's responsibility. The consensus on this seems absolute in Hungary.

The woman is responsible for childcare and increasingly also for all other services expected of a full-time housewife. She has at the same time a job in the 'socialist sector'. Her husband tries to maximize his income and other resources by finding an optimum combination of jobs in the first and second economy. His primary responsibility is that of the provider. The general rule appears to be that both man and woman save their energy during the long hours of their state job in order to be able to pursue their second income-generating or money-saving activities.[8] The result is that the actual number of hours that men spend away from home has been continuously enlarged. The husband is often away up to 16 hours a day or more.

A relatively new development is that couples pursuing an upwardly mobile dual-career lifestyle are becoming a significant minority. Three varieties of 'dual-career' families exist. In the first, the husband pursues a career, the wife has a job. In the second both partners appear to pursue careers, but the wife will relinquish hers if the husband becomes successful. In the third the couple attempt to determine the optimum combination of jobs in the first and second economy in order to reach the best possible position (status and income) as a couple. Hiring a female relative or housekeeper, making the wife's tasks at home more supervisory, becomes more common. The husband's career almost always retains priority.

Looking to the future

The situation in Hungary at the time of writing is diffuse, inconsistent and in flux. Changes are occurring in rapid succession, but the necessary adaptations are not keeping pace with these changes. Since the 1960s the rigid system whereby the party assigned and controlled educational and job mobility has gradually been discarded. Until recently, however, a minimum of job security was guaranteed. This is no longer the case and the threat of unemployment looms. Women are particularly vulnerable. They are concentrated in certain sectors of employment, where the pay and work conditions are poor. Moreover, much of the women's sector is characterized by underemployment, lack of modern machinery and techniques, inefficiency and unnecessary bureaucracy. In the new situation therefore many of the women's jobs are even less secure than men's work.

Steps are being taken to merge the first and second economies. These steps tend to overemphasize the male-dominated market side of the economy, while neglecting the redistributive function of the state in which women play a larger role (Ferge, 1989).

Three additional factors increase hardship and insecurity for dual-earner families and further curtail women's opportunities in the labour market. Prices which had been kept artificially low, especially for basic goods and services, are now rapidly rising to western levels and the impact is aggravated by high inflation. Prior to 1988 income tax was negligible and applied only to first-economy wages. Now a progressive income tax has been introduced, which applies to income in both economies. Formal wages and pensions have been increased to compensate, but not income in the second economy. Men, who have higher earning potential and employment opportunities in both economies, are less severely affected by the new taxation than women. Thirdly, people who are not fully employed in the first economy (mainly women, with low incomes) are no longer automatically covered by health insurance. As women are most affected by the new health insurance regulations, couples are further encouraged to prioritize the husband's job(s). People thus tend to cling to the security of state employment. Only 3–5 percent of all active earners are not state employed, but 75 percent of all families are somehow involved in the second economy (Kolosi, 1989). The dual-earner family pattern remains the norm, but a growing minority of families is of the 'husband sole earner' variety.

In the context of these changes people are retreating into old roles and patterns of behavior. Men's primary engagement remains paid work. Increasingly women will be employed only when necessary or if they so desire. The process, started in the 1970s, whereby childcare once again becomes the sole responsibility of the mother, continues. Public childcare facilities are already decreasing in number and becoming expensive. Other facilities, such as the provision of meals through schools and the workplace, are also becoming less numerous and more expensive. Women are retreating into earlier forms of motherhood and into the old roles of supporting partner, voluntary worker and complementary earner. In general this is accomplished in an atmosphere of relief by women, especially young women who were, of necessity raised by employed mothers.[9]

Hungary is currently more traditional than western countries in regard to gender roles (values, norms, expectations and behaviour). This trend of returning to pre-communist forms of gender roles and division of labor is the more remarkable because the developments in Hungary since 1956 have been unique among the communist states in Eastern Europe in allowing a greater freedom and more experimentation with employment. Also the so-called 'capitalists and intellectuals' have been gradually reincorporated in society, giving the society more innovative power. Conditions since the mid-1960s seemed more conducive to the development of 'modern' family patterns and gender roles than in those countries where full communist repression lasted longer. However, the extremity of the original repression after World War II, and of the suppression of the Revolution in 1956, may have resulted in a stronger attachment to traditional roles and values, perhaps as an unconscious manifestation of rebellion.[10]

It is always dangerous to speculate about future developments, and especially so in times of rapid change. However, in view of Hungary's past and current experiences and the present situation (Andorka et al., 1990; Tóth and Gábor, 1989) it seems likely that the regression to old forms will continue during the period of continuing socio-economic transition. Later a process of readjustment may set in. The employment of women and division of labor within dual-earner families could then begin to take on new forms.

Notes

1. Two contrasting hypotheses are: (1) that enforcement will lead through habituation to acceptance and internalization, followed by change in traditional values and norms; (2) that enforcement will lead to resistance, no acceptance nor internalization will take place, no change of traditional values and norms will take place.

2. Without a formal job, that is, within the 'socialist sector' or first economy, one could not become a citizen with full rights to benefits, pensions, places at childcare facilities and so on (Szalai, 1989).

3. 'Party' always refers to the Communist Party, although the formal name has been changed several times.

4. It created at the time a sensation in all of the European Communist People's Republics, and even in 1988 still formed an example of change for the leaders and economists in the USSR.

5. Although the working of the labor market was very limited and people did not have to worry about getting a job, there was fierce and often harsh competition on all levels for the 'better' jobs. The inequalities within the 'classless socialist society' have been the subject of many discussions. See for example Ferge (1979, 1986).

6. One is not paid a wage, nor bound by the customary protection of employees such as regulation of the number of working hours, certain standards of working conditions. The reason why employers used the new economic legislation was twofold: (1) many state firms could not meet the goals required by the 'Central Economic Plan'; (2) one could not hire new regular labor, or give them higher wages or pay for overtime, because the so-called 'wage fund' was no longer automatically raised by the state.

7. For example, to make clothes one needs materials and a sewing machine.

8. Time budget studies reveal that 34 percent of paid working time is not spent at the first economy or state job (Kolosi, 1989). In this figure the data on the 'secondary-economy' activities of mothers on childcare leave are not included.

9. In many private talks middle-aged, highly educated women, dedicated to their jobs but by no means 'feminists' in western terms, express their disbelief in this complete return to the patterns of their grandmothers.

10. This outcome supports hypothesis (2) (see note 1) that, due to the lack of internalization of the new enforced norms and behavior, there will be a tendency to return to old norms and behavior patterns.

References

A Dolgozó Nö (1964) [The Working Woman; a booklet by the government to inform the working woman of her new rights]. Budapest.

Andorka, Rudolf, Kolosi, Tamás and Vukovich, György (eds) (1990) *Társadalmi Riport*. Budapest: Tarki.

Berend, I.T. and Ránki, G. (1985) *The Hungarian Economy in the Twentieth Century*. London and Sydney: Croom Helm.

Clason, Christine (1977) *Beroepsarbeid door gehuwde vrouwen* [Employment of Married Women; with English summary]. Groningen: RUG.

Ferge, Zsuzsa (1979) *A Society in the Making. Hungarian Social and Societal Policy 1945-75*. Harmondsworth, Middlesex: Penguin.

Ferge, Zsuzsa (1986) 'The varying rhythm of women's situation in Hungary', paper presented at Symposium on 'Work, Family and Social Planning' Budapest.

Ferge, Zsuzsa (1989) 'Chances of social policy: is social policy needed and for what?' in Tóth and Gábor (eds), pp. 23–33.

Gábor, István (1989) 'Main issues and major trends of government employment and wage policies', in András Tóth and László Gábor (eds), *Flexibility and Rigidity in the Labour Market in Hungary*. ILO Research Series 90. Geneva: International Labour Organization.

Gadourek, Ivan (1953) *The Political Control of Czechoslovakia*. Leiden: Stenfort Kroese.

Horváth, Tamás and Sziráczki, György (eds) (1989) *Flexibility and Rigidity in the Labour Market in Hungary*. Geneva: ILO Research Series 90.

Hungarian Central Statistical Office (1990) *Statistical Yearbook 1988*. Budapest: Central Statistical Office.

Kolosi, Tamás (1989) 'The prospects facing us', in Tóth and Gábor (eds), pp. 9–23.

Kulcsár, Kalman (1984) *Contemporary Hungarian Society*. Budapest: Corvina Kiadó.

Sas, Judith (1984) *Changes in the Life Patterns of Families in Hungary*. Vienna, Vienna Centre Current Research Reports.

Spéder, Zoltan (1990) *Haushaltsproduktion und Versorgungsstrategien der Haushalte*. Budapest: Universität für Ökonomie.

Szalai, Júlia (1989) 'Social crisis and the alternatives for reform', in Tóth and Gábor (eds), pp. 33–53.

Tóth, András and Gábor, László (eds) (1989) *Hungary under the Reform (Sociological Studies)*. Budapest: Research Review.

PART TWO

IN THE FAMILY

7
British Households after Maternity Leave

Julia Brannen and Peter Moss

This chapter is about employed mothers with very young children living in dual-earner households – in Britain in the early and mid-1980s. The date is important. The late 1980s brought some substantial changes, and we conclude the chapter by considering the nature and extent of these changes, as well as the underlying continuities in the situation of employed mothers in the 1990s.

Britain in the early 1980s had a distinctive pattern of employment for women – high levels among women before childbirth and for older women whose children were at school or grown up, but low levels for women with 'pre-school' children (which in Britain means under 5) (OECD, 1988). The post-war years had seen an increasing trend for women to take jobs between pregnancies, but the predominant pattern remained for women to leave full-time work on giving birth to the first child, and then to resume employment on a permanent basis only when all their children were established at school. Less than 10 percent resumed full-time employment within 6 months of having a first child and even fewer, less than 5 percent, remained permanently in the labour market throughout their childbearing years (Martin and Roberts, 1984). The 'typical' woman, as a result of childbearing, lost 7–8 years of full-time employment (Joshi, 1987).

The other distinguishing feature was the predominance of part-time employment. Part-time employment is high, by international standards, among women workers in Britain. In the early 1980s, most mothers with pre-school children who were employed had a part-time job and most of these part-time workers were employed for very short hours (less than 16 hours a week) (Martin and Roberts, 1984). Many of these part-timers worked evenings or weekends, 'fitting in' their jobs at times when partners or relatives were around to provide care for their children.

This distinctive employment pattern reflects, to a large degree, labour market forces. Women were not needed in large numbers in the post-war labour force, at least not to work full time. At the same time, employers, and particularly employers in the service sector, recognized the benefits of employing part-timers such as women with children, and especially women with young children. These women provided a ready supply of labour for these part-time jobs, as they were prepared to accept the poor quality of most of these jobs in return for the opportunity of local work with 'flexible hours'.

But other factors played a part in women's position in the labour force. There was strong, underlying ideological opposition to women with young children being employed; such behaviour was considered harmful to children and not something that was compatible with 'good motherhood'. This position was stated by the government immediately *after* the war, during which acute labour shortages had forced a recognition of the need to attract such women into the labour force. With that imperative removed, 'the Ministers concerned' signalled a return to pre-war normality: '[We] accept the view ... that the proper place for a child under 2 is at home with his mother ... the right policy to pursue would be positively to discourage mothers of young children under two from going out to work' (Ministry of Health Circular 221/45).

This position was re-stated in a Ministry of Health Circular (37/68) of 1968: 'Wherever possible the younger pre-school child should be at home with the mother ... because early and prolonged separation from the mother is detrimental to the child.'

Opinion polls showed that there was widespread agreement with this official view. In a national survey in 1965, 78 percent of women agreed with the view that mothers of pre-school children 'ought to stay at home', while most of the remainder (15 percent) thought they 'should only go out to work if [they] really need the money' (Hunt, 1968). The 'good mother' therefore was clearly one who stayed at home while her children were young, just as the 'good father' was defined in terms of his ability to maintain steady full-time employment and his bread-winning capacity. Moreover, and paradoxically, although the growth of technology and consumerism lifted some of the material burdens attached to being a mother, this did not necessarily create new space and opportunities for women to follow other activities, such as paid work. Instead, the tasks of motherhood have expanded, rather than contracted, placing new demands on mothers and especially with respect to ensuring the emotional and psychological development of children (Chodorow, 1978; Schutze, 1988).

Hostility to the idea of 'working mothers' has its roots in two assumptions. First, it has been widely believed that young children

MANCHESTER POLYTECHNIC

Director Sir Kenneth Green MA

Faculty of Community Studies and Education
Department of Psychology and Speech Pathology
Elizabeth Gaskell
Hathersage Road
Manchester M13 0JA

Telephone 061-247 2556
(direct line)

Facsimile 061-257 3024

with compliments

If the direct line number given above is not obtainable, please telephone the Polytechnic exchange on 061-247 2000

Dear Mike,

Hope you enjoy the loot. I also enclose a poster about the conference. The reason it is so inexpensive is that Julia has ESRC funding to cover most of the expenses. She will be sending material to Carol shortly. Thanks for your help.

Sue

(under 3s in particular) need full-time parental care and would be adversely affected by regular non-parental care. While never substantiated by research, this belief has found widespread support among various health and welfare professionals; in both the 1945 and 1968 government circulars referred to above, reference was made to medical and other experts to justify the assertions made about the preferability of avoiding daycare. Secondly, it has been widely assumed that mothers are primarily responsible for the care and upbringing of children – hence, for 'parental' care read 'maternal' care.

These assumptions have influenced post-war daycare policy, under successive Labour and Conservative governments. This policy has emphasized that government has no responsibility for providing daycare for children if it is required because of their parents' employment; instead, public daycare is only justified for children with special needs or with parents who are unable to provide them with adequate care. As a consequence, public daycare has become essentially a social work resource, for children with problems or parents who are failing to cope. The corollary of believing that mothers should not go out to work has been to leave those who insisted on doing so to their own devices; certainly, government has not seen it as its role to encourage such 'perverse, even harmful', behaviour. The government-appointed committee which, in 1966, proposed a major expansion of nursery education, reflected this view when it emphasized that nursery education was not to be seen as a service to support women who wished to go out to work; not only was this implicit in their advocacy of part-time nursery schooling, but it was also made explicit in their discussion of who should benefit from the limited amount of full-time schooling that they recommended.

> The extent to which mothers of young children should be encouraged by the provision of full-time nursery places to go to work raises a question of principle. Our evidence is that it is undesirable, except to prevent a greater evil, to separate mother and child for a whole day in the nursery. We do not believe that full-time nursery places should be provided even for children who might tolerate separation without harm, except for exceptionally good reasons. Some mothers who are not obliged to work may work full-time, regardless of their child's welfare. It is no business of the education service to encourage these mothers to do so. (Central Advisory Council for Education, 1966)

Opposition to the idea of mothers with young children working remains strong in sections of the Conservative Party (and other political parties). However, from the beginning, the Thatcher government of the 1980s rejected the provision of public support for working 'parents' not on moralistic grounds, but in terms of the boundaries between public and private responsibility. Whether or not, as many believed, Conservative ministers wanted mothers in the home, what they said was quite different. They referred usually to 'parents', masking the question of gender, and put forward the view that whether 'parents' went out to work or not was a private matter; government had no interest or responsibility, and any provisions such as childcare were for parents or employers to arrange.

This response on daycare must be seen as part of a wider discourse, which has viewed the family as a private domain, and the care of children as a purely private matter; in a country where, in Margaret Thatcher's words, 'there is no such thing as society', the having of children is regarded as a private decision, the consequences of which must be borne by the individual parents involved. Resistance to any direct involvement by government has been further reinforced by the government's strong commitment to reduce the role and expenditure of government and to let market forces operate – a position that appears incompatible either with funding daycare services or introducing new statutory employment rights for parents.

In sum, therefore, a long-standing reluctance by post-war governments to become involved in daycare provision and other types of support for employed parents, which was based for most of the post-war period on ideologies about good motherhood and the needs of children, has been sustained through the 1980s on the basis of neo-liberal economic and welfare ideologies. In view of this background, it is perhaps not surprising to find that Britain provides less public support for employed mothers than almost any other country in Europe. The only existing legislative measure to support employed parents, passed in 1975 and then only after substantial opposition within Parliament and from employers (Fonda, 1976), is statutory maternity leave; however, so stringent are the qualifying conditions attached that many women are not eligible, while only six weeks of the leave period is covered by earnings-related benefit. Otherwise there is nothing – no paternity leave, no parental leave (the British government having played a major role in vetoing an EC initiative to establish minimum standards throughout the European Community), no leave to care for sick children, and no publicly funded childcare for working parents. Working mothers, or fathers, must rely on family or friends (and relatives remain the main form of childcare used by working parents), their employers or else turn to the private market to seek a place with a childminder or in a nursery or, perhaps, hire a nanny.

For women contemplating resuming employment after maternity leave in Britain in the early 1980s, the ideological and policy context was hostile and unsupportive. This is the context in which the study, described below, was set.

The study

In this chapter we have drawn upon data from a longitudinal study conducted in the first half of the 1980s. It covers several aspects of the dual-earner lifestyle at the family formation stage in the life course when both parents are in full-time employment. In the next section we discuss the evidence concerning the decision to continue to be a dual-earner household after the birth of the first child. In the following section we consider the negotiation of gender roles within the household; how far such households conform to and depart from the stereotypical 'normal' family in which the mother takes the lead role in domestic matters and the father specializes in the breadwinner role. We also consider the emotional support provided to women by their partners. In the last section, we consider the support – formal and informal – available outside the household and its effects on mothers' experience of support.

One of the principal, original aims of the longitudinal study was to investigate the effects of full-time daycare on the children of employed mothers. Three groups of children were included – those cared for by relatives, those cared for by childminders, and those cared for in nurseries, together with a fourth group who, at least initially, were to be cared for at home by their non-employed mothers. The mothers constituted the main sources of information.

The study group was composed of 185 households in which the women intended to resume their former employment on a full-time basis following maternity leave. A further group of 70 women not intending to return was also included. Both groups were selected through large employers of women, nurseries and maternity hospitals in Greater London. The mothers and children were first studied while the mothers were on maternity leave, that is when the children were 4–5 months old. The mothers were followed up on four subsequent occasions; when the children were 10–11 months (after the employed mothers' return to employment), and when the children reached 18 months, 36 and 72 months. (The chapter does not include any information from the 72-month contact.)

The households were selected on a number of criteria: that the child was the mother's first born; that the mother was living with the child's father when the child was born; that the mother was born in the United Kingdom or Ireland; and that the child would be placed in one of the three types of daycare mentioned above. All households lived in the Greater London area, and the sample was recruited into the study between 1983 and 1984.

The original intention of the study was to achieve an equal balance of women in higher-status (professional and managerial) and lower-status (clerical and manual) occupations. However while the study more than adequately represented women in higher-status jobs, it substantially under-represented women in manual employment; a high proportion was concentrated in non-manual occupations in central and local government, the health service, the financial services sector and the teaching profession. This imbalance in the sample was in part a consequence of our sampling strategy, but it was also due to the fact that because of eligibility conditions fewer women in manual work qualify for maternity leave in Britain. Where they do return to the labour market following childbirth, they tend to find new jobs.

The methodological approach involved a mix of quantitative and qualitative methods both in the fieldwork and the data analysis. Such an approach was particularly fruitful in illuminating the contradictory elements in the ideologies and practices of these dual-earner households. Further details about the methods and the sample are given in Brannen and Moss (1990).

The decision to return to work after maternity leave

Women in dual-earner households regarded going back to their former jobs after maternity leave very much as a decision rather than as a foregone conclusion. Conversely, for those not intending to return, the majority in Britain at the time of the study, not returning to work was not seen as a decision at all. Interview questions which assumed that such women explictly decided not to go back to work were treated by them as meaningless and irrelevant. Since most women in Britain in the post-war period have resigned from the labour market during pregnancy, it is not surprising that giving up work was taken for granted.

Going back to work was treated by women returners and their partners as the woman's individualistic decision rather than a joint or household strategy. Thus although, as Pahl (1984) suggests, such decisions affect the household, women's accounts did not define them as being made by the household. Even in those cases where husbands had clearly urged their wives to return to work for financial reasons, women never talked in terms of a 'joint decision'. Rather husbands were described as 'sitting on the fence' or as 'leaving it up to her'; at the most extreme, the 'good husband' was said to prefer his wife to have the option of staying at home. Overall when put on the spot, the proportion of wives who thought their husbands to be in favour of their employment (41 percent) was almost equal to those who thought them to be opposed (44 percent). The remainder were uncertain about their husbands' attitudes. Going back to work after maternity leave was seen as the woman's 'choice' even though, as was clear from other parts of the interviews with the women, the majority of those returning to work felt constrained to do so for financial reasons. Sixty-three percent in high-status jobs and 72 percent in low-status jobs gave money or housing as one of their main reasons for returning, with 58 percent overall giving it as their main reason.

Although in many cases the return to work was far from a 'free choice' made by the mother, the pretence that this was so served to reinforce the idea of the man as the 'good provider'. The other side of this cultural stereotype is the failed husband who cannot earn enough to enable his wife to stay at home if he or she wants this. This discourse, with its emphasis on returning to employment being the woman's choice, had another effect; it encouraged women to view consequences and problems as the result not of a dual-earner lifestyle but of their personal decision – and therefore for them, rather than both parents, to resolve. Men in these households were thereby freed from having to admit failure as breadwinners or accept equal responsibility for the management of the household.

In economic terms the major beneficiary of the decision was the household; returners contributed some 44 percent of net household income, earning on average four-fifths of their partners' earnings (that is around six months after the return to work) and contributing to all major items of expenditure. Nonetheless the costs of the dual-earner lifestyle were not equally distributed inside the household (Brannen and Moss, 1987). Notably the mothers saw the costs of childcare as being their responsibility, rather than a charge on total household income; many women viewed their earnings in terms of what was left after childcare costs (whether or not mothers actually paid the costs themselves), which in turn affected whether mothers felt it was 'worthwhile working' in financial terms.

Gender roles in the household

Given that it was seen as the woman's decision to return to work after maternity leave, it is not so surprising to find that the woman was also the author and manager of the dual-earner lifestyle, especially the domestic division of labour. On every indicator of childcare and housework examined, mothers with full-time jobs did substantially more than their partners, even though these fathers in general did more than fathers with partners who were not employed.

This pattern was established at an early stage. Although childcare was needed because both parents had full-time jobs, most childcare arrangements (81 percent) were made by mothers, and it mostly fell to mothers to maintain those arrangements; just over 70 percent of children were taken always or mostly to daycare by their mothers.

Mothers were more likely to take time off work if children were ill or needed taking to the doctor's. In the home, at all contacts, mothers reported themselves as doing most of a range of childcare and housework tasks – although when it came to play, fathers were reported to be much more involved. Time-budget diaries kept by the mothers showed that they spent substantially longer in sole charge of children than their partners did – over 20 hours a week more when children were 18 and 36 months old. Most mothers (77 percent) felt that they had the main responsibility for their child and his or her upbringing. Overall, in only about 10 percent of dual-earner households was there a division of domestic labour that was equal or near equal.

Women used a variety of coping methods for dealing with this situation – of managing a full-time job and most of the domestic workload. At the most extreme, some gave up employment altogether or found a part-time job. By the time children were 3 years of age, only 107 women were in full-time employment, compared to 185 who had initially resumed full-time employment after maternity leave. For those who worked on in full-time jobs, the organization of time was crucial. Women coped by concentrating on the 'core activities' of employment, childcare and housework, and making the most effective use of available time so that every minute counted. On average, mothers got up in the morning earlier than fathers, often using the first part of the day to catch up on housework or organize for the day ahead. Many cut down on social life and leisure activities. Standards of housework might be lowered or certain jobs axed altogether. More efficient working methods were applied, both in the home and in employment – better planning, the application of a routine, working more intensively. Finally, some women coped by buying in more material resources – investing in labour-saving equipment or materials or, for 10 percent, paying someone else to do part of the housework.

Just as the decision to resume work was rarely an explicit household strategy, so the division of work was rarely decided or tackled at a household level. Nearly half the mothers said there had been no discussion with their partners about how childcare and domestic work would be organized after maternity leave had finished, or else that there had been some discussion but with no conclusion. The remainder were equally divided between those who said there had been a discussion, but only leading to some unspecific conclusion ('He said he would try and do more') and those who said there had been a discussion which had produced a specific agreement. Yet this last group – about a quarter of the households – had rarely discussed allocation of the overall household workload; the focus instead was on managing specific problem areas, usually childcare rather than housework. With some notable exceptions, the domestic role of the father was that of domestic assistant, 'helping out' to a greater or lesser degree, rather than an equal participant in managing the dual-earner lifestyle. It was taken for granted in these households that the woman would carry the major responsibilities which 'traditionally' have been allocated to women. Conventions that assume that women are in charge are not considered to warrant discussion.

Women responded to this situation – where the domestic workload was rarely equally shared – in significant ways. Despite subscribing, in the great majority of cases, to a belief in equal shares in domestic work when both parents were in full-time employment, women did not insist on more instrumental support nor did they often criticize partners when such support was not forthcoming. Indeed, in response to direct questions concerning satisfaction with the contribution of their partners, for example with routine domestic tasks and childcare, women projected themselves as relatively satisfied; only one-third expressed any dissatisfaction on this issue. An examination of what they actually said indicates that they were often curt in their replies and that criticism of their husbands was generally muted or qualified.

However, elsewhere in the interviews women were more discursive, especially in talking about particular events and incidents. In these accounts women resorted to a number of strategies whereby criticism was avoided or defused. Husbands were let off lightly or they were excused on a number of grounds: by virtue of their masculine gender, by a belief in the salience of employment for the male ego; by the notion that breadwinning is the responsibility of men not women; by a lack of expertise and skill in caring and housework. Even more fortunate were those husbands who were recipients of praise. Indeed most women fell over backwards to be 'fair', a strategy whereby husbands were presented in the interviews in a favourable light: 'Although I've said he hasn't been very good, he has been very good. He's been very patient. It's unfair to say he doesn't do any work.'

As Backett (1982) observes, these strategies serve as a smokescreen for basic inequalities between men and women in the household. Underlying this reluctance to criticize are low expectations, in particular the assumption that the most that could be expected was for men to perform a subsidiary role. Dominant normative assumptions concerning gender roles and marriage lay essentially undisturbed.

Whilst women were reluctant to criticize husbands for lack of practical help, they were less restrained in articulating their thoughts concerning husbands' emotional support. Indeed, husbands were said to be the main providers of emotional support. Husbands were most frequently mentioned as confidants before the return to work – persons to whom women would turn with a personal worry. Overall, they were considered to be the most significant figures in providing support for mothers during the first three years of their children's lives. There was, however, little hard evidence to suggest why this might be so in terms of concrete examples of practical help although there was an association between the amount of childcare and housework men carried out and how emotionally supportive their wives perceived them to be. It was notable that in women's accounts of their husbands' support it was not so much what they did that was important. Rather, husbands' support appeared to be more symbolic than real – 'He's always there', 'He'd be there *if* (our emphasis) I wanted him.' Rather than equally sharing the load of work and responsibility, husbands were key figures in providing women with a sense of security – persons upon whom women felt they could rely in an emergency or crisis. It was evident that, in most cases, crises were rare and husbands' help was in practice insubstantial. Even so, women still felt they 'would' help in a real emergency.

Social support and its impact on the household

Informal support
Given a lack of childcare provision and the inequitable distribution of work inside the household, mothers may be expected to rely upon informal support from social networks. The study provides ample data on the availability of social network support, the extent women drew upon such support, and the ways they perceived and experienced it. The data suggest that the support received was limited but that women did not necessarily expect it to be otherwise.

Detailed data on the size, composition and interconnectedness of the networks of returners and non-returners were collected during maternity leave and six months after the return to work. During maternity leave it appears that, compared with returners, non-returners had larger networks in absolute and relative terms and more social contact with other mothers who had young children. Such contact is likely to provide a pool of supportive and reciprocal relationships, especially with respect to knowledge about young children and childcare. However, despite having fewer such contacts, returners were more likely to know a greater number of working mothers than non-returners; as their accounts also suggest, these were mainly acquaintances, rather than friends whom they saw regularly or knew well, and these acquaintanceships with other working mothers were frequently made by women in anticipation of their return to work. Six months later there is a similar story, with an increase in size in the networks of non-returners and an even more marked decrease in the networks of returners.

These differences between the networks of returners and non-returners are not surprising since returners had little time and energy for activities outside employment and childcare, a finding borne out by women's own accounts of their daily lives. Moreover it is also likely that returners were prepared to invest less effort during maternity leave in building up relationships with other (home-based) mothers because they knew that they would have difficulty sustaining them once they were back at work and that they could not easily engage in reciprocity.

Just as returners had fewer network resources than non-returners, they also lacked *appropriate* sources of support for the decision to resume a full-time job following maternity leave. Roughly half of those with whom returners had discussed the matter were said to be disapproving – 50 percent of parents, 51 percent of friends, 58 percent of other relatives, 50 percent of work colleagues. It seems likely that the expectation of a stigma being attached to the employment of mothers of young children, together with the rarity of such a course of action among their friends and relatives, may have deterred women from consulting many network members in the first place. In general, mothers were forced to look beyond their social networks for reassurance and for role models, namely those 'in the same boat' as themselves; such support proved difficult to find, as women's accounts indicate.

The situation with respect to the search for and the provision of childcare is somewhat different. In terms of finding childcare, 62 percent of women consulted network members, but most also sought information from other informal sources. As to its provision, in the vast majority of cases, women (since it was principally the mother's task) relied a great deal on informal sources of support: in 24 percent of cases female relatives looked after their children, while in some cases, childminders were found from among their friends. However, there appeared to be no clear normative expectation that relatives – as significant sources of childcare – were obliged to offer childcare assistance. It was notable that relatives were said to have 'offered' rather than to have been asked for help and that women were extremely 'grateful' if any help was forthcoming.

How did these households respond to the support provided (or not) by their networks? Excluding their partners, the persons regarded as most supportive over the first three years of children's lives comprise a relatively small part of the women's social networks, mainly female kin from their own or their partners' families of origin (67 percent mentioned mothers, mothers-in-law or other female relatives as being among their three most supportive persons). More specifically, apart from husbands, who as we have already described figured prominently, the main persons who women experienced as supportive in the first three years of motherhood were the children's grandmothers and other people who cared for their children, mainly childminders. Children's grandmothers were valued often for practical help, either as full-time carers or as the main source of back-up childcare.

As others have also found (Hill, 1987; Evetts, 1988), friends and other non-kin ties, with some notable exceptions, were infrequently mentioned as being supportive in practical ways; only 24 percent mentioned friends as supportive persons. Evidence from a questionnaire completed by women concerned with coping strategies in the event of returning to work reveal that the great majority wanted to know others in a similar position to themselves and with whom they could identify. Most mothers said they had found taking part in the research helpful for this very reason, with several mothers asking us to put them in touch with other working mothers in the study.

Network structure, especially size and degree of interconnectedness, might be expected to affect the availability or experience of support. We explored this issue but found no generalizable effect, though it is possible to see in particular instances the ways in which network structure might do so. For example, women who had very small 'truncated' networks and who felt supported were more likely to mention support as coming from outside their meagre networks, frequently from their children's carers (in particular, childminders). Those with other types of larger networks were more likely to experience support from persons inside their networks.

Some reasons why returners did not receive more support have already been considered. In addition it needs emphasizing that, although women did not receive a great deal of support, they did not necessarily report feeling unsupported. An explanation for this is that they did not expect a great deal of support, an issue which leads back to the question of the ways in which the return to work is socially constructed: the ideology of the mother's decision and the mother's choice.

Such ideological constructions resonate with less gender-specific notions of individual choice, including household autonomy and self-sufficiency, which are current in British society. Ideas about individual choice have a specific force at the family formation stage of the life course. Couples are expected to choose the right time to 'start a family' but they are expected to do so in certain circumstances, the notion of choice being somewhat in contradiction with the notion that it is women's 'natural' function to have children.

Ideas about household self-sufficiency and autonomy relate to the circumstances in which childbearing is socially prescribed, in particular the achievement of financial independence by the couple and the acquisition of suitable housing in which to bring up a family. New parents are expected to have entered the property-owning classes or at least to be occupiers of appropriate accommodation, namely a house and garden. The fact that the current housing situation requires two incomes to set up house while at the same time the normative ideal of 'the mother who stays at home' continues to be influential points to the tensions between the rhetoric of individual self-sufficiency and the policy and practice surrounding the dual-earner lifestyle.

The political rhetoric of individual choice in 'family life' came to the fore in the 1980s with the emphasis on individual as opposed to collective enterprise, and the sharp division between the (minimalist) sphere of state responsibility and the private, untrammelled world of the family. These ideologies are notably gender blind in that they have signally failed to address the ways in which women who resume employment after childbirth have to find their own individual solutions for their children's care and take on most of the household responsibilities and the servicing of their partners.

Formal support

This section reports findings from our study concerning support in the workplace and the help which is forthcoming from health and welfare agencies in the public sector. Such support as was available is gender specific since the society and the women themselves assume that mothers, rather than both employed parents, need support, an assumption which reinforces the reality that mothers are the principal architects and work-horses of the dual-earner lifestyle.

At the workplace, many mothers found themselves to be the only employees managing full-time jobs and bringing up young children. They rarely encountered any women 'in the same boat' who could be supportive or, simply by their presence, constitute a reminder that going back to work after childbirth was a feasible and acceptable thing to do. The few exceptional cases where women had such colleagues underlined the importance of such support in the workplace.

> 'I was lucky that this other girl had gone back to work before so she kind of paved the way. They'd got used to it! Before I'd left the attitude was "Oh, we're not going to make any special allowances".' (Social worker, aged 34)

Despite the fact that the majority of women in our study were in relatively advantaged parts of the labour market, only 28 percent reported that their employers made any allowances or special provision for working parents. Eighteen percent mentioned childcare provision, a figure which greatly overestimates the proportion in the population who are catered for in this way, since use of workplace childcare was one of the methods by which we selected the sample. Only 9 percent mentioned that they could take any time off for the care of sick children and 5 percent said that they were entitled to changes in working hours – for example, the opportunity to go part time on return from maternity leave.

By contrast, health and welfare agencies featured little as sources of support. Notably, while on maternity leave, few women discussed their decisions to return to work with 'health visitors' (health care workers who visit the home to check on infant and maternal health in the period following the birth). Nor did they expect to do so. The few helpful health visitors and health care professionals were supportive in a personal rather than a professional capacity, in most cases having returned to work themselves when their children were small.

Formal agencies in the public sector did figure more in the search for childcare though, in most cases, involvement took the form of the provision of lists of childminders by the social services departments of local government authorities. It was notable that, unlike other sources of support, women did express considerable dissatisfaction concerning the lack of advice and information publicly available to those searching for childcare. It was also the case that women, as first-time mothers, had little understanding of the paucity (and hence also the quality) of childcare provision in Britain. This is perhaps surprising to a cross-national audience but may be explained not only by the small amount of public childcare provision in Britain but also by the absence until recently of any public debate on the subject.

Women's dissatisfaction on this issue is in contrast with their lack of expressed dissatisfaction with support received from partners, family and friends. Furthermore it is likely to be seriously underestimated since the data refer to the first childcare arrangements made after the return to work and not to the many subsequent arrangements. In the three years of the study nearly half of the children had at least one change in childcare arrangements while their mothers were in full-time employment. Furthermore, it was notable that a very high proportion of mothers opted for the first available arrangement. This fact is also likely to have led to an underestimate of satisfaction since further exploration on the women's part might have revealed the very limited options available and hence increased their dissatisfaction.

The extent to which women were satisfied with support in the workplace and from health care services and professionals is dependent upon whether and to what extent they expected support from these quarters. As we have suggested, women clearly expected more public information in their search for childcare but did not expect the 'personal' decision of their return to work to be discussed. Similarly in the workplace, women did not expect provision to be made by employers for those with childcare responsibilities. Indeed many regarded concessions as 'soft options' rather than legitimate rights, especially if a woman took on a full-time job, that is a job which is seen pre-eminently to belong to a male breadwinner: 'If you work full time you have to accept that you work the same as everybody else and you shouldn't be entitled to special privileges – time off and things like that.' Reflecting the current political culture, 'good' employment practices were dismissed by some women as costly and sentimental: 'They've got businesses to run, haven't they? And businesses don't run on sentimentality.'

Whilst not everyone took such a hard line, the majority seemed overly 'grateful' for even very small concessions, including those which their employers were legally bound to provide, such as time off for medical checks in pregnancy. Such gratitude suggests that, at an individual level, women lacked confidence, especially those in a subordinate status in male-dominated organizations such as banks. It is also an indicator of low expectations of provision for working parents. Lack of confidence and low expectations are also reflected in women's zealousness in being seen as reliable and hardworking, especially in the first few months back at work. This showed itself in a reluctance to take time off when children were ill; most took only one or two days in the first six months back at work, with many making other arrangements.

Gratitude was also the theme of women's responses to informal help in the workplace. Women clutched at small tokens of help, with nearly half of bosses being portrayed as 'understanding' even though in practice few gave any practical help such as allowing women initially to return on a part-time basis. Work colleagues were more likely than bosses to be described as unhelpful (57 percent vs. 21 percent). This is perhaps surprising since it might be presumed that colleagues, who are more likely to be women than are bosses, would be more supportive than male bosses over this issue. In women's accounts it is notable that supportive colleagues were described as women with young children or those who had worked when their children were young; unhelpful colleagues, the majority, were described as 'older women' who were disapproving of mothers 'leaving' their children. Such responses may perhaps be a 'sour grapes' reaction on the part of some older women workers because, not having had the opportunity to take maternity leave themselves, they had left work before the birth of their children. Moreover, since workplaces, especially offices, can be 'gossipy' places, women feared that any special considerations they received (most of which were unofficial) would be interpreted by other colleagues as favouritism and hence as potentially divisive.

Change and continuity

In some important respects, the situation in Britain has changed since the mid-1980s. An impending labour shortage has led to the beginning of a rapid rise in employment among women with children; between 1985 and 1988, before the full impact of the trend had been felt, the employment rate among women with children under 5 rose from 29 percent to 37 percent (although it remains the case that most women in Britain still do not resume employment after maternity leave). Childcare and working mothers have received an unparalleled degree of publicity and attention, with a deluge of articles, reports and books on the subject. The present government's Inter-Ministerial Group on Women's Issues, established in 1988, has been examining childcare needs, as have many employers. Employers have shown increasing interest in providing some support through workplace crèches and financial assistance for childcare, career-break schemes and more flexible employment arrangements. Public opinion is moving towards a gradual acceptance of the employment of mothers of young children. Between 1965 and 1987 the proportion of women who agreed with the view that mothers of pre-school children 'ought to stay at home' fell from 78 percent to just under half, while the proportion who felt it was 'up to her whether to go out to work or not' rose from 5 percent to a quarter (Ashford, 1988).

Yet, while there appears to have been an improvement in the position of some employed mothers since the early 1980s, largely due to better employment opportunities and greater responsiveness by some employers, in certain important ways change has been minimal and marginal. The issue remains defined in terms of 'working mothers' (Lewis, 1991), with solutions sought which assume that mothers are primarily responsible for children. The implications for men of the emergent two full-time-earner lifestyle have been virtually ignored. Childcare is still not seen as a 'men's issue' and while measures such as career breaks and flexible working may, in theory, be equally available to fathers, little attention is paid to the fact that few fathers take them up.

The issue is also still seen as a question to be sorted out by market forces. It is not part of an overall policy to maximize human resources (Ruggie, 1984). The solution for parents seeking to combine employment and parenthood remains a private one. Despite changing circumstances, the Conservative governments of the 1980s and early 1990s have refused to concede any public responsibility in the provision of childcare (except for the regulation of the private market) or any public intervention in employment to extend the rights of parents. Government on the surface encourages employers and others to act, and tries to set an example in its own role as employer, but rejects responsibility for the structural changes required to make childcare and other services more widely available.

In the absence of government intervention, employed parents must rely to a disproportionate extent on their personal coping strategies and resources. In practice, this means that women manage the dual-earner lifestyle on their own or with a bit of goodwill from others. This is inevitably a recipe for inequality. As long as men continue to take a lesser share of domestic responsibilities, and show little interest in cutting down on overtime or adopting 'flexible' working practices such as career breaks and part-time work, women will be unable to compete on equal terms with men.

Inequality also divides women: women with highly prized job skills or in areas of the country with labour shortages are likely to receive more support from employers than those with few skills or in areas of high unemployment. Inequality also extends across households: higher-income households can 'buy in' services while those with low incomes cannot. Although there are no official statistics, there is much anecdotal evidence of substantial increases in the use of private servants – nannies and domestics. Ultimately such solutions depend on the supply of cheap labour, prepared to provide domestic services at cheap rates. How long such a supply will be maintained, before the onset of a new 'servant problem', will depend on economic perform-ance, the availability of alternative sources of employment and immigration controls. Also available to high-income households is the growing number of private nurseries. Those offering reasonable standards of care in a city like London are expensive. They cost well over £100 a week, higher than the fees at a 'public school'. For households without sufficient income, the private solutions available remain the old ones – grandmothers, childminders and jobs that 'fit in' with men's working hours.

In Britain, the dual-earner household is increasingly common. Yet the dominant ideological rhetoric, the everyday practices of mothers and fathers and the institutional context have not responded to this emergent household type; the issue continues to be defined as the problem of 'working mothers'. Without change at all levels and in the definition and labelling of the issue, managing the dual-earner lifestyle will remain a problem, and a problem to be solved by women themselves.

References

Ashford, S. (1988) 'Family matters', in R. Jowell, S. Witherspoon, and L. Brook (eds), *British Social Attitudes: The 1987 Report*. Aldershot: Gower.

Backett, K.C. (1982) *Mothers and Fathers: A Study of the Development and Negotiation of Parental Behaviour*. London: Macmillan.

Brannen, J. and Moss, P. (1987) 'Dual-earner households: women's financial contributions after the birth of the first child', in J. Brannen and G. Wilson (eds), *Give and Take in Families*. London: Unwin Hyman.

Brannen, J. and Moss, P. (1990) *Managing Mothers: Dual-Earner Households after Maternity Leave*. London: Unwin Hyman.

Central Advisory Council for Education (1966) *Children and their Primary Schools, Vol 1*. London: HMSO.

Chodorow, N. (1978) *The Reproduction of Mothering: Psychoanalysis and the Sociology of Gender*. Berkeley: University of California Press.

Evetts, J. (1988) 'Managing childcare and work responsibilities', *Sociological Review*, 36 (3): 501–31.

Fonda, N. (1976) 'Current entitlements and provisions: a critical review', in N. Fonda and P. Moss (eds), *Mothers in Employment*. Brunel University Management Programme.

Hill, M. (1987) *Sharing Childcare in Early Parenthood*. London: Routledge & Kegan Paul.

Hunt, A. (1968) *A Survey of Women's Employment*. London: HMSO.

Joshi, H. (1987) 'The cost of caring' in J. Millar and C. Glendinning (eds), *Women and Poverty*. Brighton: Wheatsheaf.

Lewis, S. (1991) 'Motherhood and employment: the impact of social and organizational values', in A. Phoenix, A. Woollett and E. Lloyd (eds), *Motherhood: Meanings, Practices and Ideologies*. London: Sage.

Martin, J. and Roberts, C. (1984) *Women and Employment: A Lifetime Perspective*. London: HMSO.

OECD (1988) *Employment Outlook, September 1988*. Paris: OECD.

Pahl, R.E. (1984) *Divisions of Labour*. Oxford: Blackwell.

Ruggie, M. (1984) *The State and Working Women: A Comparative Study of Britain and Sweden*. Princeton, NJ: Princeton University Press.

Schutze, Y. (1988) 'The good mother: the history of the normative model of "mother love"', in *Growing Up in a Modern World*. Proceedings of an International Disciplinary Conference on the Life and Development Of Children In Modern Society, Vol. 1. Trondheim, Norway.

8

Financial Affairs: Money and Authority in Dual-Earner Marriage

Rosanna Hertz

The relationship between 'money' and authority is a significant yet neglected problem in the sociology of the family.[1] Until recently, this relationship was assumed to have a particular direction: whoever earned the income would have the greatest influence in family decision-making. However, changes in the labor force participation rate of married women have raised questions about both the direction and the consistency of this relationship. If authority in household matters is closely linked to the source of the income itself, we would expect to find that increases in wives' contributions to family income would result in different authority patterns between spouses: to wit, as wives' incomes approach equivalence with their husbands, relative equality in decision-making over expenditures (and perhaps other facets of household affairs) should result.[2] However, research on dual-earner couples has thus far failed to generate consistent evidence in support of equilibration. Traditional patterns of authority in the family and allocation of household responsibility seem to be remarkably durable even in the face of changes in the relative contribution of income by husbands and wives.

Failure to detect changes in the structure of authority in the family associated with new patterns of wives' employment can be the product of several things. The traditional wives' role may be so powerful as to withstand even a direct assault on one of its basic premises: that wives do not contribute materially to the maintenance of the family. Women's earnings, no matter how large, could be 'written off' as marginal, ephemeral, or supplementary. Alternatively, we may fail to see a change in authority relations because we have used imprecise or incorrect measures of authority. That is, when employing survey items which refer to, but do not adequately define, 'control over spending' we may be missing subtle but real shifts in authority. In the past scholars have reduced the definition of authority in financial matters to one of implementation (such as who pays the bills) but who shapes the premises on which the decisions are made is not simply a question of who handles the budget or who pays the bills. This ignores the distinction made, for example, by Safilios-Rothschild (1970) between 'orchestration' and 'implementation.' That is, authority may actually reside in the ability to establish the premises and the categories of household finances (orchestration) not simply in the physical activities (implementation); alternatively real authority may reside in the capacity to determine long-term financial strategies. Similarly, the labor market ideology that wages are payment for *individual* work legitimizes the practice of the breadwinner (male) retaining control of the family funds and avoiding housework. Wives share this equation: they insist upon *their* right to control their wages when they enter the paid work force (Luxton, 1980; Hunt, 1978).

Taken together these explanations point to two important omissions in research on money and authority: detailed investigation of how dual-earner couples handle money and how they attribute meaning to money in family life. Before we can determine the nature of the relationship between money and authority, it is essential to draw back the curtain that has concealed this aspect of family life from public view.

There are at least two reasons why sociologists *and* economists should be interested in knowing more about how families handle money. The first has to do with *who* makes decisions about financial matters. The traditional division of labor within the family assumes that men concentrate on earning a living while women maintain the home in order to maximize economic utility. The implicit gender stereotype of most economic theory leads us to believe that for efficiency's sake a household's decision-making process should be guided by the preferences of a single individual – presumably the individual who generates most of the household income is entitled to make decisions (Becker, 1976, 1981). However, growth in the percentage of dual-earner marriages would suggest that how financial decisions are made is now more likely to be a joint product of the preferences of all household members who generate income, regardless of whether it is more efficient for both spouses to participate (Horney and Mcelroy, 1981; Morris, 1990). Certainly this has been argued by those who have studied dual-earner couples earning roughly comparable wages (Blumstein and Schwartz, 1983; Hertz, 1986).[3] Thus, we are led to question what effect changes in labor force participation have on the way households handle money, especially how they partition income into spending versus savings. More importantly, we are led to wonder what the *process* of money-handling and allocation looks like in diverse households.

The second reason has to do with the kinds of information couples use to make specific decisions and the criteria they use to arrive at a methodology for decision-making. Imperfect information is, of course, an aspect of reality to which both economists and sociologists will admit. However, the causes *and* the consequences of imperfect information ought themselves to be seen as a critical subject for inquiry. That is, whether we refer to the actual distribution of income to consumption and savings or to the methodology for arriving at that distribution, we know very little about the kinds of information couples use or the kinds of information search they engage in prior to making decisions.

The objective of this chapter is to draw attention to what we know and what we need to know about money and authority in dual-earner families. I start in the first section by reviewing the extant empirical literature from the United States and the United Kingdom on the topic. In the second and third sections, I provide an overview of preliminary findings from my own research in an attempt to cast light on some of the more subtle but complex issues involved in household financial management in the USA. The final section builds on the preceding three to suggest questions to guide future research.

Prior research

Although researchers have historically attributed a great deal of significance to the role of money in the status system of the family, few studies have investigated *both* the division of labor in financial affairs and the symbolic meaning couples attach to money in their relationship. (For exceptions see Brannen and Moss, 1987; Wilson, 1987.) Evidence that increases in women's contributions to household income have not resulted in a consistent movement toward equilibration in authority over finances, has led researchers to speculate that something else must be going on in husband–wife relations to negate or undercut wives' claims to parity. Unfortunately, without studies of both the details of how money is handled and the way that couples make rules about money in their lives, we cannot adequately explain either the empirical phenomenon or its implications for prevailing theory. For this reason then, it is essential to go beyond descriptive typologies for classifying money handling systems (e.g., Pahl, 1983) into the development of a more organic linkage between (1) money as the material or economic basis of family life and (2) money as a symbolic reflection of authority relations in marriage.

Finances and authority: material dimensions

There are two core material dimensions to the relationship between finances and authority in marriage. The first has to do with the relative contributions of husbands and wives to total family income. The second refers to the influence of extra-familial factors – specifically, class and gender stratification – on the opportunities for money to alter authority relations. The relevance of each dimension to research on financial arrangements is discussed below.

Despite the centrality of money to theories of power and authority in the family, little attention has been paid to the weight attached to relative incomes in the balance of authority between husbands and wives. Even in terms of the prevailing theoretical perspectives, it has never been especially clear how much income is necessary to tip the traditional balance of influence away from husbands and toward wives.[4] Since men generally earn more, wives do a larger share of housework in order to maximize economic utility (Becker, 1976). By contrast, Huber and Spitze (1983) argue that the more money wives earn, rather than the income gap between spouses, influences the amount of housework husbands do. In other studies, however, it has been argued that even full-time, permanent employment with an income approaching the husband's does not guarantee that a wife's contribution will be defined by the couple as anything more than a 'supplement' or 'pin' money. Steeped in a cultural and familial ideology which reinforces a gender-based division of labor, these wives are reluctant to emphasize their financial earning power even when they earn as much as their husbands (Stamp, 1985; Brannen and Moss, 1987; Rosen, 1987). Therefore, they retain primary responsibility for the home. Finally, other studies have found that the larger the proportion of family income the wife contributes, the more likely it is that her husband will also contribute housework and childcare time to the family (Heer, 1958; Ferree, 1987, Hochschild and Machung, 1989). However, if he holds traditional beliefs about gender roles the closer the income gap between husband and wife the more inadequate he may feel as a breadwinner and the more likely he is to feel underpaid (Mirowsky, 1987). Although at some point it may be appropriate to engage in a 'calculus of contribution', the inherent confusion in the theory suggests that it is important first to compare couples' methods for handling money across different ratios of contribution, that is, where wives earn less than their husbands; the same as the husbands and, if possible, more than their husbands.

When we turn to extra-familial influences, it is surprising to discover how little we know about the way couples in different social and income classes as well as different cultures handle and make sense of their finances. Despite the accumulation of Anglo-American family studies about different income groups which mention aspects of financial arrangements – working-class (Rubin, 1976; Luxton, 1980; Halle, 1984), middle-class (Fowlkes, 1980; Zussman, 1985), upper middle-class dual-career couples (Rapoport and Rapoport, 1971, 1976; Hunt and Hunt, 1977; Pepitone-Rockwell, 1980; Hertz, 1986), and upper-class couples (Ostrander, 1984) – there has yet to emerge a systematic effort to compare the relationship between finances and authority across social classes. Bird's (1979) work perhaps comes closest, although social class comparisons were not the focus of her investigation. As a result, we are left with few answers to a hotly contested question at the core of family sociology: the relative influence of class and gender in explaining authority relations in the family.

This point is perhaps best illustrated in Ostrander's (1984) study of upper-class American couples. She found that, despite inheritances and external sources of wealth that made wives equal to their husbands as contributors to family income, they deferred to husbands in managing and investing their contributions. Without class variation in her sample, Ostrander was compelled to discount class as an explanation and concluded that gender roles seemed to permeate even the most affluent families. In a somewhat similar vein, I found that it was at least as common for dual-career wives to give their husbands authority over family financial matters as it was for couples to share authority over their earnings – despite the fact that wives' earnings equaled those of their husbands and wives' professional training and competence made them fully capable of handling the finances (Hertz, 1986). Pahl (1983) and Luxton (1980) have shown, with respect to working-class families, that women are at least as likely to manage the money as their husbands. Ultimately, however, the major earner has the right to decide what to do with the paycheck. (See Blumstein and Schwartz, 1983, who discuss this as a general feature of American couples; Hunt, 1980, who makes the same point about British working-class couples and Wilson, 1987, who compared British couples from different social classes.) Rubin (1976), Pahl (1980, 1983), and Wilson (1987) suggest that there may be links between the income level of a household and the type of financial arrangement couples select. Women are more likely to manage the money when there is little or no discretionary income. Among higher-income levels husbands are more likely to make major decisions, even though their wives may administer the money (Rubin, 1976; Edgell, 1980). Thus, in the few studies of affluent families it seems to be the case that traditional gender roles prevail and influence the distribution of authority over finances; but in working-class families, where traditional gender roles should be expected to hold greatest sway, gender appears to be less important in the delegation of responsibility over financial management.

Yet we cannot assume that the relationship between the relative financial contributions of husband and wife to the household and the structure of decision-making in the family is universally similar. In

India the pattern of authority is determined within the context of the extended family. Thus, for example, a wife's contribution to family income gives her bargaining power with her mother-in-law, not her husband. (See Sekaran, this volume.)

Absent from these studies is an explicit effort to document the linkages between income generation and expenditure, *and* the linkage between 'money' as object or commodity and 'money' as symbol. Without such research, we can have little hope of understanding the relationship between financial matters and authority in families. It is equally important that future studies be conducted among couples from different social classes and in different societies in order to assess the relative influence of gender and class in marital relations.

Familial decision-making: the power structure[5]

While much is known about income differentials *between* families, little attention has been paid by sociologists to how income is distributed *within* families. We assume that all family members share the same economic fate and the same socio-economic status. Some family members cannot be rich while others are poor (Young, 1952). A further corollary is that all family members are supposed to be equal beneficiaries of the household income (despite the fact that not all members earn wages). Using data from the British Family Expenditure Survey 1977, Piachaud (1982) found instead that the distribution of income within families is highly unequal. He suggests that expenditure patterns bear no simple relationship to the division of paid work and income.

Sociological analyses of power within marriage have used measures constructed from replies to questions about which partner was responsible for making specific decisions. This literature focuses primarily on the outcomes instead of the process by which decisions are made. (Safilios-Rothschild, 1970, and McDonald, 1980, provide decade reviews.) Most studies, cited below, find a positive correlation between level of income and responsibility for decision-making. Typically, the greater proportion of household income which a spouse contributes, the greater part that partner will play in decision-making. The husband's marital power increases as his relative income increases, and it is at its greatest when the wife is not earning (Blood and Wolfe, 1960).

This literature assumes (a) that family members active as wage earners tend to exercise greater authority than non-wage earners and (b) more recently, that the individual who earns the higher amount of money in the case of two-paycheck couples (Bird, 1979) will have greater say and responsibility for decisions. The primary focus of these studies has been on housework and childcare arrangements between spouses (Blood and Wolfe, 1960; Nye and Hoffman, 1963; Safilios-Rothschild, 1970; Young and Willmott, 1973; Walker, 1970; Meissner et al., 1975; Pleck, 1977; McDonald, 1980; Robinson et al., 1976; Berk and Berk, 1979; Gerstel and Gross, 1984). Each study asks only a few questions about financial arrangements – typically, who pays the bills and makes decisions around major and minor family purchases.[6] Deciding how money will be allocated between various family members and understanding the mental work of keeping track of inflows and outflows of monetary resources has received only patchy attention. Researchers studying the division of labor in the home have not examined the topic of money in the detail that has been the cornerstone of major work on other aspects of family life such as the social organization of housework (cf. Berk and Berk, 1979), food preparation and cooking (DeVault, 1991), and sexual activity (Kinsey, et al., 1948, 1953). Understanding the process by which couples make decisions about financial matters will shed light on the power structure within the family.

Finally, in order to understand how financial arrangements may structure power and authority relations between spouses it will be necessary to distinguish what aspects of financial matters each spouse controls. For the past decade, British researchers (Gray, 1979; Pahl, 1983; McRae, 1987) have examined how different allocative systems lead to more control over certain kinds of expenditures by one spouse or the other. For example, one spouse may have the final say over major long-term and short-term financial decisions, such as deciding the amount available to spend on different categories of consumption, while the other spouse may be concerned with putting the decisions into operation, such as allocating the money among food products. (Cf. Safilios-Rothschild's, 1970, distinction between implemented and orchestrated power.) These British studies have focused primarily on the working classes and give us only rudimentary glimpses at the division of labor couples construct for handling of money.

Finances and authority: the symbolic dimension
How do couples come to construct the meaning of money in marriage? The work of resource allocation entails developing ways of figuring out how money should be spent and saved, who should make the decision (or it should be a joint decision). From the decisions that couples make (and the stories they tell about how they came to those decisions), it is possible to derive the 'rules' that couples use either implicitly or explicitly. The symbolic role of money and the authority to determine how it should 'in general' be allocated involves a close examination of the *rules* which couples employ to make decisions or, having made decisions, *to justify them*. The emphasis on symbols and

rules is based upon the recognition that each specific decision may be viewed as 'unique' (once in a lifetime), but past decisions serve as precedents for later ones so that over time, rules emerge that guide future decisions.

Silent understandings and the work women do[7]

Couples do create strategies for administering money. But as much as spouses may talk about wishing they could find a blanket formula for balancing present spending and future expenses most strategies on a daily basis are closer to improvisation than to articulated policy. Most couples believe they are inadequate forecasters and that others know secrets that no one taught them. The power of the paycheck as the only kind of work that counts for a say in decision-making remains problematic. I will confine this section to three principal topics: (1) how dual-earner couples describe the dilemma of handling money; (2) what they do to cope with it; and (3) what we can learn about the things they do and don't do with money.

Money matters

Independent of the manner in which they deal with income and outflow or with spending and saving, the couples I studied were similar in two ways. First, they are convinced that their current money-handling practices are more irrational and uncontrolled than they would like them to be. Secondly, they are reluctant to explore ways to gain more insight into – or control over – the handling of money. For instance, couples wish they had formulas to help them better predict whether (and how much) to spend or to save. Money-handling is a baffling and perplexing process that couples don't feel they really understand – and that leads to aggravation, worry, and a yearning to be more in control. It remains so because it is not a topic of frequent conversation between couples – and sometimes even *within* couples.

Money belongs to a 'class of silences' or aspects of life that aren't talked about. Probing the relationship between money and authority is difficult because money is treated as a 'sacred' topic and not easily discussed. Financial status is usually revealed indirectly by one's lifestyle, not directly in discussions of income. Our consumption patterns may announce what we are worth, but specific discussions about money are as off-limits today as discussions about sex were in the 1950s. People seldom discuss their financial situations unless it is a matter of public record, and even then they tend to be close-mouthed about what they do with their money. While we may have a general idea of an assistant professor's salary or the range within a salary grade, people seldom reveal specific figures. General discussions may take place among people who know they are in the same economic situation and share the same problems or circumstances, but quite often they depend on external information about one another's earnings – and, therefore, mastering money remains a remarkably private and mysterious affair (Blumstein and Schwartz, 1983).

This is not to suggest that people do not create 'systems' or 'strategies' for handling their money or for tracking their expenses. They do. And those systems vary in complexity: from the attempt to exert discipline over a limited set of behaviors to extremely detailed analyses. For example, a 30-year-old man with an associate's degree explained what he felt to be an important spending control he and his wife had devised:

> We try to go out [grocery shopping] with lists . . . I used to go out meandering through the store buying this and that. I try to do it not hungry either.

A 46-year old woman whose combined family income totalled $65,000 a year explained that:

> Less than a year ago I just thought that we had no idea where the money is going and it just seemed like we should be more on top of it. My idea was we put the checks in my account – because he also didn't pay his bills on time and I would get really upset. It actually gave us a better picture of where the money was going.

And then there is the man who is a financial manager in a manufacturing company who began computerizing his family's records ten years ago:

> So at that point I started up some spread sheets. I got sort of an income statement on spending which is on an annual basis and after tax. . . . And I roll that out into a twenty year grid . . . Inflates it for inflation and anticipates raises. So I get an idea of the normal flow of bucks. Then I have a section that's got [children's college] tuitions in it. I inflate that at a greater rate than the rest of it, unfortunately, which is a killer. And then other spending like a car every ten years. . . . So I have a formal system that will allow me to change any dimension.

Yet, aside from casually observing the lifestyles (or purchasing habits) of their (presumed) financial peers and occasionally perusing 'how-to' columns in the newspaper, none of the couples interviewed thus far explored the topic in detail with parents or siblings. They regret that financial arrangements (such as how much to spend and how much to save) were not visible aspects of their parent's household – a 'how-to' part of home life like cooking and passing on family recipes – so they could watch how it was done. They do not query their peers to see how they 'do it' and they rarely pay someone else (for example a money management 'expert') for guidance. The private aura surrounding household finances leads people to believe their financial circumstances are unique. For example, an administrative assistant with a bachelor's degree wondered how her friends were able to afford yearly European vacations:

> But I have no sense of what those people make or how they really spend their money. Sometimes I wonder whether people at similar levels with kids or something – how they manage and if we're being careless. I don't know on a scale if we're being more careless or we're in fact worrying about it more than a lot of people do. I have no sense of that.

In one of the few instances of 'learning from others', one working-class woman talked about how a girlfriend's mother provided her with a model for saving money:

> But seeing Cindy's parents, I mean, it was really something positive that they worked toward [saving for retirement]. They had no money back when the kids were little and then I just saw this happen over the last few years. And it just seemed to make more sense: they could do it [save] because she always put the $5.00 away before she bought the food and stuff.

But, despite the important lesson she felt she had learnt from observing her friend's parents, she echoed the more general quandary couples described:

> I'm curious to know how other people do it. Do they have other savings accounts? Do you have one savings account that your real savings are in and do you have another savings account that's just a cushion? That's stuff that you don't really read about in magazines.

Although the tendency not to seek information or guidance in money-handling is a complex topic in itself two general factors have emerged from the interviews that help explain the situation. The first has to do with what respondents learnt or, more importantly, did not learn from their parents. The second is the value attributed to different forms of labor. Each factor is discussed in subsequent sections.

Learning about money and teaching about money
Few respondents could recall having been 'schooled' in money-handling by their parents. They certainly recalled a standard of living and patterns of parents' employment; but little in the way of technique was passed down and even less in the way of detail about their family's 'real' economic status was revealed to them as children. Though parents did not teach them how to handle money, they did learn values about money – particularly to distinguish between household tasks that were paid and those that were unpaid. They pass these 'lessons' to their own children in indirect ways. Childhood lessons became the basis for differentially valuing adult contributions, which I will discuss

in the next section. One popular approach is to give children an allowance. With literally each dollar they give, parents try to teach children to think about the dilemmas of spending and saving. Discussing her seven-year-old son one mother said:

> He wants to take his whole allowance and blow it on a soda. I really want to teach him that you don't do that. Set aside a certain amount that you are going to spend and save the rest.

While older children may be expected to work outside the home to save for future expenses like college tuition, younger children whose understanding of the future is more limited are expected to delay gratification and save for personal things parents do not consider essential. For example, young children – regardless of social class – are encouraged to save for expensive items like video games and sneakers as well as less expensive ones such as baseball cards and Barbie doll clothes. Some children even pool allowances with siblings to buy expensive items like video game cartridges. In the process, however, most children learn more about individual consumption and initiative than about collective/familial responsibility to divide household resources equally or fairly. No children in this study contribute income to the household.

Saving for items parents won't buy is also supposed to teach children about *working* for the things *they* want. Certain household chores are transformed into paid activities. It is ironic that the first paid work most children do is housework considering that it will become unpaid labor for almost all of them. As children become young adults paid labor becomes synonymous with working outside the home.

Not all housework tasks are included within the domestic market of child labor. When I asked parents what their children had to do to earn an allowance, I was told that some activities had a monetary value and others did not. How parents decide which tasks are paid and which are unpaid (but still expected) deserves closer scrutiny. It appears that some parents distinguish between tasks that are part of the core of family life and tasks that are more peripheral. Only the latter are attributed a monetary value. For instance, helping to prepare meals and clearing the table after dinner are unpaid chores. Cleaning the basement, pulling weeds, and throwing out the garbage are paid tasks. Other parents distinguish between the personal or private domain and the common or family domain. Taking care of oneself (for example putting away one's own toys and making one's own bed) is paid. Helping with household chores (folding the laundry, carrying in wood for the stove) is unpaid. All parents use money explicitly or implicitly as a form of social control. In the following example the controlling function of money is made clearly explicit:

Mother: And there are certain things they have to do for their allowance. Even before the allowance they had to make their [own] beds and they had to be dressed by a certain time, have their teeth brushed by a certain time and all of that. [Now] they have to take out the garbage for their allowance. They have to not only clear the table, which they had to do before, but they also have to sponge down the table and push in the chairs.
RH: So these are additional things they have to do for their allowance?
Mother: It is not simply doing chores. It is a whole cooperation kind of thing to keep the household running smoothly. I think if I really thought about that I would probably have some ambivalence about that cause I don't think a kid should get paid for keeping a household running smoothly. But it is sort of my method for getting a fire lit under him when he is spacing out.

Under the guise of education, monetary incentives teach children proper social and moral values (Zelizer, 1989). Overall, teaching children about the value of money through spending and saving part of an allowance is a direct goal that contemporary parents feel is important. However, indirectly and less consciously children are learning that some activities/tasks have a monetary value whereas others do not.[8] But more broadly, there is a contradictory message between what children learn inside versus outside the home. Within the home they are taught that things with the greatest value have no price tag. By contrast, outside the home they face a world where the price tag determines value. Finally, they are also learning that money is power and it can be used for control.

Valuing labor and apportioning votes

While parents assign monetary value to the various chores performed by their children, they are less clear about how to evaluate the chores they perform in the home and how to calculate the value of individual contributions and, with that calculation, how to allocate votes or influence over spending and saving. That is, each decision over what to spend and what to save represents a mini-referendum on the rights or power of family members – not only on *what* is important but also on *who* has the right to vote – and should one have a determining vote and should anyone have a veto.

From my interviews, it is clear that paid work is more highly valued by both husbands and wives than either volunteer work *or* unpaid household labor. Even though some people noted that their volunteer work was more interesting, it is the paycheck that gives them a sense of economic worth *and* a claim to influence over family finances. They feel it entitles them to rights about how money will be used (see Hertz, 1986, 1990).

Similarly, couples mention, though rarely calculate, how their own labor aids in savings. For instance, people talk about saving money by doing things themselves (for example painting the house, hauling the trash to the dump.) If it is a service that they once bought they can attach a monetary figure to the task. 'I saved $100 a year by discontinuing the town trash service.' But these services that couples forgo to save money are purchased outside the home. They are normally not household chores that wives traditionally have done. In other words, when spouse labor is a service which the couple have never purchased in the past (as in caring for children or elderly parents), the substitution does not factor into people's thinking. In this regard, women's labor is a 'gift' made to their husbands, children, and aging parents. A housekeeper's thriftiness is rarely assigned a monetary value. The value of her labor is rarely balanced against his earnings. Consequently, women who contribute domestic labor nonetheless feel like second-class citizens because they contribute less money. They also contribute less savings because they give gifts (that is, care for family members). Because they contribute less to family income and savings, they feel less entitled to buy personal things for themselves. So they sacrifice their personal desire to purchase clothes or to engage in hobbies in favor of expenditures on husbands' sports and leisure activities and/or more general spending on children.

The traditional jobs of the wife – cooking, cleaning and childcare – diminish the wife's economic value when they become purchased services. Similar to findings in my earlier work on dual-career couples, when spouses pool their paychecks the costs for childcare are usually subtracted from the wife's salary instead of being evenly divided between the two spouses (cf. Brannen and Moss, 1987). Even though the money may be pooled, the wife's contribution is not considered as her gross income but rather as her gross income minus childcare and house-cleaning costs, which reduces the value of her work, and therefore her worth, considerably. Women who earn their own paycheck do not feel guilty spending money on their children even though they all report, with varying degrees, feeling guilty about spending money on themselves. Those most likely to feel guilty spending money on themselves are women who contribute less than 25 percent of the household income. One woman, a secretary who worked part-time, explained to me that she no longer felt 'personally rich.' When I probed for the meaning of this phrase she explained that when she was first married she worked full time and contributed equally to the household income but now two young children and the high cost of childcare have diminished her sense of feeling entitled to spend the 'family money' on herself. Even though the woman below believes that 'intellectually,' as she puts it, she makes an important contribution to her children's childhood on days when she is with them full time, she explains how her part-time income figures into the household:

Wife: I have my paycheck and I cash it and it's basically gone. It goes for childcare and a few other things so I never feel like I have a license to just go out and buy something. [This perspective is supported in her husband's interview.]

RH: So your check goes for childcare?

Wife: That's the way I see it though it's not literally the way it happens. But that is sort of the way I see it in my head. When I figured out what we could afford for childcare I compared it against what I make because I work – not really because we both work. But the way I see it in my mind because I am working for this amount of time – that is how much I make an hour and this is how much I can pay an hour for childcare.

RH: So the way you think about it is the cost of childcare plus a couple of extras?

Wife: Yeah. Maybe the groceries.

RH: How come you don't think about it as half his childcare expense and half yours?

Wife: I guess I think of it as either the choice to work or stay home and if I stayed home there would be no childcare cost. It's also more of a job than a career for me . . . I feel the responsibility for providing for the family has been taken over by him at this point. So I guess I see my job in a sense as more of an elective since I am contributing fairly little to the running of the house. In other words what I'm making is basically paying for childcare.

This analysis points to an apparent paradox. Husbands' and wives' contributions to the home are not symmetrically valued: both the ability to purchase a service to substitute for their own labor and using their own labor to save money reflect gender role expectations. That is, she is always expected to care for children. If she works outside the home it is an additional income but if she substitutes a paid worker or daycare center it is an added expense. By contrast, if he works outside the home he is not expected to repair the car engine but if he does it is an added saving. Whereas children learn lessons that distinguish between individual and collective/familial responsibility, adults reinforce a gender-based division of labor which is embedded in the symbolic ways couples calculate and differentially categorize money and its substitution.

Financial arrangements among dual-career couples[9]

Money remains a taboo issue between many couples because when people talk about money, they are simultaneously talking about authority relations. Authority relations should reflect how much people earn, and the form of budgeting should symbolize how power is distributed in the family. If the questions of how money should be handled and, more important, why one person should make decisions about how it will be used are never confronted directly, authority relations can remain hidden or obscured. But when women earn as much as or more than their husbands, traditional authority relations may be challenged. When each partner has an income, the woman is more likely to develop substantial autonomy than women who do not have an income. Husbands and wives with independent incomes may not necessarily create new methods for handling financial affairs, but the possibility is available to them.

Findings from my dual-career research indicate that the development of new familial accounting systems is an empirical indicator of a change in authority relations between husbands and wives. However, who controls the discretionary income is no longer a simple determinant of which spouse makes decisions or which partner pays the bills, or even how much will be discretionary. Instead, the restructuring of the accounting system – specifically, women's autonomous use of discretionary money – may question men's traditional authority over familial decision-making.

Pooled versus separate accounting systems

In my study of dual-career couples finances between spouses were handled in two different ways: roughly half the couples pooled their finances and the other half kept separate accounting systems.[10] Those couples who pooled their finances blurred the distinction between 'his' money and 'her' money. Husbands in these cases were the ones who paid all the bills and made the major financial decisions. By contrast, couples who have separate accounts compute basic expenses and each spouse contributes a separate amount to a common pot – either a share proportionate to income or an equal sum. Each spouse keeps the remaining income in a separate account, to spend at his or her own discretion.[11]

On the surface, these two models may appear to be simply minor variations in approaches to household accounting. However, there appears to be a relationship between the relative earnings of spouses and the type of accounting system they devise. I caution that these findings are exploratory; the sample is small. However, the finding is a highly suggestive one: the separate accounting system is used more often by families in which wives earn as much as or more than their husbands, whereas pooled accounting systems are more common when wives make less than their husbands.

The explanation for this apparent correlation resides in the link between economic roles (work roles) and the distribution of authority in the family. Men have traditionally derived their authority from status and resources acquired outside the family and have transformed that status and those resources into authority within the family. In the separate accounting model, wives act like their husbands, translating external status into familial authority over the allocation of money.

With less money held collectively, the amount controlled by each spouse increases. But equally important, women are asserting the same authority over discretionary income that men have traditionally had; they feel that neither one should have authority over the other's discretionary money. Controlling discretionary money bestows greater autonomy, especially for women. In this case, participation by both spouses in the labor force produces a more egalitarian family model. Put simply, the separate accounting system is an internal representation of extra-familial roles.

In the pooled model, by contrast, female participation in the labor force may not alter the traditional familial authority structure. This model attempts to minimize the external inequality in the labor market (income disparities due to either industrial pay-scale difference or to level of career development) by pooling resources. More to the point, this collective familial model limits the autonomy of one or both spouses.[12] Whereas the wives who keep separate accounts have developed a 'money consciousness' – that is, they actively decide how to spend, save and invest their own money – the women who pool finances report that their husbands handle it.

Understanding the origin of these arrangements is the key to understanding money as an expression of the underlying authority relations between husbands and wives. In working-class families, arguments about money have to do with 'coming up short' at the end of the month (Rubin, 1976; Luxton, 1980). (For instance, is it the wife's fault that she managed the money poorly and this is why there is no meat on the dinner table or is it the husband's fault that he does not earn enough to pay for it all?) Dual-career couples argue instead about the 'rights' to that money. They ask who has the right to determine how the income will be spent, if both husband and wife are perceived as significant and central breadwinners. One woman, married four years, addressed this question:

> When we decided to get married, we had a very, very financial-type discussion. You know, where neither of us wanted to give up the rights to go out – like I'll go out and spend $400 on a suit and I don't want to hear about it; and Bill the same thing – he'll go to Florida and spend $1,000 on golf and he doesn't want to hear about it – so we both knew that we had to have enough money on our own, and this [separate accounting system] seemed like the fair way to do it.

I suggest that it is the notion of marriage that determines the type of accounting system the couples choose. The couples in this study describe their marriage differently. Pooling couples conceptualize marriage as 'the merger of two individuals' based on 'unlimited trust'. These older notions of marriage are now being questioned by couples who use separate accounting systems. Those couples who separate their money do not speak about trust directly. They speak about autonomy and retaining individual control. Conversely, pooled couples speak about trust without reference to autonomy.

Some couples who now have separate accounting systems did not begin with this system. Instead, money arguments led to a shift in financial arrangements. A woman who shifted after ten years of marriage to a separate accounting system told the following story:

> The money was all in one joint account, and I found that I was always coming up short. And I figured that I was busting my tail at work and at home and that I should have money left for me. I didn't at all. Over the years my discretionary income was subsidizing his expense account at his office, and I finally decide, 'Nope, you can sink on your own.' Now it is wonderful I have that income. And now he says, 'How am I going to pay my half of the Marshall Field's bill.' And I say, 'It's your problem.'

This example implies a breakdown in trust though in this wife's account she did not speak in these terms. According to her a mushrooming career and significant salary increases were the catalysts behind the change.

A separate accounting system accommodates different attitudes about money, so that couples do not have to agree about either the value of money or how to spend it. However, partners do not necessarily approve of or ignore differences in outlooks or money management styles.

> Burt is much more compulsive in terms of money management than I am. He balances his checkbook and I never do. When my bills come in the mail, he gets terrible annoyed if I don't pay them on time. It's just not a part of me to pay bills on time . . . He likes things orderly, and I like to do things my way.

Money and independence

Regardless of whether people pool their finances or keep them separate, secure careers and large incomes have also had two additional consequences for a couple's lifestyle. For women that takes the form of independence and for men their wives' incomes have allowed some of these men to make career changes.

For women being able to support oneself is a crucial element of independence in the relationship. A woman's choice to remain in an existing marriage or to be married at all no longer needs to be based on financial considerations. Money, as one woman testified, makes a difference for dual-career wives in that it places women on an equal footing with men:

> I'm in the relationship because I want to be, not because somebody's taking care of me. If I want to take a walk, I can take a walk and not worry about being able to take care of myself. From my view point it certainly does give

me some independence. I feel like I don't have to say, 'Well, you're bringing in the money that's putting food on the table, that's keeping me alive.' I'm putting in money, too.

Money – specifically two substantial incomes – also allows for career change for men because it liberates men from being the sole financial providers for the family. Men are free to make career changes without breadwinner worries. Even though the man quoted below paid a price in terms of his autonomy, he established his own business:

I think Lisa probably feels she made a significant investment in terms of my building my business. If it weren't for her income, which we lived on, and her encouragement, this couldn't have happened. That is a direct example of the freedom I have had because of my wife's income. Because of the investment on her part, she likes to know what is going on with the business.

Women in this study had not made career shifts that included starting their own companies but it is possible that in the future his income will support the family, while she establishes herself in a business.

The mere fact of women earning independent incomes has not necessarily led to a revolutionary change in authority relations between husbands and wives. What happens to that income and how couples view it becomes equally important. In general, those couples who have chosen separate accounting systems have made a step toward altering the traditional balance of marital authority. Having money has allowed the development of substantial autonomy for each spouse; the wife is no longer subject to collective discretion. In contrast, when pooled accounting systems have been selected, authority relations between husbands and wives seem to have undergone only limited change. Wives in these relationships absolved themselves of financial responsibilities. Thus, the existence of two incomes in itself does not make the crucial difference; rather, the mechanisms devised to deal with this money are a focal point for husband–wife relations among dual-career couples.

Future research on dual-earner couples: financial arrangements as a missing piece of the puzzle

This chapter has attempted to pose an important empirical and theoretical question: What is the relationship between the relative financial contributions of husbands and wives to total family income and wealth and the structure of authority and decision-making in the family? Rather than assume a direct and non-problematic linkage between authority and the source and amount of 'money,' I have argued that it is important to examine how money flows into, through, and out of the family. Six interrelated questions about the relationship between money and authority should be investigated in future research:

1 Does the pattern and process of husband–wife decision-making remain stable in the face of alterations in either total family income or the relative contribution of marital partners, or does it change in response to the latter and, if so, how?
2 What are the critical decision points with regard to the allocation of resources, between the 'arrival' of money and its 'departure' in the form of expenditures?
3 How do couples (as dyads and as individuals) give meaning to the role of finances in their lives? That is (a) what rules do they construct for generating, allocating, and expending their income; (b) what status or value do they attach to money-handling roles (e.g., income producer, money manager, and consumption manager); and (c) what are the categories of expenditure into which they partition income and wealth?
4 Does the relationship between 'money' – as an *object* to be handled and as a *symbolic representation* of husband/wife relations – and authority vary with the income level of the family or its social class and cultural milieu?
5 Do women and men perceive and value money differently? If so, how do these differences reflect a particular structural arrangement between the sexes based upon a sexual division of labor?
6 How do differences in national and/or cultural context, particularly where the dominant pattern of family life is extended not nuclear, alter husband/wife authority relations?

Conclusion

For too long we have assumed that in the contemporary family all members, but most particularly spouses, have an equal say over the social distribution of benefits and resources. Following the classic study by Blood and Wolfe (1960) a dominant though under-investigated theme in family sociology has been an emphasis on the relationship between income and authority. Most recently, feminist scholars have begun to revisit this topic as married women become permanent labor force participants whose paycheck is essential to their families' well-being in industrialized countries. Yet under what conditions the wife's paycheck gives her equal bargaining power remains to be empirically uncovered as additional layers of family life continue to be peeled back.

Focusing on household finances as a dynamic system through which work, family, and gender relations may be studied will lead to a more sophisticated conceptualization of the subtle outcomes of relative income rather than merely examining the correlations between income and authority. In order to analyze the relative influence of class and gender in marital relations, a fine-grained comparative study is needed to generate consistent evidence of social change in the home brought about by women's labor force participation.

Notes

I thank Dafna Izraeli, Sue Lewis, Helen Hootsmans, Elliot Mishler, and Robert Thomas for critical comments on parts of this chapter. The research proposal and initial data collection for my present study began as part of a post-doctoral fellowship under Elliot Mishler's guidance at Harvard Medical School. The collegial and supportive work environment he created has become an invaluable part of my professional life. During 1990 different sections of this chapter were presented at the Center for Research on Women at Wellesley College, the Fourth International Interdisciplinary Congress on Women at Hunter College, and the American Sociological Association in Washington, DC.

1. Colloquially, the term money refers to both income and wealth. My research on relations between authority and how families manage their finances also includes both. This is unclear in other empirical studies.

2. Carolyn Bell (1974) provided the first analysis of American husbands' and wives' incomes using Bureau of Labor Statistics data. Most scholars report that on average women's contribution to the total family income is between 25 and 27 percent; these figures have supposedly changed little despite the growth of women's employment outside the home. Bell argues that as a result of quoting this average amount women's contributions are typically dismissed. She demonstrates that in fact the average is a simplification of a more diverse reality.

3. While most sociological studies described in this chapter challenge the utility model, other studies emphasize money as a way to puncture the myth of the family as a haven by revealing its market traits (Millman, 1991). Similarly, recent studies of divorce (Weitzman, 1985; Arendell, 1986) demonstrate marked differences in the earning potential and economic status of men and women post-divorce in order to highlight the increasing impoverishment of women and their children. These studies can be viewed as a critique of the sentimental model of the family. See also Zelizer (1989) for an interesting discussion of the changing social meaning of domestic money in the United States between 1870 and 1930.

4. In the majority of American dual-earner couples, the wife earns less than half what her husband did in 1981. According to census data analyzed by Bianchi and Spain (1983: 14), 'a significant share of dual-earner couples included wives who earned 75 percent or more than their husbands. Wives earned more than their husbands in 16 percentage of dual-earner couples, and the same as their husbands in another 2 percent of couples. The wife earned twice what her husband earned in 1.6 million, or 6 percent, of dual-earner couples. Interestingly, almost 40 percent of the 4.0 million couples with a wife as primary earner fell into this category.' (Examining wives' occupational distribution, 36 percent of wives who earn more than their husbands are professionals or managers.) It is important to note that dual-earner couples are classified as 'husband primary' if the husband

provided more or the same income as the wife and 'wife primary' if the wife had at least $1 more earnings than her husband.

5. In the literature on family sociology, power and authority continue to be used interchangeably (cf. Safilios-Rothschild, 1970 for a critique of this point.) Although I believe this leads to some important sources of imprecision in analysis (e.g. it fails to distinguish between coercion and legitimate authority), I will use the terms synonymously in this chapter. Safilios-Rothschild (1970: 540) states that family power is a multi-dimensional concept that can be 'measured through the outcome of decision-making, the patterns of tension and conflict management, or the type of prevailing division of labor.'

6. Hiller and Philliber (1986), in one of the most interesting studies on division of labor, find that money management is the only regular household task either done by or shared by a majority of husbands. Two-thirds expected to take equal responsibility for managing money. While couples are willing to share in the traditional roles of their spouse, they do not expect to relinquish primary responsibility for their own traditional roles in marriage. One-third of the couples agreed that housework is the wife's job, and 43 percent agreed that income earning is the husband's job.

7. This section is a preliminary analysis of an on-going study on financial arrangements within marriages. The sample will compare dual-earner couples from the working class, middle class and upper class where the wife earns less than, equal to and more than her husband. This will allow me to examine the relationship between gender and class.

8. However, I would also note that we need to check if those tasks are gendered or would be if children did not do them, e.g. paying kids to shovel the walk, which is normally a male activity on division of labor surveys.

9. The material from this section is reported in greater detail in my book *More Equal than Others* (Hertz, 1986). See specifically Chapter 5 (pp. 84–113). Twenty-one corporate dual-career couples were interviewed in-depth for this study from a sample of Chicago organizations. Husbands and wives were interviewed separately in order to ensure that each spouse would have privacy to comment on their own money views and those of their spouse. The median family income was $90,250 in 1981, placing them in the salaried ranks of America's upper middle class. Women's median income was $40,200 and men's median income was $47,500. In this study 52% of the couples had separate accounts.

10. My findings correspond most closely to Pahl's (1983) typology. We both refer to a shared/pooled system as one where spouses do not distinguish between 'his or her money.' What I am calling the separate accounting system she terms the independent management system. While we agree upon the descriptive typology I add that it is the couples' ideological views of marriage and gender roles that determines the selection of accounting system by each couple. Pahl (1989) attempts to refine her earlier typology to distinguish between the management and control of money by having two typologies, the first being the system of money management and the second, the control of finances.

11. Although I expected to find that couples with children would be more likely to have a communal or pooled accounting system, this was not the case. Of those couples who pooled their incomes, three had no children and eight had children. Of those couples who had a separate accounting system, four had no children and six had children.

12. Praeger (1982) discusses conflicts between individualistic and shared principles in marital property law, arguing that the individualistic model rewards self-interested choices that can be detrimental to marriage. Praeger argues for what I call the pooled system.

148   *Dual-Earner Families*

References

Arendell, Terry (1986) *Mothers and Divorce: Legal, Economic and Social Dilemmas.* Berkeley: University of California Press.

Becker, Gary (1976) *The Economic Approach to Human Behavior.* Chicago: University of Chicago Press.

Becker, Gary (1981) *A Treatise on the Family.* Cambridge, MA: Harvard University Press.

Bell, Carolyn Shaw (1974) 'Working women's contributions to family income', *Eastern Economic Journal*, 1 (2 and 3): 185–201.

Berk, Richard and Berk, Sarah F. (1979) *Labor and Leisure at Home: Content and Organization of the Household Day.* Beverly Hills, CA: Sage.

Bianchi, Suzanne M. and Spain, Daphne (1983) 'Wives who earn more than their husbands', *U.S. Bureau of the Census*, Special Demographic Analyses, CDS–80–9. Washington, DC: US Government Printing Office.

Bird, Caroline (1979) *The Two-Paycheck Marriage.* New York: Pocket Books.

Blood, Robert O. and Wolfe, Donald M. (1960) *Husbands and Wives.* New York: Free Press.

Blumstein, Philip and Schwartz, Pepper (1983) *American Couples.* New York: Morrow.

Brannen, Julia and Moss, Peter (1987) 'Dual earner households: women's financial contributions after the birth of the first child', pp. 75–95 in Julia Brannen and Gail Wilson (eds), *Give and Take in Families. Studies in Resource Distribution.* London: Allen & Unwin.

DeVault, Marjorie (1991) *Feeding the Family.* Chicago: University of Chicago Press.

Edgell, Stephen (1980) *Middle Class Couples.* London: Allen & Unwin.

Ferree, Myra Max (1987) 'The struggles of supermom', in C.E. Bose, R. Feldberg and N.J. Sokoloff (eds), *Hidden Aspects of Women's Work.* New York: Praeger.

Fowlkes, Martha R. (1980) *Behind Every Successful Man: Wives of Medicine and Academe.* New York: Columbia University Press.

Gerstel, Naomi and Gross, Harriet (1984) *Commuter Marriage.* New York: Guilford Press.

Gilligan, Carol (1982) *In a Different Voice: Psychological Theory and Women's Development.* Cambridge MA: Harvard University Press.

Gray, A. (1979) 'The working class family as an economic unit', in C. Harris (ed.), *The Sociology of the Family.* Keele: Keele Sociological Review Monograph.

Halle, David (1984) *America's Working Man: Work, Home, and Politics among Blue-Collar Property Owners.* Chicago: University of Chicago Press.

Heer, David (1958) 'Dominance and the working wife', *Social Forces*, 36: 341–7.

Hertz, Rosanna (1986) *More Equal than Others: Women and Men in Dual-Career Marriages.* Berkeley: University of California Press.

Hertz, Rosanna (1990) 'Financial arrangements among dual-earner couples: money matters and distributive justice', Paper presented at the American Sociological Association Meeting, Washington, DC.

Hiller, Dana V. and Philliber, William W. (1986) 'The division of labor in contemporary marriage: expectations, perceptions and performance', *Social Problems*, 33: 191–201.

Hochschild, Arlie and Machung, Anne (1989) *Second Shift: Working Parents and the Revolution at Home.* New York: Viking Penguin.

Horney, M.J. and Mcelroy, Marjorie (1981) 'Nash-bargained household decisions: towards a generalization of the theory of demand', *International Economics Review*, 22 June: 333–49.

Huber, Joan and Spitze, Glenna (1983) *Sex Stratification: Children, Housework and Jobs.* New York: Academic Press.

Hunt, Janet G. and Hunt, Larry L. (1977) 'Dilemmas and contradictions of status: the case of the dual-career family', *Social Problems*, 24: 407–16.

Hunt, Pauline (1978) 'Cash-transactions and household tasks: domestic behaviour in relation to industrial employment', *Sociological Review*, 26(3) Aug.: 555–71.

Hunt, Pauline (1980) *Gender and Class Consciousness.* London: Macmillan.

Kinsey, Alfred C., Pomeroy, Wardell and Martin, Clyde (1948) *Sexual Behavior in the Human Male.* Philadelphia: Saunders.

Kinsey, Alfred C., Pomeroy, Wardell, Martin, Clyde and Gebhard, Paul (1953) *Sexual Behavior in the Human Female.* Philadelphia: Saunders.

Luxton, Meg (1980) *More Than a Labour of Love.* Toronto: Women's Press.

McDonald, Gerald (1980) 'Family power: the assessment of a decade of theory and research, 1970–1979', *Journal of Marriage and the Family*, 42(4) Nov.: 841–54.

McRae, Susan (1987) 'The allocation of money in cross-class families', *The Sociological Review*, 35(1) Feb.: 97–122.

Meissner, Martin, Humphreys, Elizabeth W., Meis, Scott M., and Scheu, William J. (1975) 'No exit for wives: equal division of labor and the cumulation of household demands', *Canadian Review of Sociology and Anthropology*, 12: 424–39.

Millman, Marcia (1991) *Warm Hearts and Cold Cash: How Families Handle Money and What this Reveals about Them.* New York: Free Press.

Mirowsky, John (1987) 'The psycho-economics of feeling underpaid: distributive justice and the earnings of husbands and wives', *American Journal of Sociology*, 92 (6) May: 1404–34.

Morris, Lydia (1990) *The Workings of the Household.* Cambridge, MA: Basil Blackwell.

Nye, Ivan F. and Hoffman, Lois W. (eds) (1963) *The Employed Mother in America.* Chicago: Rand McNally.

Ostrander, Susan (1984) *Women of the Upper Class.* Philadelphia: Temple University Press.

Pahl, Jan (1980) 'Patterns of money management within marriage', *Journal of Social Policy*, 9 (3) July: 313–35.

Pahl, Jan (1983) 'The allocation of money and the structuring of inequality within marriage', *Sociological Review*, 31(2) May: 237–62.

Pahl, Jan (1989) *Money and Marriage.* London: Macmillan Education.

Pepitone-Rockwell, Fran (1980) *Dual-Career Couples.* Beverly Hills, CA: Sage.

Piachaud, David (1982) 'Patterns of income and expenditure within families', *Journal of Social Policy*, 11(4) Oct.: 469–82.

Pleck, Joseph H. (1977) 'The work–family role system', *Social Problems*, 24: 417–27.

Praeger, Susan Westerberg (1982) 'Shifting perspectives on marital property law', pp. 111–130 in Barrie Thorne (ed.), *Rethinking the Family: Some Feminist Questions.* New York: Longman.

Rapoport, Rhona, and Rapoport, Robert N. (1971) *Dual-Career Families.* Harmondsworth, Middlesex: Penguin Books.

Rapoport, Rhona and Rapoport, Robert N. (1976) *Dual-Career Families Re-Examined. New Integrations of Work and Family.* New York: Harper & Row.

Robinson, J., Juster, T., and Stafford, F. (1976) *Americans' Use of Time.* Ann Arbor, MI: Institute for Social Research.

Rosen, Ellen Israel (1987) *Bitter Choices: Blue-Collar Women in and out of Work.* Chicago: University of Chicago Press.

Rubin, Lillian Breslow (1976) *Worlds of Pain: Life in the Working-Class Family*. New York: Basic Books.

Safilios-Rothschild, Constantina (1970) 'The study of family power structure: a review of 1960–1969', *Journal of Marriage and the Family*, 32 (4) Nov.: 539–51.

Stamp, P. (1985) 'Research note: balance of financial power in marriage: an exploratory study of breadwinning wives', *Sociological Review*, 33: 546–66.

Walker, Kathryn E. (1970) 'Time spent by husbands in household work', *Family Economics Review*, 4(2) June: 8–11.

Weitzman, Lenore (1985) *The Divorce Revolution*. New York: Free Press.

Wilson, Gail (1987) 'Money: patterns of responsibility and irresponsibility in marriage', pp. 136–54 in Julia Brannen and Gail Wilson (eds), *Give and Take in Families: Studies in Resource Distribution*. London: Allen & Unwin.

Young, Micheal (1952) 'Distribution of income within the family', *British Journal of Sociology*, 3: 305–21.

Young, Micheal and Willmott, Peter (1973) *The Symmetrical Family*. New York: Pantheon.

Zelizer, Viviana A. (1989) 'The social meaning of money: "special monies"', *American Journal of Sociology*, 95: 342–77.

Zussman, Robert (1985) *Mechanics of the Middle Class: Work and Politics among American Engineers*. Berkeley: University of California Press.

9
Dual-Earner Families in the United States and Adolescent Development

Lucia Albino Gilbert and L. Suzanne Dancer

> Women have long been nameless. They have not been persons. Handed by a father to another man, the husband, they have been objects for circulation, exchanging one name for another. That is why the story of Persephone and Demeter is the story of all women who marry: why death and marriage were the only two possible ends for women in novels, and were frequently, the same end. For the young women died as a subject, ceased as an entity. For this reason, then, women who began to write another story often wrote it under another name. They were inventing something so daring they could not risk, in their own person, the frightful consequences. (Heilbrun, 1988: 121)

Adolescents in the US today are growing up at a time when more and more women are daring to write their own lives. Women in the US now experience greater economic freedom and personal opportunity than ever before.[1] In the first stages of the feminist movement women pushed for equality in the world of work; now some twenty years later many women are also asking for equality in the world of the family (Bernard, 1981a, 1981b). These changes in women's lives have had and continue to have enormous impact on men. Many women are asking men to be partners in a different kind of marital relationship, one in which both partners involve themselves in occupational and family roles. In response, men too are changing although many still resist modifications in traditional male behavior and privilege.

The dual-earner pattern as the modal family form in the US grows out of these changes in women's and men's lives, and the accompanying modifications in roles traditionally assigned on the basis of gender. In this chapter we first provide an overview of the literature on the dual-earner family in the United States in which we give particular consideration to the heterogeneity among dual-earner families and to key variables associated with women's employment. We then turn to possible influences of growing up in a dual-earner family on female adolescents' self-concepts and choices.

We chose to focus on female adolescents in this chapter, and not both male and female adolescents, because the processes are likely to be non-parallel for women and men and because women's lives appear to be changing more dramatically than men's at the present time. Historically women's lives were determined by men (Hare-Mustin and Marecek, 1990); it is only recently that women are in a position economically and politically to define themselves and hence to create new possible selves for all women.

The dual-earner family in the United States

Women's and men's lives in the US have altered quite dramatically in the past twenty-five years. Young women and men today (age 25 to 29) are just as likely to have four or more years of college, and more women are in the paid workforce than ever before (Spain, 1988). In 1987, 45 percent of the total US labor force was female (US Department of Labor, 1989). Also, women now constitute nearly 39 percent of the professional labor force, compared with 26 percent in 1960. Current norms not only assume that single and married women and men will work but also consider work and career as an important component of women's and men's identity (Betz and Fitzgerald, 1987). Today, only 10 percent of American families fit the traditional model of a two-parent family with children, a wage-earning husband, and a homemaker wife. Even among two-parent families, the proportion where the husband is the only wage-earner has dropped to 20 percent; for ethnic minority families it is even lower (Spain, 1988; US Department of Labor, 1989). Of married women with children under 6 years old, 56.1 percent are in the labor force, and of these 69.4 percent are employed full time. For married women with children under the age of 18, these percentages increase to 65 percent employed and 72.9 percent employed full time (US Department of Labor, 1989). The average working wife with full-time employment contributes approximately 40 percent of the family's annual income (US Department of Labor, 1989).

Modifications are also occurring in men's roles, albeit less dramatic than those reported in women's lives. A number of studies indicate that men in the US today base their self-evaluations less on work-related issues, and more on family-related issues, than in previous times (Gilbert, 1985; Pleck, 1985, 1987). Barnett and Baruch (1987) reported that men (and women) who use both employment and family relationships in defining their adult lives experience psychological and physical health benefits. Thus, adult men and women are becoming increasingly similar in the ways they define well-being, although there is still considerable disparity in how roles are actually performed. Wives in dual-earner families, for example, do significantly more of the household work and parenting than do husbands (Pleck, 1985; Thompson and Walker, 1989).

Although employment appears to benefit both women and men, the overall effects of employment appear more beneficial for men than women, most likely because men earn more and have more opportunities for advancement, and because women carry more of the home and family responsibilities (Repetti et al., 1989; Thompson and Walker, 1989; Walker and Wallston, 1985). Despite fuller participation in the workforce, for example, women still encounter certain constraints in occupational placement and advancement related to gender stereotyping (Spence et al., 1985). Also, within the culture, the structure of work remains unaltered and families are expected to accommodate to the demands of employment. Despite these realities, however, how roles are combined and the quality of these roles are more important indicators of well-being than is role occupancy per se (cf. Baruch and Barnett, 1987; Crosby, 1987). A case in point is employment. Whether a married woman with a preschool-aged child works outside the home is less important in predicting her well-being than are such factors as her spouse's involvement in home roles, employers' family-related policies, job satisfaction, and so forth.

Involvement in home and work roles
Although most women with families have entered the workforce, widespread resistance to women's significantly altering their traditional care-taking responsibilities persists. An early indication of this resistance was the 'politics of housework' which, in effect, put women in the position of working outside the home and doing everything else they used to do as well. Women achieving parity with men within the family and within the culture, however, requires that men alter patriarchal views of women's work and involve themselves in family work.

Men's level of involvement in family work in dual-earner families has received increasing attention by researchers (e.g., Crouter et al., 1987; Pleck, 1985). Overall, the findings indicate that men's participation in family work continues to increase, more so in the area of parenting than in the area of household work (Dancer and Gilbert, 1990; Pleck, 1983, 1985, 1987). When both parents of preschoolers are employed, studies indicate that fathers and mothers spend about the same total time in direct interaction with their children as do parents in families in which only the husband is employed (Jump and Haas, 1987; Scarr et al., 1989). In dual-earner families, men's involvement in household work, although increasing and significantly higher than that of men in single-earner families, shows a good deal of variation. On the average wives still do more than husbands, but many husbands do as much as wives and some do more (Gilbert, 1985, 1988; Pleck, 1985). Gilbert (1985) specifically investigated husbands' involvement in housework and parenting in a sample of dual-career families. Wives and husbands in approximately one-third of the sample participated fully in both parenting and household activities and one-third shared in parenting only. Wives did most of the parenting and household work in the other third of the families. Reports from other researchers parallel these findings (Thompson and Walker, 1989).

In families in which wives are employed full time, marital satisfaction is best predicted by husbands' involvement in family work and their support for the wives' employment (Baruch and Barnett, 1987). A case in point is a recent study by Perry-Jenkins and Crouter (1990). These investigators used Peplau's (1983) model, which links specific role behaviors to cognitions and affect, to investigate the relationship between men's attitudes about the provider role, particularly regarding the issue of who should be responsible for the financial security of the family, and men's contribution to household work and their marital satisfaction. As predicted, husbands having 'co-provider' orientations involved themselves more in family work and reported higher marital satisfaction. Thus, men who felt a congruency between their role beliefs and the enactment of roles within the home were more satisfied with their marriage. Similar findings were reported by Ross and her colleagues (cited in Thoits, 1987) in their investigations of marriage patterns in dual-earner families. The lowest distress levels occurred in marriages in which both spouses were employed, both wanted to be employed, and both shared the housework and childcare. The greatest distress for both spouses was found in marriages in which the wife was reluctantly employed and took full responsibility for family work.

Childcare
Parenting in the US is still typically equated with mothering. Research on the increased use of paid childcare initially focused on comparisons of children reared in traditional and dual-earner homes. Results indicated that children are not at added risk if they receive child or day care instead of parental care for some portion of the day, and that in some ways they may benefit from it (Hoffman, 1989; Scarr et al., 1989). Both girls and boys, for example, appear to develop less stereotypic gender role attitudes; in blue-collar families, sons of employed mothers have generally obtained higher scores on measures of cognitive development and socioemotional adjustment (Hoffman, 1989).

Research interest next moved to investigations of the kinds of care provided and definitions of optimal care. Most recently, attention has also focused on the broader issues of day care and the family and work environments, specifically employer benefit policies and the structure of occupations, and how that impacts on family life and spouses' well-being (Zedeck and Mosier, 1990).[2] Given current employment benefits and policies, for example, women are better able than men to ask for and receive the accommodations necessary for combining work and family responsibilities (for example maternity leave, flexible schedules). Present policies generally reflect a traditional workplace culture in which women leave the workplace and men continue unencumbered by family responsibilities. As Congresswoman Pat Schroeder noted, 'If the father would want to take off [to stay home with a newborn infant], if he even mentions it, it's like he has lace on his jockey shorts. You don't do that in America' (1985: 16).

Generally role conflict and day-to-day stress associated with parenting are lowest when: (a) employers of both spouses have benefit policies which are family-responsive; (b) one spouse feels she (or he) will not have to do all the accommodating; (c) husbands make a commitment to involve themselves in parenting; (d) traditional ideas that a child should be reared full time by the mother are redefined by the spouses; and (e) suitable childcare is located (Gilbert, 1988).

The dual-career family

Most dual-earner families in the US are either dual-job families in which both partners consider their employment a job or they are career-job families in which the male spouse's employment is considered a career and the female spouse's a job. In 1969, the Rapoports first used the term 'dual-career family' to describe yet a third type of dual-earner family, one which at the time was considered revolutionary. In these families both spouses pursued a lifelong career, relatively uninterrupted, and also established and developed a family life that often included children. The uniqueness of the dual-career lifestyle came partly from the assumption that the husband and wife both engaged in occupational and family work and that they shared home and paid work roles in a relatively egalitarian manner.

Despite the assumption of egalitarianism, considerable variation exists within the dual-career category (Gilbert, 1985). Some partners achieve a role-sharing marriage, while others remain fairly traditional in role behaviors within the home. Useful to understanding this variation is Peplau's (1983) classification of marital roles into three types: traditional, modern, and egalitarian. These three types basically differ on two dimensions – power (the extent to which the husband is more dominant than the wife) and role specialization (the extent of role specialization between the spouses). According to Peplau, 'Traditional marriage is based on a form of benevolent male dominance coupled with clearly specialized roles [assigned on the basis of gender]. Egalitarian marriage rejects both of these ideas. Modern marriage represents a middle position' (1983: 252).

Numerous studies indicate that many dual-career marriages are far from egalitarian (see Thompson and Walker, 1989). In an in-depth study of men in dual-career families, Gilbert (1985) found three marital types, which she labeled traditional, participant/modern, and role-sharing/egalitarian; these types parallel the traditional, modern, and egalitarian types identified by Peplau. In a traditional dual-career family, the responsibility for family work is retained by the woman, who adds the career role to her traditionally held family role. In the participant or modern type, the parenting is shared by the spouses, but the woman retains responsibility for household duties. In this situation, as in the modern marriage identified by Peplau (1983), male dominance is muted and gender-based role specialization is less extensive. In role-sharing or egalitarian dual-career families, both spouses are actively involved in both household duties and parenting.

Factors influencing the type of marital role pattern adopted in dual-career and other dual-earner families can be divided into three major categories – personal factors, relational factors, and environmental factors (cf. Gilbert and Rachlin, 1987; Gilbert, 1988). Personal factors include personality characteristics, attitudes, values, interests, and abilities. Examples of relational factors are sources of power in the relationship (for example salary, education) and tasks that need to be done to maintain the family system. Finally, environmental factors refers to the structure of occupations, benefit policies provided by employers, societal norms and attitudes, and social networks and support systems. Satisfaction with the particular pattern adopted depends on these same factors, as well as on the degree of congruence and mutuality between spouses (Thoits, 1987).

The available evidence shows that children in dual-career and other dual-earner families generally are more independent and resourceful and have a wider range of role models than children raised in more traditional homes (Gilbert, 1985, 1988; Kimball, 1988). They appear to benefit from greater contact and interaction with both parents and less exposure to stereotypic gender-role behavior in the home. Both Kimball (1988) and Carlson (1984) reported that children see both parents as doing what they want to be doing and, thus, being happier and more content when they are with the family. Kimball's interviews with 42 children reared in egalitarian dual-earner families and 41 reared in traditional single-earner families also indicated that the former group of children, more than the latter group of children, intended to duplicate role sharing in their own future marriages. Knaub (1986) surveyed adolescent and young adult children, male and female, reared in dual-career families. Respondents, who ranged in age from 13 to 24, rated their families high in closeness and especially noted feelings of mutual concern and suppport. Benefits frequently mentioned included children's perceptions of both parents as positive role models, their exposure to a broad range of values and experiences, the family's financial security, and the children's opportunity to develop independence. Time constraints was the most frequently mentioned problem.

In summary, the dual-earner family is the modal family form in the United States. But the dual-earner family is not a single pattern – there are dual-job and dual-career patterns, among others, as well as variations in how spouses combine work and family roles within each pattern (for example, traditional, modern, and egalitarian). Overall, women's sharing in the provider role has not been paralleled across the board by men's sharing in home roles, although men show increasing participation, more so with regard to parenting than household work.

Influences on adolescents' expectations and choices

Thus far we have considered literature on the dual-earner family itself. Now we turn more specifically to the possible influences on daughters of growing up in a dual-earner family, knowing that considerable variation occurs within the dual-earner family form. Of particular interest is the identification of factors which might enhance female adolescents' visions of possible selves.

Choices about life roles are not made in a vacuum. They are formed and shaped by the reality of women's and men's lives within their culture. Recent research underscores the importance of understanding how gender-role socialization within families and educational institutions influences decisions about career and life choices (for example, Block, 1984; Eccles, 1987; Hare-Mustin and Marecek, 1990; Jacklin, 1989; Tittle, 1981). Parents' beliefs, values, and behaviors with regard to adult roles can particularly influence the self-concepts and goals of their children (Antill, 1987; Eccles et al., 1982; Hanson and Bozett, 1987; Jacklin, 1989; Tittle, 1981).

Markus and Nurius (1986) described the concept of possible selves. Possible selves represent individuals' ideas of what they might become, what they would like to become, and what they are afraid of becoming. Theoretically, individuals could create any number of possible selves. In actuality, the set of possible selves derives from individuals' experiences within their particular sociocultural and historical context and the models, images, and symbols which that culture provides them. 'Possible selves thus have the potential to reveal the inventive and constructive nature of the self but they also reflect the extent to which the self is socially determined and constrained' (Markus and Nurius, 1986: 954). Pat Schroeder, mentioned earlier in the chapter, is a popular and skillful member of the US House of Representatives with a highly visible and supportive spouse and children. She no doubt created powerful possible selves for women when she declared her candidacy for the presidency of the United States in 1988.

Particularly important to the creation of particular possible selves are: (1) the ability to transform a desire for a possible self into a vision for the self which is healthy, active, and strong; and (2) a set of plans and strategies that the individual feels able to implement (Markus and Nurius, 1986). As Heilbrun (1988) noted in the introductory quote to this chapter, traditionally all women had the same end – marriage and children – or one possible self. The purpose of her book, *Writing a Woman's Life*, is to encourage women to write their own lives – to create new images and possible selves of women.

Eccles's (1987) model of educational and occupational choice makes explicit the connection between individual differences on attitudinal variables and expectancies and socialization experiences. Two features of her model are particularly pertinent to the concept of possible selves described earlier. These are perceived field of options and complexity of choice. Clearly the narrower one's perceived field of options, the more limited one's choices. Parents can influence the options considered through modeling, encouraging, or providing certain kinds of experiences, and so forth. For example, children reared in gender-role traditional environments may eliminate or fail to consider options which fall outside of a narrowly defined area and, consequently, limit their choices to the traditional male-dominated or female-dominated fields.

The second feature of the model related to possible selves is complexity of choice. According to Eccles (1987), the decisions made by adolescents occur within a complex social reality which presents the individual with a number of choices, each with long-term and short-term consequences. Occupational choices may be influenced by such factors as the job market, indications of sexual discrimination or 'glass ceilings,' the nature of family-responsive programs provided by employers, or the fear that family life or marriage would have to be sacrificed.

Adolescents' views of work and family

Katz (1979) noted that adolescence offers one of the best times to examine attitudes toward gender roles and perhaps to influence these attitudes in view of the reality of women's participation in the labor force. A number of studies indicate that women's and men's decisions about life roles are moderated by a somewhat different set of factors. Most men who have access to educational opportunities assume they will enter careers, marry, and have children. Little thought is given to how these adult roles will be combined or to how marriage and children will influence chosen career paths. In contrast, women's career commitment and occupational choices are often influenced by considerations of future relationships with men and the rearing of children (Archer, 1985; Catalyst, 1987; Farmer, 1985; Tittle, 1981).

Tittle's (1981) study of middle-class urban eleventh-graders indicated that most expected to work full time after completing their formal education. When it came to combining work and family, however, 95 percent of the males but only 20 percent of the females expected to work continuously regardless of marriage and children. Aproximately 80 percent of the girls expected to work full or part time when children were between 3 and 12 years old. Archer (1985) reports that both the girls and boys in her sample of 96 adolescents from grades 6, 8, 10, and 12 desired careers but girls alone anticipated conflict with home roles which would require them to withdraw from the workforce. The major dilemma for girls was associated with the assumption that husbands would not involve themselves in family work and that support systems for their combining work and family continuously would be lacking. The author speculated that these girls may have internalized the view that working women carry most of the family responsibility and have little societal support for sharing these responsibilities by observing their parents' behaviors.

Farmer (1985) studied the same age group as Archer but used a much larger sample of ninth- and twelfth-graders and included measures of respondents' perceived support. Three aspects of environmental support were assessed – parent support for their school achievement, teacher support for their career plans, and views of support for working women from future husbands and society. As anticipated, the mediating effect of environmental support on motivational dimensions (aspirations, mastery, and career commitment) was stronger for young women than young men in the study.

Finally, Catalyst (1987) conducted a study with students from six diverse campuses to explore their attitudes about career and family roles for women and men. Responses indicated that most students, female and male alike, wanted satisfying careers and meaningful family lives, but that they had a very limited understanding of the realities involved such as salary expectations, parental leave policies, and difficulties typically experienced by working parents.

Maternal employment and its effects on daughters: emerging perspectives

In a recent update of earlier reviews on dual-earner families, Hoffman (1989) reached the same conclusions she had reached previously: maternal employment per se is not generally related to child outcomes. Instead, maternal employment 'operates through its effects on the family environment and the child care arrangements, and these are moderated by parental attitudes, family structure, and other variables' (1989: 289). At the same time, research on maternal employment does consistently document that among children of employed mothers, gender-role attitudes are more egalitarian than among children with nonemployed mothers. Moreover, comprehensive reviews of research data on maternal employment show that daughters of employed mothers were often reported to be more self-confident, to achieve better grades in school, and to pursue occupational work themselves more frequently than the daughters of nonemployed mothers (Hoffman, 1984, 1989).

A factor which appeared to contribute to these earlier findings was the importance of mothers as a female model of achievement for daughters (Eccles et al., 1982; Hackett et al., 1989; Scarr et al., 1989). Leslie (1986), for example, explored assessments of the rewards and costs of employment and parenthood in a large sample of eleventh- and twelfth-grade girls and the impact of these assessments on their plans for organizing their adult lives. The critical variable investigated in the study was the daughter's perceptions of what being an employed or nonemployed mother had been for her own mother. Overall, daughters of employed mothers rated employment as more rewarding and children as less costly to careers than did daughters whose mothers were full-time homemakers. Those daughters who saw their mothers as disliking employment were the most likely to perceive employment as costly for themselves. For daughters reared in both types of family, the assessed cost of employment was a significant predictor of future life roles, indicating that daughters' perceptions of mothers' experiences were influential. In a similar kind of study, Sandburg et al. (1987) assessed the career choices of 68 middle-class girls during childhood and then again during adolescence. Girls who preferred careers in male-dominated professions were more likely to identify with an employed mother than were girls who wanted to marry or who wanted to enter traditional female occupations.

The emerging perspectives The literature is replete with studies similar to the ones just described. Unlike the situation today, however, these investigators assumed female career aspirations and preferences for employment were unusual or atypical. In the 1990s full-time employment is normative for women, even after childbearing. Most mothers are employed and many prefer to be employed. Such a fundamental change in assumptions about maternal employment calls into question the usefulness of continuing to focus on the effect of maternal employment itself on daughters' gender-related choices. Whether a mother works becomes meaningless as a predictor when most mothers work. Instead, variables influenced by women's employment appear to hold particular importance for daughters' developing self-views. Thus women's greater economic independence and increased status in the family and in the society at large are likely to influence girls' possible selves. A second influential variable, particularly in terms of parental modeling and values, might be fathers' involvement in family work.

Maternal employment and paternal involvement in home roles

Hoffman (1989) wondered if the consistent finding that children of employed mothers hold less stereotypic attitudes about gender roles than do children of nonemployed mothers may be explained partially by the intermediating effect on the parental division of labor vis-à-vis home roles. Two aspects of fathers' behaviors appear relevant in this regard – role-modeling and motivations for involvement in home and family roles. That is, the male parent in dual-earner families, not unlike the female parent, may also model less stereotypic behavior, which in turn provides the child with alternative images of adult roles and how they can be combined. Also important may be the father's actual involvement with the child, the motivations for this involvement, and the effects of these kinds of experiences.

Processes responsible for fathers' involvement with children in dual-earner families may differ from those in single-earner families (Crouter et al., 1987; Gottfried et al., 1988; Hoffman, 1989). Participation in childrearing and household work by fathers in single-earner families appears to be motivated by individual preferences and motivations quite independent of changes in gender-role preferences and behaviors. Fathers' greater involvement with children in single-earner families, for example, was reported to be related to perceived competence in childrearing (Crouter et al., 1987) and attitudes toward the quality of parenting fathers themselves received (Barnett and Baruch, 1987). Fathers in single-earner families are also more likely than those in dual-earner families to involve themselves in play activities with the child and are less likely to carry out childcare and household tasks (Pleck, 1987).

The motivations of fathers in dual-earner families, in contrast, may also be embedded in the marital and family situation itself. That is, regardless of, or in addition to, personal preferences the realities of a dual-earner lifestyle may demand husbands' participation in parenting and household work. As we mentioned earlier in this chapter, wives who are employed typically push for husbands' increased participation in parenting and household work, particularly if wives prefer to be employed (Ross et al., 1983). In families in which wives are employed full time, marital satisfaction is best predicted by husbands' involvement in family work and their support for the wives' employment

(Baruch and Barnett, 1987). These dissimilar motivations for father participation in single-earner and dual-earner families may differentially impact on children's gender-role development.

Thus, although fathers in single-earner families may spend more time with children than in the past, the division of labor in the family remains basically unchanged and falls along gender lines. In contrast, fathers' participation in family roles in the dual-earner family could reflect a merging of spouses' roles. As already mentioned, men's participation in family work continues to increase, more so in the area of parenting than in the area of household work (Dancer and Gilbert, 1990; Pleck, 1983, 1985, 1987). When both parents of preschoolers are employed, studies indicate that fathers and mothers spend about the same total time in direct interaction with their children as do parents in families in which only the husband is employed (Jump and Haas, 1987; Scarr et al., 1989).

Female adolescent development, family context, and pattern of father involvement

The studies on adolescents' attitudes and intentions about work and family considered in previous sections of the chapter either investigated high-school and college students in general or made comparisons based on mother's choices and behavior. By and large these kinds of studies have not considered either (a) family context/structure, that is the variation of the nuclear family in which the adolescents actually grew up; or (b) pattern of father involvement, that is fathers' choices and behaviors about parenting and household work. Two studies by the authors explicitly took family context into account and these are now described briefly.[3]

Family context   Our interest focused on adolescents' perceptions of their involvement in occupational roles and their intention of integrating occupational and family roles. The studies examined background and process variables thought to relate to career decisions and life goals. The background variable was family context (that is, single-earner traditional family or one of two kinds of dual-earner families). Process variables included parents' patterns of combining work and family (traditional, modern, or egalitarian) and daughters' intentions regarding work and family integration and desired educational attainment, and their perceptions of parents' choices and satisfactions.

The early stages of this research involved the development of a psychometrically sound instrument, the Orientations to Occupational–Family Integration scales or OOFI scales, to assess respondents' views of whether and how occupational and family roles would be combined in their own lives (Gilbert et al., 1991). Two scales of the OOFI are relevant here: (1) the Female Traditional Scale (FTR) which reflects the view that although both women and men may be employed, the woman primarily holds responsibility for the home and children and the man for providing economically; and (2) the Role-Sharing Scale (RS) which reflects the view that occupational and family roles are integrated, both within the respondent and within the respondent's prospective marital partner.

The OOFI, once developed, was used to investigate perceptions of work and family roles in middle-class samples of young women who were university juniors and seniors (Study One) and high-school juniors (Study Two). On the basis of background information obtained from students in Study One, and from students and their parents in Study Two, respondents were classified into one of three types of families or contexts: traditional single-earner (SE), dual-worker (DW), and dual-career (DC). Dual-career families were defined as ones in which both spouses worked full time in positions which required substantial education, had clear development stages, and entailed a high degree of commitment; other combinations of full-time employment were defined as dual-worker.[4] Single-earner families were defined as those in which the father was employed full time and the mother not employed or employed less than half time.

In both studies, family context was found to be related to responses on the OOFI and to responses on career-related and parent-related variables as well. As predicted, young women reared in dual-earner (that is, DW and DC) families reported a lower commitment to a traditional orientation, a greater commitment to role-sharing in marriage, a higher commitment to continuous employment, and a higher desired educational level than those reared in traditional single-earner families. In addition, the DC and DW groups differed on the two career variables, employment commitment and educational level desired, with the DC group scoring higher on both.

The pattern of responses on the mother and father variables showed less consistent differences between the SE group, on the one hand, and the DW and DC groups on the other. Instead, DC and DW respondents differed on nearly all of the mother and father variables. Daughters from DC families saw both mothers and fathers as more satisfied, more influencing the daughter's choices, and in a positive way; parents were rated as higher in marital happiness and as holding higher vocational aspirations for daughters. DC respondents, more so than DW and SE respondents, also rated their own choices as similar to those of their mothers. The lowest ratings on the mother and father variables for the three family contexts generally occurred for the DW group. This pattern occurred for both mother's and father's satisfaction, influence on daughter, and marital happiness. Although daughters generally perceived parents to be quite happy in their marriages, DW girls as a group saw their parents as less happy than did girls in DC and SE families.

Daughters' ratings on these variables may reflect the greater overload experienced by wives in dual-worker families because roles are not appreciably redefined between spouses and possibly because of husbands' ambivalence about wives' employment. The dual-worker families in our samples mostly represented families in which husbands were in careers and wives in jobs. Personal decisions of spouses and disparate occupational demands may make it more difficult for these families to achieve a more egalitarian marriage although the balance they do achieve may be equitable from the vantage point of one or other spouse.

In summary, the results from the two studies fit the emerging views on the effects of maternal employment. High-school-aged and college-aged women who grew up in families where the integration of occupational and family roles was likely to be modeled, and probably encouraged, described self-views which reflected these experiences. Moreover, respondents from all three family contexts saw parents as influential in their choices about work and family roles.

Family context and pattern of father involvement   The emerging perspectives on maternal employment predict that employment by wives not only influences family context or structure, but through family structure also influences husbands' involvement in family work. Our second study with high-school girls included indices of each parent's pattern of involvement in family work and thus provided a test of these predictions. Information was gathered from each parent about their involvement in a subset of household and parenting activities. Fathers (and mothers) described their degree of involvement in six household and eight parenting activities (these are listed in Table 9.1) as well as their overall degree of involvement in these two areas. Responses were made on a 5-point Likert scale that ranged from 'husband is almost entirely responsible' (1) to 'wife is almost entirely responsible' (5).

The possible influence of fathers' pattern of involvement on daughters' perceptions and choices was then looked at in three ways. First, comparisons by family context were made for fathers' involvement on each household and parenting task. As anticipated, these comparisons yielded highly significant differences for overall involvement in household activities and on most of the specific household activities. Men in DC families, relative to men in SE and DW families, described themselves as most involved in household tasks, especially in

Table 9.1   *Housework and parenting activities rated by fathers for their level of day-to-day involvement*

Housework activities
        House cleaning
        Food shopping
        Preparing meals
        Washing clothes
        Making investments
        Paying bills

Parenting activities
        Attend conferences
        Take child to appointments
        Make decisions about social activities
        Help with homework
        Attend child's activities
        Talk with child about concerns
        Discipline child
        Leisure time with child

house cleaning, preparing meals, and washing clothes; SE men were least involved, with DW men being intermediate. The reverse pattern occurred for making investments. Also as anticipated, family context made little difference to men's involvement in parenting. The only difference was on spending leisure time with children; SE men indicated higher involvement in this activity than the DC and DW men.

Second, correlations were calculated between daughters' scores on two measures of gender-role attitudes included in the study (attitudes toward women scale, AWS, and Ideal Marital Roles Scale, MRS; Spence et al., 1973, 1980) and fathers' involvement in household work. Greater father involvement was expected to co-vary with more liberal scores from daughters. A similar pattern was not anticipated for parenting activities because, as noted earlier, fathers as a group are becoming more involved as parents although the motivations may differ for those in dual-earner and single-earner families. The correlations between daughters' scores on the two gender-role-related measures (AWS and MRS) and fathers' involvement in the four household tasks specifically related to housework fit with our theoretical expectations. For all four household activities the correlations were significant, although low in magnitude, indicating that greater father involvement was related to less traditional views. In contrast, no pattern was apparent in the correlations for parenting activities. With a few exceptions, these correlations were close to zero.

Both family context and pattern of father involvement were considered in the last approach to the data. Based on both partners' responses to the two general items, 'How do you and your spouse handle household tasks?' and 'parental responsibilities?,' families were categorized by pattern of fathers' involvement according to the conceptual categories described by Peplau (1983) – egalitarian, modern, or traditional within the DW and DC family contexts, and modern or traditional within the SE family context (for descriptions of these categories, see p.155). Daughters' OOFI scores were then calculated for each subgrouping.

Table 9.2 summarizes DW and DC daughters' scores on the Female-Traditional and Role-Sharing scales of the OOFI by level of father involvement in each family context. As can be seen from the table, the number of respondents in each category was quite small and precluded

Table 9.2 *Summary of OOFI means by two-parent family context and pattern of father involvement*

| Family context | Pattern of involvement | OOFI scores | |
		FTR	RS
Dual-career	Traditional ($n = 5$)	*3.33*	3.63
	Modern ($n = 9$)	2.91	3.98
	Role-sharing ($n = 7$)	2.36	*4.19*
Dual-worker	Traditional ($n = 7$)	2.31	*4.14*
	Modern ($n = 11$)	*3.33*	3.89
	Role-sharing ($n = 3$)	2.83	3.50
Single-earner	Traditional ($n = 7$)	*3.31*	2.72
	Modern ($n = 32$)	3.23	*3.32*

OOFI = Orientations to Occupational–Family Integration; FTR = Female traditional commitment; RS = Role-sharing commitment.

All responses are on a 5-point Likert scale which ranged from a low of one to a high of five. Scale scores were divided by the number of items on each scale.

Means italicized are the highest means in that column.

additional analyses. The pattern of the means was as anticipated, however. For girls in DC families, the highest commitment to role-sharing was for those reared in role-sharing family environments (item mean score of 4.19; items were rated on a 5-point scale which ranged from 1 to 5). Those reared in a more traditional dual-career family environment expressed a lower commitment (mean of 3.63). The DW family situation appears to be quite different in its possible effects. For this group, a higher commitment to role-sharing (mean of 4.14) was reported by daughters reared in a more traditional dual-worker environment where the mother does most of the household work in addition to her full-time employment, than by daughters from a role-sharing dual-worker environment where husbands fully participate in home roles (mean of 3.50 but based on only three participants). The stress girls in dual-worker families may recognize in their mothers' lives, as well as mothers' instructions to daughters to marry more liberal men than their fathers, may encourage these daughters to want something more equitable for themselves. Of the three family contexts, girls in SE families reported the lowest commitment to role-sharing regardless of pattern of father involvement.

These preliminary data provide some indication of how fathers' (and conversely mothers') pattern of involvement in household work and parenting may influence daughters' decisions about integrating work and family as adults. A good deal more additional research must be conducted to better understand how patterns of father involvement indirectly influence daughters through family context as well as how they independently relate to aspects of daughters' development. One of the principal longer-term questions relates to the shifting of men's roles and self-definitions. Because family roles have not typically been included in the study of men's well-being, the effects of quality of experience in family roles on fathers' psychological distress and well-being, and thus on children's development, are not well understood. Additional study of these variables is also needed with sons. Fathers' influence on sons' life choices and self-concepts may be quite different. There is a greater resistance to men taking on women's work than vice versa. Moreover, for men who want a greater care-giving role, approaches must be developed to overcome the influences of the workplace and society that discourage and devalue men's involvement with their children.

Closing remarks

Four themes emerge from our overview of the dual-earner family and the possible influences of this modal family form on children: first, the dual-earner family is not a single pattern and, within each pattern, there are variations in how spouses combine work and family roles (for example traditional, modern, and egalitarian); secondly, variables associated with mothers' employment status, such as parental attitudes, parents' modeling in the home, and opportunities within the society at large, appear more influential in children's choices for themselves and visions of possible selves than mothers' employment per se; thirdly, girls and boys reared in dual-earner families hold less stereotypic views of women's and men's roles, attributes, and abilities than those reared in traditional single-earner families; and finally, patterns of father (and mother) involvement in family work, and the family context in which it occurs, may particularly influence children's views of gender roles and the accompanying self-concepts and images of themselves as women and men which they subsequently develop.

Erikson (1968) described young adults as striving to achieve a self-definition which not only gives them a sense of knowing where they are going but also is met with support and approval from the significant others in their lives, particularly parents and other influential adults. According to Erikson, attaining a sense of inner identity represents the ability of individuals to adapt their special skills, capacities, and strengths to the prevailing role structure of society. In the past this meant that women and men lived separate lives. The emergence of the dual-earner family as a modal family form, within the larger context of women's increased opportunities and status in the USA and elsewhere, represents a changing role structure. Individuals today, regardless of sex, must consider their life choices within the broader framework of combining occupational work and family rather than of precluding one or the other. Increasing numbers of women and men are developing possible selves in which the demands of work and family are natural and not competing. The available research indicates that many adolescents today, particularly young women, hold this view (see Catalyst, 1987).

Parents' role-modeling and interactions with their children, and the visions they hold for their children's adult lives, appear highly important to this process. In several of the studies we described young women reared in role-sharing dual-earner homes envisioned themselves and their future spouse combining work and family in a way similar to their parents. However, because individual lives occur within a larger social context, changes in public attitudes and institutional arrangements, as well as new laws and public policies, become integral to such visions and to the ability of individuals to achieve them successfully. Societal change may be occurring too quickly for some, but these changes are not occurring quickly enough for many girls and boys limited by their society to less than full lives.

Notes

1. The research reviewed and the data presented in this chapter reflect the experiences of predominately Caucasian respondents who reside in the USA. Generalizations to other populations may not be appropriate.

2. Unlike other industrialized countries, in the United States employers determine the extent and type of benefit to most workers. However, through tax incentives, the government could encourage employers to provide benefits such as dependant care and other kinds of family-responsive programs. At this time there is no federal incentive program for dependant care.

3. Karen M. Rossman and Brian L. Thorn assisted with Study One and Sue Lucas with Study Two. Their valuable assistance is acknowledged with much appreciation.

4. There are important differences between families in which the wives' employment is a career and the wives' employment is a job, differences which may in turn affect men's participation in family work. The most obvious of these are the differential demands, commitments, and responsibilities of involvement in a career versus a job and the differences in self-concepts and life goals of women and men pursuing the two respective lifestyles.

References

Antill, J.K. (1987) 'Parents' beliefs and values about sex roles, sex differences, and sexuality: their sources and implications', in P. Shaver and C. Hendrick (eds), *Sex and Gender*, pp. 294–328. Beverly Hills, CA: Sage.

Archer, S.L. (1985) 'Career and/or family: the identity process for adolescent girls', *Youth and Society*, 16: 289–314.

Barnett, R.C. and Baruch, G.K. (1987) 'Social roles, gender, and psychological distress', in R.C. Barnett, L. Biener, and G. K. Baruch (eds), *Gender and Stress*, pp. 122–43. New York: Free Press.

Baruch, G. K. and Barnett, R. C. (1987) 'Role quality and psychological well-being', in F. Crosby (ed.), *Spouse, Parent, Worker*, pp. 63–84. New Haven, CT: Yale University Press.

Bernard, J. (1981a) *The Female World*. New York: Free Press.

Bernard, J. (1981b) 'The good provider role: its rise and fall', *American Psychologist* 36: 1–12.

Betz, N. and Fitzgerald, L.F. (eds) (1987) *The Career Psychology of Women*. Orlando, FL: Academic.

Block, J.H. (1984) *Sex Role Identity and Ego Development*. San Francisco: Jossey-Bass.

Carlson, B.E. (1984) 'The father's contribution to child care: effects on children's perceptions of parental roles', *American Journal of Orthopsychiatry*, 54: 123–36.

Catalyst (1987) 'New roles for men and women: a report on an educational intervention with college students'. (Available from 250 Park Ave. South, New York, NY 10003.)

Crosby, F. (ed.) (1987) *Spouse, Parent, Worker: On Gender and Multiple Roles*. New Haven, CT: Yale University Press.

Crouter, A.C., Perry-Jenkins, M., Huston, T.L. and McHale, S. M. (1987) 'Processes underlying father involvement in dual-earner and single-earner families', *Developmental Psychology*, 23: 431–40.

Dancer, L.S. and Gilbert, L.A. (1990) 'Participation in family work in dual-career, and traditional families', paper presented at the annual meeting of the American Psychological Society, Dallas, TX (June).

Eccles, J.S. (1987) 'Gender roles and women's achievement-related decisions', *Psychology of Women Quarterly*, 11: 135–72.

Eccles, J., Adler, T.F. and Kaczala, C.M. (1982) 'Socialization of achievement attitudes and beliefs: parental influences', *Child Development*, 53: 310–21.

Erikson, E. (1968) *Identity, Youth, and Crisis*. New York: Norton.

Farmer, H.S. (1985) 'Model of career and achievement motivation for women and men', *Journal of Counseling Psychology*, 32: 363–90.

Gilbert, L.A. (1985) *Men in Dual-Career Families: Current Realities and Future Prospects*. Hillsdale, NJ: Lawrence Erlbaum.

Gilbert, L.A. (1988) *Sharing It All: The Rewards and Struggles of Two-Career Families*. New York: Plenum.

Gilbert, L.A. and Rachlin, V. (1987) 'Mental health and psychological functioning in dual-career families', *The Counseling Psychologist*, 15: 7–49.

Gilbert, L.A., Dancer, L.S., Rossman, K.M. and Thorn, B.L. (1991) 'Assessing perceptions of occupational-family integration', *Sex Roles*, 24: 13–16.

Gottfried, A.E., Gottfried, A.W. and Bathrust, K. (1988) 'Maternal employment, family environment and children's development: infancy through the school years', in A. E. Gottfried and A.W. Gottfried (eds), *Maternal Employment and Children's Development: Longitudinal Research*, pp. 11–58. New York: Plenum.

Hackett, G., Esposito, D. and O'Halloran, M. S. (1989) 'The relationship of role model influences to the career salience of educational and career plans of college women', *Journal of Vocational Behavior*, 35: 164–80.

Hanson, S.M. and Bozett, F.W. (1987) 'Fatherhood and changing family roles', *Family and Community Health*, 9: 9–21.

Hare-Mustin, R. T. and Marecek, J. (1990) *Making a Difference: Psychology and the Construction of Gender*. New Haven, CT: Yale University Press.

Heilbrun, C.G. (1988) *Writing a Woman's Life*. New York: Balentine Books.

Hoffman, L.W. (1984) 'Work, family, and the socialization of the child', in R.D. Parke (ed.), *Review of Child Development Research*, vol. 7, pp. 223–81. Chicago: University of Chicago Press.

Hoffman, L.W. (1989) 'Effects of maternal employment in the two-parent family', *American Psychologist*, 44: 283–92.

Jacklin, C.N. (1989) 'Female and male: issues of gender', *American Psychologist*, 44: 127–33.

Jump, T.L. and Haas, L. (1987) 'Fathers in transition: dual-career fathers' participation in child care', in M.S. Kimmel (ed.), *Changing Men: New Directions in Research on Men and Masculinity*, pp. 98–114. Beverly Hills, CA: Sage.

Katz, P. A. (1979) 'The development of female identity', *Sex Roles*, 5: 155–78.

Kimball, G. (1988) *50/50 Parenting*. Lexington, MA: Lexington Books.

Knaub, P.K. (1986) 'Growing up in a dual-career family', *Family Relations: Journal of Applied Family & Child Studies*, 35: 431–7.

Leslie, L.A. (1986) 'The impact of adolescent females' assessments of parenthood and employment on plans for the future', *Journal of Youth and Adolescence*, 15: 29–49.

Markus, H. and Nurius, P. (1986) 'Possible selves', *American Psychologist*, 41: 954–69.

Peplau, L.A. (1983) 'Roles and gender', in H. H. Kelley, E. Berscheid, A. Christensen, J.H. Harvey, T.L. Huston, G. Levinger, E. McClintock, L.A. Peplau, and D.R. Peterson, *Close Relations*, pp. 220–64. New York: Freeman.

Perry-Jenkins, M. and Crouter, A.C. (1990) 'Men's provider role attitudes: implications for household work and marital satisfaction', *Journal of Family Issues*, 11: 136–56.

Pleck, J.H. (1983) 'Husbands' paid work and family roles: current research issues', in H. Lopata and J.H. Pleck (eds), *Research in the Interweave of Social Roles: Jobs and Families*, pp. 251–333. Greenwich, CT: JAI Press.

Pleck, J.H. (1985) *Working Wives/Working Husbands*. Beverly Hills, CA: Sage.

Pleck, J.H. (1987) 'American fathering in historical perspective', in M.S. Kimmel (ed), *Changing Men: New Directions in Research on Men and Masculinity*, pp. 83–97. Beverly Hills, CA: Sage.

Rapoport, R. and Rapoport, R.N. (1969) 'The dual-career family', *Human Relations*, 22: 3–30.

Repetti, R.L., Matthews, K.A., and Waldron, I. (1989) 'Employment and women's health: effects of paid employment on women's mental and physical health', *American Psychologist*, 44: 1394–1401.

Ross, C.E., Mirowsky, J. and Huber, J. (1983) 'Dividing work, sharing, work and in-between: Marriage Patterns and Depression'. *American Sociological Review*, 48: 809–23.

Sandburg, D.F., Ehrhardt, A.A., Mellins, C.A., Ince, S.E., and Meyer-Bahlburg, H.F.L. (1987) 'The influence of individual and family characteristics on career aspirations of girls during childhood and adolescence', *Sex Roles*, 16: 649–67.

Scarr, S., Phillips, D., and McCartney, K. (1989) 'Working mothers and their families', *American Psychologist*, 44: 1402–9.

Schroeder, P. (1985) 'Should leaves for new parents be mandatory?', *The New York Times*. 29 Dec.: 16E.

Spain, D. (1988) 'Women's demographic past, present, and future', paper presented at the Radcliffe Conference on Women in the 21st Century, Cambridge, MA (October).

Spence, J.T., Helmreich, R.L. and Stapp, J. (1973) 'A short version of the attitudes toward women scale (AWS)', *Bulletin of the Psychonomic Society*, 2: 219–20.

Spence, J.T., Helmreich, R.L. and Sawin, L.L. (1980) 'The male–female relations questionnaire', *JSAS Selected Documents in Psychology*, 10 (87).

Spence, J.T., Deaux, K., and Helmreich, R.L. (1985) 'Sex roles in contemporary American society', in G. Lindzey and E. Aronson (eds), *Handbook of Social Psychology*, 3rd edn, Vol. 2, pp. 149–78. Reading, MA: Addison-Wesley.

Thoits, P.A. (1987) 'Negotiating roles', in F.J. Crosby (ed), *Spouse, Parent, Worker: On Gender and Multiple Roles*, pp. 11–22. New Haven, CT: Yale University Press.

Thompson, L. and Walker, A.J. (1989) 'Women and men in marriage, work, and parenthood', *Journal of Marriage and the Family*, 51: 845–72.

Tittle, C.K. (1981) *Careers and Family: Sex Roles and Adolescent Life Plans*. Beverly Hills, CA: Sage.

US Department of Labor (1989) 'Facts on US working women', Women's Bureau, 200 Constitution Ave. NW Washington DC 20210–9990.

Walker, L.S. and Wallston, B.S. (1985) 'Social Adaptation: a review of dual-earner family literature', in L. L'Abate (ed.), *Handbook of Family Psychology*, pp. 698–740. Homewood, IL: Dow Jones-Irwin.

Zedeck, S. and Mosier, K.L. (1990) 'Work in the family and employing organization', *American Psychologist*, 45: 240–51.

10
Dual-Earner Families and the Care of the Elderly in Japan

Jeanette Taudin Chabot

Kimiko's story

Kimiko Watanabe is thirty-four years old.[1] She studied journalism at the University of Tokyo, Japan's most prestigious university and is currently employed at a European embassy in Tokyo. Her husband, Masahiro, was a classmate; theirs was a so-called 'love marriage'.[2] They have one daughter, Hiroko, aged five.

Masahiro works for one of the largest advertising agencies in Japan. He joined the firm immediately after his graduation from university. Although the tradition of lifetime employment is gradually giving way,[3] Masahiro has no intention – at the moment – of looking for a job with another firm. It would be difficult to find a more prestigious company to work for in his field, and he earns a generous salary cushioned further by 'bonuses' distributed twice yearly.[4] His company was a pioneer in introducing the five-day work week and therefore he has both Saturdays and Sundays free, although about once a month, on a Sunday, he plays golf with business associates.

During the week he is rarely home before midnight. He either works overtime or entertains business contacts. If he has to stay in town after eleven o'clock at night for business purposes (including entertaining clients), then the company covers the taxi fare home, which is US $90 per ride. Masahiro prefers a taxi ride home late at night to a longer and more tiring train journey earlier in the evening.

Masahiro takes his daughter to kindergarten every morning, and on two occasions when Kimiko was on an extended business trip he took several days' leave from work to take care of Hiroko. He rarely eats dinner at home during the week, let alone sharing the housework. On weekends he may help with shopping or take Hiroko to a neighborhood park, but he does not participate in household chores. Their apartment is small and Kimiko seems to prefer that he 'stay out of her way' rather than 'meddle with the housework'. During the weekend, if he is not playing golf, he takes long walks and browses through book shops and record shops.

After graduation, Kimiko started work as an executive secretary for the president of a large multinational company. For the first twelve months she was thrilled with her job. She could make good use of her English with her American boss. She was given quite an extensive range of responsibilities, including coordinating meetings, keeping up with business correspondence, screening visitors, translating, and receiving people. 'Important' people walked through her office and chatted with her on their way to her boss. She also attended luxurious dinners and receptions as an interpreter. As a bilingual executive secretary, a rare commodity in Japan, her starting pay was even higher than that of her husband. She knew that her job was glamorous by every standard in Japan – for a woman.

However, after the initial excitement of the 'foreign' setting and contact with business world celebrities, Kimiko came to realize that despite being a graduate of what is probably the most competitive university in the world, her status was after all only that of a secretary. In addition, although she earned a good salary, her job offered no possibilities for promotion. Accordingly, after four years with the company she began looking for another job and soon found her current position at a European embassy in Tokyo. She was to be in charge of regional development, a position which involved helping various Japanese firms to organize symposia, conferences, and trade fairs in fields related to the European country for which she worked. The Japanese were quick to recognize the possible implications of the integration of the Common Market in 1992, so the embassy was a stimulating place to work. She could continue making good use of her knowledge of the English language and, more importantly for her, she had a wide range of direct responsibilities and could shape the projects herself. She was also required to travel considerably within Japan and occasionally to Europe, something that proved to be a mixed blessing.

A year after Kimiko started working at the European embassy two significant things happened; she became pregnant and her husband was transferred to Sapporo, the farthest point from Tokyo within Japan. Because she was pregnant and therefore required extra medical attention which might have been difficult to obtain in a strange place, she decided not to follow her husband, but to move in with her parents who live in Yokohama, just outside Tokyo. Many Japanese husbands live separately from their families for several months or even years when they are relocated and so her decision to stay in Tokyo did not seem unusual.

Kimiko liked her new job tremendously. When her daughter, Hiroko, was born her mother took care of her and also made Kimiko's dinner when she returned from work. Kimiko took care of her daughter as often as possible, but without her mother she would not have been able to take business trips. Her husband came 'home' about four times that first year, and she flew to Sapporo once to visit him. Kimiko was finally beginning to find a balance between work and family life which gave her a sense of satisfaction.

After a year and a half of separation Masahiro began to insist that Kimiko and Hiroko come to live with him in Sapporo, pointing out that all his colleagues had their wives to take care of them. He even wanted to buy a house in Sapporo, since it seemed that he might stay there for some time. Kimiko resisted. By this time she had determined never to give up her career, realizing that meaningful work played a central role in her life. Consequently, tension mounted between Kimiko and her husband. When Masahiro hinted that she should 'come over here, or else . . .', she even considered divorcing him, rather than relinquishing her career in Tokyo to become a full-time housewife in Sapporo. She was convinced it would be impossible to find such a satisfying job there. Moreover, even if a reasonable job were available, she would be unable to replace the type of childcare her mother was providing.

Before Kimiko was forced to decide Masahiro was seriously injured in a car accident in which two other passengers were killed instantaneously. Masahiro was hospitalized in Sapporo for four months, during which time Kimiko flew to Sapporo every weekend. When her husband was discharged from the hospital his company sent him back to Tokyo, thus resolving their earlier problem.

Kimiko found an apartment close to her parents as she still relied on her mother to babysit. It was difficult to make a new start as a family. When the daughter, who was then three years old, asked 'When is this uncle going away?' Masahiro immediately retorted that had Kimiko talked about him more often to their daughter she would never have made such a comment. Even though Kimiko considered herself lucky to work a five-day week, she found running a full household burdensome and tiring. She would spend almost the whole weekend cleaning, doing the laundry, shopping for the week's groceries and playing with her daughter. In addition, after having become accustomed to managing by herself, she found it annoying to have to explain her actions and to consult her husband. Now she usually works normal hours (9–5, plus three hours' commuting per day). She rushes to pick up her daughter from her mother, cooks dinner, eats dinner with her daughter, and reads to her. By that time, it is nine o'clock. She has about an hour to herself in the evening, usually reading until her husband comes home. She is often already asleep when he arrives.

Hiroko attends a kindergarten which is close to Kimiko's parents' house from 8.30 a.m. until 2.30 p.m. Either Kimiko's sixty-five-year-old mother or her retired seventy-one-year-old father, is at home for

Hiroko at about three o'clock when she is brought home by her kindergarten teacher. For the parents' days (when parents are expected to spend the day at kindergarten), either Kimiko or Masahiro (whenever Kimiko is unavailable because of business trips) has always attended. If Kimiko cannot be home by seven in the evening Kimiko's mother gives Hiroko dinner and when Kimiko is away on a business trip, Hiroko may even sleep over at her grandmother's home.

Unlike professional women in many other industrialized countries Kimiko is in no position to hire help for household chores and childcare. Japan is a very homogeneous country in which differences in income and educational background are minimal. It is virtually impossible for the average dual-earner family to hire regular domestic help. Japan has very tough immigration laws which prohibit people from poorer foreign countries working in Japan. Although many restaurants and construction sites do hire workers from other countries, such as the Philippines and Pakistan, it is illegal to do so. Very limited space in private homes also makes it impractical for private families to illegally hire foreign help for live-in childcare. Japan has a shortage of laborers at this moment, and the possibility of a change in policy to legalize the hiring of foreign workers is under consideration. However, as Japan is an island with no experience as a multiracial country, it is feared that a large influx of foreigners might create considerable social strain. In any case, the government is resisting the legalization of foreign laborers at the present time. Accordingly Kimiko does not have the option of 'importing' cheap foreign help as a substitute for her mother to care for Hiroko.

Kimiko's mother has never complained about taking such extensive care of her granddaughter. Kimiko knows, however, that caring for Hiroko severely restricts the grandmother's own social life and leisure activities. She has also noticed that her mother looks tired. Yet an even more strenuous time for both Kimiko and her mother is still to come. Next year when Hiroko starts elementary school she will return home at 1.30 p.m., placing a heavier burden on Kimiko's mother, which will last for the entire first year. From the second grade the school hours will be longer, until 3 or 4 p.m., depending on the grade. Kimiko hopes that her mother will be able to sustain this pace for at least another four or five years. For Kimiko, Hiroko's attendance at elementary school means that she will have to be available for even more parents' days and evening meetings to discuss her daughter's academic progress, as well as to receive the teacher when she pays home visits. Kimiko will also be responsible for ensuring that her daughter does her homework diligently. She would also like her daughter to take piano lessons but in Japan it is usually the responsibility of the mother to make sure that the child practices every day at home. Recently Kimiko has started to insist that Masahiro takes days off to care for Hiroko when she is on long business trips.

Masahiro wants to have another child. Kimiko realizes that if they are to have any more children, they should not wait much longer. She would like Hiroko to have a brother or a sister but also feels that she is fully stretched and that she could not feasibly cope with a heavier workload. Kimiko knows that she cannot count on a substantial increase in her husband's contribution to housework or childcare and that she would have to rely on her mother to take the full burden of raising another child from infancy at a time when she feels she should be doing something to cut down on her mother's workload. Therefore Kimiko has decided against having another child, despite the fact that she considers being Hiroko's mother to be the most fulfilling part of her life. She has already told Masahiro about her decision and he was clearly not happy to hear it. The issue still crops up from time to time.

Kimiko has one older sister who is married and has two children. She lives with her husband's parents, who take care of her children while she works part time. She started working after the children were in elementary school and her current working hours do not inconvenience the family life in any substantial way. She does most of the housework and all of the cooking for her three-generation household. What she enjoys most of all about her part-time work is the privacy she has being away from her in-laws and the extra cash at her disposal. Kimiko's sister is actually a more typical case of a married woman working outside the home in Japan, than Kimiko.

Masahiro's parents, who live on the other side of Tokyo, are slightly older than Kimiko's parents. Masahiro is their only son and in a few years' time he would like to live with his parents. Kimiko feels strongly that if the time comes when her parents are unable to take care of one another, she would like to live with them and take care of them. She would then have to give up her career. She would not give it up to live with her husband, nor would she give it up to become a housebound mother for her daughter. Yet she will give it up for her parents, who raised not only her but also her daughter. She said that

> without my parents, particularly my mother, I wouldn't have been able to have a career, because of the childcare problem. They have supported me unconditionally in every way they possibly could, and in doing so they enabled me to do what I really wanted with my life – to have a career and a child. In fact I owe more to my parents than to my husband.

In effect she has exchanged the childcare problem for a potential eldercare problem.

In answer to the question of what she would do were her husband's parents to require live-in help and Masahiro insisted on moving in with them, she replied,

> When my husband says 'Let us move in with my parents', he means *we* move in, *he* would continue working, and *I* would have to give up my career to take care of them. I wouldn't give up my career to care for his parents. Were I to do so, and then my own parents needed the same kind of help, I wouldn't be available to provide it. I cannot do that to my parents who did everything they could to enable me to achieve what I really wanted to do in my life. Besides, Hiroko isn't close to Masahiro's parents; she was not raised by them. If my husband really insists on moving in with his parents, we will have to separate then, I guess.

In fact, if they want to buy a house of their own within reasonable commuting distance, Kimiko and Masahiro may have to decide with which set of parents to live even before any of the parents become dependent on them. Although they earn good salaries, it would not be possible to finance both land and a house from their earnings and the amount that they can borrow. Real estate prices are extremely high and are still rising in Tokyo and its environs. As both sets of parents own their houses and land, Kimiko and Masahiro may decide to build a larger house on one of the properties and live with the parents who provide the land. This is a very common arrangement in Japan. Where they build their house will determine with which set of parents they will live.

This is the situation that Kimiko and Masahiro Watanabe face in 1990. Although they represent the elite of Japanese society in terms of education and jobs, the problems with which they are struggling are widely encountered by Japanese dual-earner couples.

Women in the Japanese labor market

About half of all Japanese women are employed, and they constitute 40 percent of the total labor force. Almost two-thirds of the employed women are married. Only 11 percent of the labor force works part time although the proportion is increasing rapidly (Steinhoff and Tanaka, 1988). Women comprise 71 percent of part-time workers. The popularity of part-time work, particularly for mothers of young children, is illustrated by Kimiko's story. The long working day exacerbated by excessive commuting time, the need to travel extensively and often to relocate, which are characteristics of more demanding jobs, create a situation where it is extremely difficult for both parents to pursue full-time careers, even in the context of support from extended family. Japanese women are almost as well educated as men in that 35.4 percent of women attend college compared to 38.2 percent of men (Iwao, 1989). However, in Japan, as elsewhere, women are underrepresented in senior positions in the workplace. Currently however, there is a shortage of labor, from menial labor to managerial positions.[5] The number of women with managerial titles increased by 50 percent between 1982 and 1987 (Solo, 1989). Women's labor force participation will be increasingly important in the 1990s if the pace of the Japanese economy is to be maintained. The recent increase in the elderly population has also intensified the demand for women's labor to care for relatives both in the home and in the labor market, where women staff social welfare agencies. These agencies are increasing rapidly, albeit not fast enough to keep up with demand (Okifuji, 1982a).

Men's participation in childcare and domestic work is limited and hired domestic help is not readily available. In this context it is common for employed mothers, like Kimiko, to be supported by childcare assistance from their parents or parents-in-law. In addition there are nurseries and kindergartens, both public ones which are subsidized according to income and more expensive private ones. There are also the so-called baby hotels, where infants can stay for 24 hours a day. These are commercial and very expensive and so their use is limited. It is socially acceptable and even considered desirable to send one's children to kindergartens, which are viewed as places for education. The nurseries, however, tend to be viewed as places where poor people who *have* to work send their children, although this image is beginning to change. These nurseries have limited opening hours and are therefore of limited use given the long commuting hours in Japan. The number of nurseries is considered adequate, although the distribution is not ideal. The government is now working on extending the opening hours of nurseries, as well as increasing provision for handicapped infants and children. In the light of these provisions and the readily available help from extended family, childcare is less problematic for dual-earner couples than the issue of eldercare.

Care of the elderly is quickly becoming the number one problem for career women in Japan. Women who, like Kimiko, rely on parents or parents-in-law to assist in childcare, feel an increased sense of gratitude and obligation to care for these parents in their declining years. In 1985, the Zensen Federation (union of textile, apparel, and supermarket workers) pressed for legislation that would grant employees (men and women) up to one year of unpaid leave to care for family members at home. Although phrased to refer to any family member, the proposed legislation was intended primarily for the care of the elderly. The Federation was not successful in its attempts. There are some local governments, such as the Osaka Prefectural Government, and some department stores which offer unpaid leave, but this is for a limited period of between one and two months. Such a short period is not sufficient to resolve the problem since the elderly may require full-time care for several years.

The elderly in Japan

Until the end of World War II, the law stipulated that the oldest son should inherit the entire family estate and take care of his parents. After the war, the legislation was changed and inheritance shared equally amongst all the children. The eldest son is no longer legally obliged to take care of his parents. Social customs die slowly however, and the expectation that the oldest son should take care of his parents persists. Where he is not in a position to do so, other children are then expected to take over.

Until recently there were few institutions for the elderly, (defined as people above sixty-five), and those that existed were of a poor standard. In recent years more apartments with special facilities for the elderly are being built and the social stigma associated with staying in an institution or with sending one's parents to one is diminishing. Also more elderly people now live alone or with their partners only. In 1979 80 percent of the elderly lived with their children (van der Burgt-Franken, 1990). In 1989, only 50 percent of the elderly lived in extended families. Nineteen percent lived as couples and 14 percent lived alone.

Despite the decline in the number of elderly people living with their children, it remains most common for sick and frail relatives to be cared for by family. In 1985, of the 480,000 bedridden elderly in Japan, 270,000 were cared for by family members at home, 100,000 were hospitalized, and 110,000 were in special intensive care nursing homes. In 90 percent of the cases where the family was involved, family members, mainly wives of sons, were responsible for taking care of the elderly (*Asahi Shinbun* [newspaper], 9 January 1985). It is estimated that approximately half of 740,000 senile people who require extensive nursing care will still be taken care of by (female) family members in their homes in 1990 (*Asahi Shinbun*, 9 January 1985). The number of senile people is expected to climb to 1.85 million by the year 2014 (Koseisho, 1988). Outside help at reasonable prices in the form of district nurses, meal service, or help with bathing is still very limited. With the trend towards higher life expectancy, the period that requires such extensive care also lengthens.

Life expectancy in Japan is 84 years for women and 79 for men. In contrast to the West, where the 'graying' of the population was gradual and took place over almost a century, in Japan the process began after World War II and proceeded rapidly. For instance in 1950, 4.1 million people, or about 5 percent of the population, were elderly. In 1980, the number rose to 10.43 million, representing 8.8 percent of the population; by the year 2000 the percentage is expected to be 14 percent and 24 percent in 2020. Thus it will take only thirty years for the proportion of elderly in Japan to climb from 7 percent to 14 percent, while in France it took over 115 years and in Sweden, 90 years (Mori, 1983). Furthermore the role of older people in society has changed. A century ago 80 percent of the population was engaged in agriculture. In an agrarian society older people perform useful functions and there are several adults in each household to care for young children and the sick elderly. Following World War II, Japan changed dramatically from an agrarian to an industrialized society with the nuclear family as an increasingly prevalent form of household. In 1920, 51.2 percent of employed persons of fifteen years and over were engaged in agriculture, in 1960 the figure was 30.1 percent and the number still continues to decline (Bureau of Statistics, 1987). A rapidly declining birth rate also contributes to the overall demographic changes (see Table 10.1).

Table 10.1   *Demographic changes*

	Birth rate (per '000)	Natural increase rate (per '000)	Total fertility rate
1950	25.47	14.44	3.65
1970	15.26	10.04	2.13
1987	11.95	9.07	1.69

Source: Bureau of Statistics (1989: 53)

The three-generation family

Despite the growing number of nuclear families, there are still many three-generation households – 47.4 percent of the households in 1983 (Kaneko, 1984). The acute housing problem contributes to this phenomenon. Because land prices have soared in the last ten years, it has become almost impossible to buy a house with one family's normal income. This has led to the consolidation of resources between two generations. If the parents own land with a small or dilapidated house, the children will take a loan to build a new house on the parents' land. Sometimes they can afford to have two almost independent apartments within one house, where only the Japanese-style bathroom is shared. In other circumstances the parents will retain one room of their own and share all facilities and lead one household life. About 26 percent of the elderly who live with their children share their room with someone else in the household (Kagoyama, 1978). If the parents own no property, the father's entire retirement money may provide a significant part of the mortgage for the house or apartment for the three generations. In that case, the elderly people who provided the mortgage expect to be supported by the child in whose name the house is registered.

The fact that there are so many three-generation households in Japan at this moment is a double-edged sword for working women. While the woman's in-laws or her own parents are healthy, they provide excellent childcare and household services that are irreplaceable in the commercial market. Their support enables the younger women not only to earn money or achieve job satisfaction, but also to enjoy some privacy from their in-laws. Problems arise later when even energetic and ambitious working women such as Kimiko who can manage the period of raising children successfully often have to succumb to family pressures and leave the labor force when their parents are elderly and require care.

Care of elderly parents: the role of the daughter-in-law

Japanese children grow up observing that their parents make many financial 'sacrifices' for them. In a society where education has a high priority, parents often spend a sizeable part of their savings to give their children the best education possible. This can be a considerable amount as the Japanese save the most, per capita, in the world: about 16.5 percent of their income, compared to 1.3 percent by the West Germans (*Mainichi Shinbun* [newspaper] 21 November 1985). They also contribute heavily to the luxurious wedding parties that have become a social custom. It could be argued that the parents are in fact providing for their old age by the money they invest in the education, weddings, or housing of their children. Nevertheless, the social and personal expectations of both the parents and children are that parents should be cared for personally by their children in their old age.

When the older wife is no longer able to care for her husband, it is almost always the daughter-in-law who takes over. Only if the elderly couple live with their own daughter, does she care for them. In some cases where a daughter-in-law falls ill (often from the exhaustion of taking care of her in-laws) her husband (the real son) may take over caring for his parents and spouse. In such, still rare, cases a husband would do as much of the household chores and family caring as possible but he is usually assisted by hired nursing help, if this can be afforded, or by a social worker.

The daughters-in-law who often spend years caring intensively for in-laws have, until recently, had no automatic legal rights to the inheritance of their husband's parents. According to recent law, a divorced wife who cared for her in-laws is now entitled to a portion of the husband's share of the inheritance after their death.

Changing patterns of marriage

As it is the norm for sons (or rather their wives) to care for aged parents, only sons or eldest sons are usually not matched in arranged marriages, with women from daughters-only households. In agrarian villages where the daughters-in-law are expected not only to live with their in-laws but also to work on the land, there is such an acute shortage of brides that some men have resorted to arranged marriages with women from South Asian countries. Even in cities, where wives often do not live with their in-laws for the first ten years of marriage, more and more women are refusing to marry so as to avoid the destiny of 'sacrificing their freedom'. Although traditionally in Japan the social expectation to get married at a certain age (for women around the age of twenty-four, for men about twenty-eight) has been very strong in the past, many women now choose to stay single or at least postpone marriage and childbirth until as late as possible (see Table 10.2). As a result many men who would like to get married are not able to find marriage partners. The shortage of brides has contributed to the tremendous commercial success of 'bridegroom schools' which were launched in 1989.

Table 10.2   *Percentage of women married, by age group (1965–85)*

	20–24 years old	25–29 years old
1965	31.4	79.6
1985	17.9	67.6

Statistics in the form reported in Japan.

Source: Bureau of Statistics (1987: 83)

'Bride schools' where cooking, sewing, and etiquette are taught, have long been familiar in Japan, but 'bridegroom schools' are new. They teach men how to talk to women and what to talk about. They teach psychology and table manners, in order that women may find the men attractive enough to marry.

For many women who have already chosen to marry, have children, and continue working, the care of the elderly is one of the greatest challenges they face in their lives. Two bestselling books dealing with this theme were *Kokotsu no hito* (Twilight Years) by Sawako Ariyoshi (1982) and *Onna ga shokuba wo saru hi* (The Day the Woman Leaves her Workplace) by Noriko Okifuji (1982b). In both works, the central female characters give up their jobs after heroic and superhuman efforts to sustain their careers while caring for a senile father-in-law in one case and for a bedridden father in the other.

Women are increasingly reluctant to relinquish their careers to care for elderly in-laws or parents. Furthermore, it is not economically feasible for so many women to leave the labor force for this purpose. Some Japanese women are refusing to marry, or to have children, so as to reduce their burden. However, this does not always solve the problem of eldercare, as many single career women spend all their free time and earnings on their own aged parents. Measures such as flexible working time, longer paid or unpaid leave from work and more daycare centres and homes for the elderly may lighten women's burden. Nevertheless the cultural expectation that eldercare is a daughter-in-law's or a daughter's responsibility persists, creating considerable tension among dual-earner families.

The problems anticipated by Kimiko as her parents and parents-in-law grow older preoccupy a whole generation of women who have managed, with the support of the extended family, to combine a career with marriage and motherhood, but who now face the more daunting challenge of eldercare. Although there is some progress in the availability and acceptability of alternative care for the elderly, women's traditional obligation to care for aged parents-in-law or parents continues to create a dilemma for many dual-earner women later in the family cycle.

Notes

1. The names used in this chapter are not the real names of the people described, but their story is true. The case study is taken from a series of interviews and was selected because it illustrates dilemmas commonly faced by dual-earner women in Japan.

2. The so-called love marriages in Japan are marriages in which partners have found each other without intermediaries. Intermediaries (university mentors, superiors at work, relatives, etc.) play an important role in introducing young (and sometimes not so young) people to each other for the purpose of making a match.

3. Although many Western and Japanese people believe that lifetime employment is a Japanese tradition, in fact it was introduced after World War II and exists only in large organizations. Small subcontractors to large companies, which employ the great majority of the labor force, were never able to offer such a luxury to their employees. However, it is a new trend in Japan that even employees of big organizations, where lifetime employment guarantees exists, change jobs.

4. The Japanese receive relatively low base salaries. Each organization normally distributes 'bonuses' twice yearly, depending upon the profits. A bonus is a way of distributing profit among employees. This system gives flexibility to the company and often motivates the employees.

5. In the last two years the closing of small companies for lack of employees has aroused much media attention. There is a definite shortage of labor to accommodate

Japan's booming economy at this moment. Many restaurants and construction sites hire illegal workers from South East Asia and many newspaper delivery people are also foreigners who cannot even read Japanese. Considering how highly automated and robotized Japanese factories are, Japan's distribution system and service industries offer very labor-intensive services which seem unnecessary in Western eyes. Some people think that the current labor shortage will have adverse effects on the Japanese economy; others think this situation will lead to structural changes resulting in greater economic efficiency.

References

Ariyoshi, Sawako (1982) *Kokotsu no hito* (Twilight Years). Tokyo: Shinchosha.

Bureau of Statistics Management and Coordination Agency (1987) *Final Report of the 1985 Population Census*. Tokyo: Government Printing.

Bureau of Statistics Management and Coordination Agency (1989) *Japan Statistical Yearbook 1989*. Tokyo: Government Printing.

Iwao, Sumiko (1989) 'Youth, women, and society', paper delivered in The Hague during a conference organized by the Embassy of Japan under the same title.

Kagoyama, Takashi (1978) 'Koreisha no seikatsu kozo to seikatsu jittai' (Life structure and actual lifestyle of the elderly), *Jurist*, 12 (Autumn): 24–8.

Kaneko, Isamu (1984) *Koreika no shakai sekkei* (Designing an Old Age Society). Tokyo: Academia shuppansha.

Koseisho (Ministry of Welfare) (ed.) (1988) *Kosei Hakusho* (White Paper on Welfare). Tokyo: Government Printing.

Mori, Mikio (1983) *Rojin mondai towa nanika* (What Are Old Age Problems?). Tokyo: Minerva shobo.

Okifuji, Noriko (1982a) *Gin no sono* (Silver Garden). Tokyo: Shinchosha.

Okifuji, Noriko (1982b) *Onna ga shokuba wo saru hi* (The Day the Woman Leaves Her Workplace). Tokyo: Shinchosha.

Solo, Sally (1989) 'Japan discovers woman power', *Fortune*, June: 64–9.

Steinhoff, Patricia G. and Tanaka, Kazuko (1988) 'Women managers in Japan', pp. 103–21 in Nancy J. Adler and Dafna N. Izraeli (eds), *Women in Management Worldwide*. Armonk and London: M.E. Sharpe.

van der Burgt-Franken, Alexandrien (1990) *Orientatie op de thuiszorg in Japan* (Orientation on the House Care in Japan). Zoetermeer: Brederaad.

PART THREE

WORK AND THE FAMILY: IMPLICATIONS FOR ORGANIZATIONAL POLICY

11
Beyond 1992: Dutch and British Corporations and the Challenge of Dual-Career Couples

Helen Hootsmans

Double Trouble or Company Strength? The Question for the 90s

Preparations for the unification of the twelve European Community countries in 1992 present an excellent opportunity for corporations to reassess the efficacy of traditional models of work to meet the needs of a changing workforce. A time of transition opens many doors, at the same time offering leaders a cover for making strategic and far-reaching changes.

The European Act of 1987 calls for the free mobility of people, goods and capital in Western Europe by January 1993. The goal of uniting Europe is complicated by diverse language, cultural and historical backgrounds. The practical harmonization of the various health, social welfare and tax systems will involve further problems. It is not yet clear how much harmonization of either social policy or corporate policy and culture is desirable or possible. Nevertheless, the need to fit into the wider European Community context requires a certain level of introspection and adaptation by organizations. The increase in the number of dual-earner couples throughout Europe requires that this adaptation should include recognition of the importance of the interface of work and family for both men and women. Top management in Europe as elsewhere has traditionally been comprised of single-earner males. Dual-career couples, who share a deep commitment to simultaneously maintaining their personal relationships and their careers, now form a small but steadily growing segment of the dual-earner population (Hootsmans, 1986). As these dual-career couples are increasingly represented on corporate management teams, they are suitably positioned to serve as reference points for work and family issues, as change agents and as implementers of new policy.

Given the diversity of the European Community context, and the complexity of the myriad unification issues, this chapter is no more than a preliminary overview of current corporate practice and policies of potential value to dual-career couples. Following a brief sketch of the European Community context, Britain and the Netherlands will serve as primary references for the overview. While Britain more closely resembles the United States than the Continental Community countries with regard to general working conditions, the Netherlands represents a middle point, both leading and lagging behind in various facets of the work and family interface.

The need for more fundamental change in organizations will be addressed with particular reference to issues of relocation, communication and alternative career paths. In a time of transition, it is relevant to signal current developments and directions for future focus. The key questions remain how attuned are corporations to the expectations, capabilities and possibilities of the new dual-career workforce and to the demands of a competitive global market? How willing is management to risk initiating and supporting change in work and family issues?

The context for European unification

Female labor force participation
Female participation rates vary across the European Community. Figure 11.1 shows women's share of the total employment in the twelve member states.

A large proportion of European women are employed part time (see Table 11.1). There is considerable variation, however, both in what constitutes part-time work and in its prevalence in the different member states (see Cook, chapter 12 of the present book). Whereas in France, 12.2 percent of the women employed part-time work less than 10 hours per week, in Britain, 23.8 percent work less than 10 hours. Six percent of British women work 31 hours or more in comparison with 12.6 percent in France (Barrère-Maurisson et al., 1990).

The different occupational sectors remain largely sex segregated throughout the Community (Commission, 1989: 47) with the percentage of women in management positions consistently low throughout Europe (Kops, 1986).

Substantial changes in the pattern of women's employment are anticipated during the 1990s as a consequence of demographic shifts. As a result of the drop in the birthrate in the 1970s in the United Kingdom, for instance, the number of 16–19-year-olds will decrease by approximately one-quarter by the mid-1990s and by 1995 retirement from the workforce will far exceed the influx of young people (NEDO,

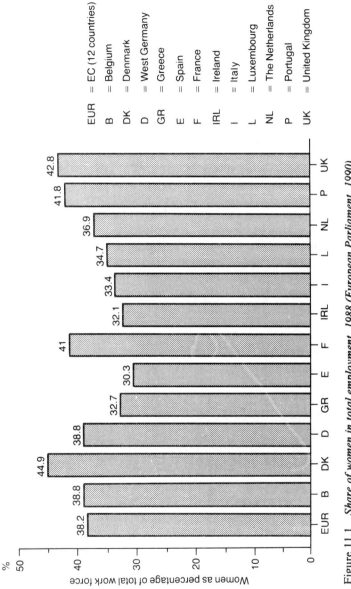

Figure 11.1 *Share of women in total employment, 1988 (European Parliament, 1990)*

Table 11.1   *Proportion of women in part-time work in five EC countries, 1986*

	Women in part-time work (% of all employed women)
Belgium	21.1
Denmark	43.9
France	23.1
The Netherlands	54.2
United Kingdom	45.0

Source: Emancipatieraad, 1989; UK data from OECD, 1986

1989). These trends are mirrored throughout the European Community. The slowing down of population growth has been most pronounced in what was formerly West Germany, but Italy, Belgium, Luxembourg, Denmark, the Netherlands and Portugal have also had low birthrates over the last decade (Berry-Lound, 1990). The shortage of labor resulting from these developments together with increasing competition within the single European market makes women's participation in the workforce an economic necessity (Commission, 1989: 38). There is a growing awareness among employers of the need to look beyond the traditional male recruitment pool for new employees and specifically for management potential (VNO, 1988; SoZaWe, 1989a, b; Hansard, 1990). The situation may be further complicated by the influx of workers from Eastern Europe since the fall of the Berlin Wall. While it should take some years to upgrade their skills and qualifications, this may occur just at the point at which demographic shortages should be creating more opportunities for women. It remains to be seen which sector of the reserve labor force, women or (former) East Europeans, industry will seek as its first supplement.

Equal opportunities legislation and statutory regulations

The Commission for the European Communities, the official governing body for the EEC, has provided two significant instruments as the backdrop for corporate work and family connections in Europe. The European Equality Directives cover equal pay for men and women (1975), equal treatment at work (1976), equal treatment in social security (1978) and in pensions (1986). These directives are of primary importance as the foundation for national legislation and as steps towards harmonization.

The second instrument, the Community Charter of Fundamental Social Rights for Workers, adopted by eleven member states on 8–9 December 1989, offers an even wider framework for socio-cultural changes in the long term. The most direct references to the work and family interface in this social charter are to be found in section 16 which states:

> Equal treatment for men and women must be assured. Equal opportunities for men and women must be developed. To this end, action should be intensified to ensure the implementation of the principle of equality between men and women as regards in particular access to employment, remuneration, working conditions, social protection, education, vocational training and career development. Measures should also be developed enabling men and women to reconcile their occupational and family obligations. (Commission, 1990a: 7)

Described as one of the most important human rights documents of the century (Kassalouw, 1990), the European Social Charter's purpose is to

> be at once a solemn statement of progress already made in the social field and a preparation for new advances – that the same importance may be given to the social dimension of the Community as to its economic aspects, in the construction of the large market of 1992. (Commission, 1990a: 2)

Responsibility for its implementation lies with the social partners (government, management and unions), the individual national states as well as the Commission itself. The action program to implement the Social Charter comprises some 50 proposals to be brought before the Council of Ministers by 1992.

Objections to these proposals, and particularly to the proposal for equal treatment of full-time and part-time workers, was stated as a reason why the UK still had not ratified the Charter as of December 1990 (Russel, 1990). Economic objections are strong. If the Commission's proposal becomes law, Britain will have to address the question of national insurance contributions, pensions, unemployment and health benefits for an estimated 2.4 million part-time workers (NWW, 1990).

Government regulations and provisions
At the level of national government, statutory regulations play a large role in regard to work and family issues. Two key statutory regulations benefiting working couples concern maternity leave and parental leave. There is considerable variation in these provisions across the member states (see Table 11.2).

Childcare
Table 11.3 provides an overview of public childcare provisions available in the European Community.

Within the European Community, France provides the most

Table 11.2   *Maternity and parental leave*

	Maternity leave	Parental leave
Germany	6 weeks before birth, 8 weeks after (12 for multiple births). 100% of earnings	18 months. Low flat-rate payment for 6 months; payment then depends on family income, so higher-income family gets less
France	6 weeks before birth, 10 weeks after (longer for 3rd+ and multiple births). 84% of earnings	Until child is 3. No payment unless 3 or more children; then low, flat-rate payment
Italy	2 months before birth, 3 months after. 80% of earnings	6 months. 30% of earnings
Belgium	14 weeks altogether; 8 weeks must be taken after birth, the other 6 weeks can be taken before or after. 75% of earnings (82% for first month)	None, but workers can take leave for family or personal reasons
Netherlands	16 weeks altogether; 4–6 weeks can be taken before birth, 10–12 weeks after. 100% of earnings	6 months unpaid part-time, min. 20 hrs per week. Partial payment for civil servants[a]
Luxembourg	6 weeks before birth, 8 weeks after (12 for multiple births). 100% of earnings	None
United Kingdom	11 weeks before birth, 29 weeks after. 90% of earnings for 6 weeks, low flat-rate payment for 12 weeks, no payment for remaining weeks	None
Ireland	14 weeks altogether; 4 weeks must be taken before birth, 4 weeks must be taken after and the other 6 weeks can be taken before or after. 70% of earnings (tax free). Mothers can request additional 4 weeks unpaid leave	None
Denmark	4 weeks before birth, 14 weeks after. 90% of earnings (up to maximum level)	10 weeks. 90% of earnings (up to a maximum level)
Greece	16 weeks, to be taken before or after birth. 100% of earnings	3 months per parent. Unpaid
Portugal	90 days altogether; 60 days must be taken after birth and the other 30 days can be taken before or after. 100% of earnings	24 months. Unpaid
Spain	16 weeks altogether; 10 weeks must be taken after birth and the other 6 weeks can be taken before or after. 75% of earnings	12 months. Unpaid

[a] These data updated 1991.

Source: Commission of the European Communities (1990b: 8)

Table 11.3   *Places in publicly funded childcare services*

	Date to which data refer	For children under 3 (%)	For children from 3 to compulsory school age (%)	Age when compulsory schooling begins (years)	Length of school day (including midday break) (hours)	Outside school hours care for primary school children (%)
Germany	1987	3	65–70	6–7	4–5[a]	4
France	1988	20	95+	6	8	?
Italy	1986	5	85+	6	4	?
Netherlands	1989	2	50–55	5	6–7	1
Belgium	1988	20	95+	6	7	?
Luxembourg	1989	2	55–60	5	4–8[a]	1
United Kingdom	1988	2	35–40	5	6½	(–)
Ireland	1988	2	55	6	4½–6½[b]	(–)
Denmark	1989	48	85	7	3–5½[a,b]	29
Greece	1988	4	65–70	5½	4–5[b]	(–)
Portugal	1988	6	35	6	6½	6
Spain	1988	?	65–70	6	8	(–)

The table shows the number of *places* in *publicly funded* services as a percentage of all children in that age group; the percentage of *children* attending may be higher because some places are used on a part-time basis.

Provision at playgroups in the Netherlands has not been included, although 100% of children under 3 and 25% of children aged 3–4 attend and most playgroups receive public funds. Average hours of attendance (5–6 hours per week) are so much shorter than for other services that it would be difficult and potentially misleading to include them on the same basis as other services; however playgroups should not be forgotten when considering publicly funded provision in the Netherlands.

? = no information   (–) = less than 0.5%

[a] School hours vary from day to day.
[b] School hours increase as children get older.

Source: Commission of the European Communities (1990b)

comprehensive childcare program. The country's post-World War I natal policy aimed to compensate for steep population losses by encouraging women to have children and to enter paid employment. This has been matched with the belief that early group care and education are beneficial to children. France's wide provision includes crèches for infants and toddlers and neighbourhood preschools for 3–6-year-olds and some 2-year-olds. These are normally open from 8.30 a.m. to 4.30 p.m. Working parents can pay extra to bring children at 7.30 a.m. and collect them at 6 p.m. Drop-in nurseries (one day a week) and home-based providers complete the picture (Cadden and Kamerman, 1990).

Assumptions about the needs of children (see Lewis, Chapter 1 of this volume) underlie the differences in approach between countries. Triest argues that

> In Holland mothers are a given fact; in Belgium, children are a given fact. Consequently, if full-time mothers are available, the Dutch will set up a society around them, while in Belgium the premise is that children exist, but that does not prevent people from organizing their own lives. (1990: 17)

This is reflected in different levels of childcare provision in the two countries. The Social Charter offers the long-term framework for change. Governments provide the legislation heading in that direction. What then is the status of corporate provision in relation to the social dimension of the Charter? Are companies anticipating the goals and taking actions in their own interest ahead of government implementation or are they waiting until the questions are settled by government mandates or collective agreements?

Corporate policies to facilitate the combining of work and family

The specific focus for corporate change reflects both the point at which legislation, statutory regulations and collective agreements cease and the phase of organizational preparations for the single European market. Thus, for instance, the need for companies to provide childcare or parental leave is greatest where government mandates or collective agreements do not exist. Similarly, as the first priority for business is its competitive position in the market, the timing for work and family issues to be addressed as part of the human resources discussion varies from country to country and among the different sectors of industry. Comparisons between organizational policies in different countries have to be evaluated in relation to these starting points in each country.

This section concentrates on benefits and work-time options of special relevance for working couples: childcare, eldercare, maternity and parental leave, career break schemes, part-time work at senior levels, job sharing and telecommuting in the Netherlands and Britain. These arrangements all challenge the notion of what constitute 'normal' working conditions.

Corporate benefits

Childcare   While the need for childcare is high in both Britain and the Netherlands as public provision is minimal, corporate response differs.

The Netherlands was exceedingly late in addressing this issue, but childcare support in one form or another is now heading onto the standard list for working parents in the large companies. For instance, one commercial care provider has 34 facilities across the country with 1,250 places for some 135 business clients (SKON, 1991), and a trade union study of 635 facilities sponsored by organizations noted a 19.5 percent participation rate for the profit sector (FNV, 1989). Forty percent of the 150 collective agreements (covering 80 percent of employers) treating childcare have led to some sort of provision. However, realization of agreed goals can take up to two years, and at the end of 1990, only an estimated 5,000 of the projected 10,000 child places were available (FNV Vrouwensecretariat, 1991). An alternative to purchasing a place in a nursery in the Netherlands is to participate in a day home care project (whereby children are cared for in the home of the provider). Companies often use this approach when no other daycare is available or to reduce costs for part-time employees as many childcare facilities charge full-time rates for part-time use. A newer approach is a direct subsidy to the employee. All in all, there is considerable progress in this area but nevertheless the current total provision is still far from adequate.

In Britain too there is an upsurge of interest in corporate childcare initiatives but examples of good practice, such as a chain of workplace nurseries opened recently by a major bank (Hansard, 1990) are rare. Despite much media attention for such initiatives, only 3 percent of employers provided some form of childcare assistance in 1989, although 15 percent were considering doing so and this may be rising (Berry-Lound, 1990). The childcare support by the small minority of companies includes on-site or shared off-site nurseries, financial assistance, childcare vouchers redeemable for approved childcare expenses, after-school and holiday play-schemes and information and referral systems (Hansard, 1990).

While there is evidence of the cost-effectiveness of corporate childcare provisions (Truman, 1986; FNV, 1989; de Steenwinkel, 1990), the value of different types of provision needs further evaluation from the parents' perspective. A limitation of the majority of the existing corporate provisions in both countries is that they focus on healthy preschool children. The harmonizing of working schedules with school vacations has received some attention both in Britain and the Netherlands (NWW, 1989b; FNV Vrouwensecretariaat, 1990), but employers have given less thought to issues of caring for sick children. Fathers' responsibilities for children are also slow to be acknowledged. In the Netherlands, children of a male employee are low on the priority list for childcare unless the father is a single parent. Implicit here is the assumption that the structure of professional work and the world of the career man remain unchanged (Gilbert, 1985). Until social fatherhood exists for men as social motherhood does for women, it will be difficult to change this assumption (Clason, 1990).

Eldercare   Before the end of the century one out of every four persons in many member states will be over 60 years old (Commission, 1989: 568). Nevertheless eldercare, described as the 'perk of the nineties' in the US (Friedman and Gray, 1989), has barely been considered as a corporate issue in Europe. A survey of 2500 British organizations for the Institute of Personnel Management found the issue of eldercare had received scant attention (Berry-Lound, 1990). In the Netherlands the issue of leave for long-term care of a family member, partner or companion is beginning to appear in the collective agreements. In practice employers are generally supportive in times of crisis (Hootsmans, 1990). One potential solution for the future may be to combine childcare and eldercare as in the example provided by a US shoe company (Watts, 1990). There has been some experimentation with placing childcare facilities in homes for the elderly in the public sector in Britain and Netherlands.

Maternity and parental leaves   The need for corporate provision of maternity leave, like childcare, varies with the level and adequacy of statutory provision (see Table 11.2). In Britain, where the maternity leave provisions have several limitations (see Brannen and Moss, Chapter 7 of the present book), a survey of over 2,000 organizations found that 22 percent offered more than the statutory minimum (Metcalf, 1990). The United Kingdom also lags behind other states in statutory or collective agreements on parental leave or leave to care for a sick child. There are, however, a few examples of companies offering paid or unpaid leave (Hansard, 1990).

In the Netherlands the public sector has had the most experience with parental leave although a few Dutch companies were already offering unpaid leave from six months to two years when the government mandated six months' unpaid part-time leave in January 1991. One Dutch multinational now offers an innovative parental leave package, allowing the choice of one or a combination of the following alternatives for a maximum of four years:

  flexible working hours;
  part-time work (minimum 20 hours);
  work at home, including the possibility of telecommuting;
  full-time unpaid leave.

Whether parental leave is paid or unpaid and the degree of its acceptance in practice are crucial factors influencing fathers' decisions regarding this option. These factors warrant future research in both private and public sectors as they affect the possibility for sharing in partnership.

Career break schemes   Concern about the loss of highly trained female staff has led to the development of career break schemes in Britain. Pioneered by a major bank these initiatives are now being adopted by a number of organizations in the public and private sectors. These schemes offer a variation of periods of leave, usually five years or less, and the company often expects the women (and very exceptionally men) to work for at least two weeks a year to keep in touch with the world of work. Training and updating of skills are normally provided on the employees' return. These schemes are of value to employers in retaining valued staff, especially as the leave-takers are not considered employees and receive no benefits while on leave. Truman (1991) points out that in practice, the schemes are elitist and geared almost exclusively toward women. Career break schemes are beginning to emerge elsewhere in Europe, where they often include the retention of some benefits or company facilities. In the Dutch context, as in Britain, the schemes are targeted at women. Until these schemes become culturally acceptable for either partner, they are unlikely to do more than create a 'Mommy-Track' (Schwartz, 1989) (see Cook, Chapter 12 of this book).

Overall the costs of motherhood in career terms remain high. To reduce the cost dual-career couples frequently delay having children until after the wife has 'proven' her value to the company and is ensured an opportunity to return to the career track (Hootsmans et al., 1988b). Inherent in this practice is the possibility that postponement will lead to the decision not to have children, or to the discovery that it is no longer possible to do so. The delay involves considerable stress for 'undecided' couples (van Luijn and Parent, 1990).

A second European trend is for women to return to work early after childbirth. Despite increases in the length of time for maternity leave, women in senior positions often do not take advantage of these benefits for fear of appearing insufficiently motivated and jeopardizing their career opportunities (Lewis and Cooper, 1989). Company culture can thus represent a barrier to the successful implementation of policies intended to assist in the transition to parenthood.

In the past business played a major role in controlling the family life of its employees by the working conditions and housing offered as well as by regulations and company culture. While objecting to any intrusion of family into the workplace, business continuously intruded into the family sphere (Barrère-Maurisson, 1987). The trends toward delayed childbirth and taking minimum maternity leave demonstrate that any family intrusion into the work sphere still clashes (or is perceived to clash) with company culture.

Work-time options

Part-time work at higher levels   Part-time work has been a largely female response to the need to manage work and family tasks. It is normally not a matter of choice but the only possible option. The majority of part-time workers in all European states are women at low salary levels.

In the Netherlands part-time work at senior levels (minimum 32 hours) is currently under discussion. Although the issue was raised in the 1970s (Schoemaker and Bartelings, 1978), widespread implementation did not follow. The public sector has been more amenable to this idea and so more professionals work reduced hours in government employment than in private corporations. The Dutch Post-Telegraph-Telephone Company (now privatized) is the best known example for policy and promotion of part-time work at higher levels (Schimmel, 1989). While most companies have categorically rejected the notion of part-time work at senior levels, incidental examples exist (Hubregste, 1987; van Vonderen, 1989; Deminent, 1989; Hermanussen et al., 1988; Wijsman, 1990). Even though management continues to view part-time employees as less motivated than their full-time colleagues, the topic is now on the agenda and some companies are reaching the stage where they can imagine that flexible systems, including part-time work, could be developed at higher levels (de Vries, 1990). The trend toward project work and new areas such as automatization have created possibilities for four-day work cultures. For part-time work to be relevant to dual-career couples, however, the value of the function must be maintained whether fulfilled by a male or a female.

Job sharing   This option, whereby two or more people share the responsibility for one function, was originally conceived for responsible positions (Smith, 1988; also Cook, Chapter 12 of the present book) and is thus of particular interest to dual-career couples. Within the European Community it is best known in Britain where it was first introduced in the public sector (Ohren, 1989; Hootsmans, 1990). A 1987 survey of 96 local authorities signaled an increase in the number of senior and managerial positions being shared (Ohren, 1989). Private companies are now beginning to see how this option can reduce training and turnover costs and considering its use in management positions (NWW, 1989a; Hansard, 1990).

Elsewhere in the European Community the potential of job sharing (Olmsted and Smith, 1989; Walton, 1990) currently exceeds its use. In the Netherlands job sharing is employed primarily at secretarial and administrative levels in business and at the elementary school level in education (Hootsmans, 1990; Fuldhauer, 1991).

Telecommuting Despite earlier predictions (Toffler, 1981; Kupfer, 1988; Kelly, 1988) telecommuting – the use of information technology to enable employees to work at home while linked to the central office by computer – has not taken over Europe, nor has its use to date been restricted to the much lauded advantage for 'mothers at home with children' (Blanpain, 1990). It appears to be best established in the United Kingdom and Germany.

British examples in the private sector include a software firm established in 1962 to meet the needs of female technical professionals who wished to combine caring for children with keeping up to date and learning new skills in their fields, and also a multinational computer firm employing 300 telecommuters with full employee status and opportunities for career progression (Huws et al., 1990). German cases include accountancy and insurance companies whose employees have the option of telecommuting for all or part of their working week. Apart from family needs, the avoidance of traffic congestion is a factor motivating such schemes (Coenen, 1989; Huws et al., 1990).

Teleworking of itself does not provide an adequate solution to the problems of combining work and parenthood (Kohler et al., 1988; see Cook, Chapter 12 of the present book). When British and German telecommuters were questioned about aspects of their working lives which they most wanted to change, they pinpointed better childcare facilities, improved communication with employer and colleagues, more social benefits and better pay (Huws et al., 1990). Given the current organization of work, telecommuting offers only a partial or temporary solution in specific phases of a life career. Its real potential for dual-career couples may well be as part of a combined package of flexible options. When the 'powershift' is finally made to a more complete information society, telecommuting will then have a major role to play (Toffler, 1990).

Future areas for focus

The following three areas are of especial concern to dual-career couples as they affect both short-term and long-term possibilities for equity in relationships and in work situations. The valuing of women's contributions and the recognition of dual-career partnerships are essential in all three instances.

Relocation

Today's question is no longer who goes where and when, but who goes where with whom? Moreover with the unification of Europe, relocation will take on a new meaning. Relocation problems arise with transfers both inside and outside national boundaries. Just as American companies transferring employees across the country discovered a need for spouse assistance (Winfield, 1985), French companies moving personnel from Paris to Alsace-Lorraine, another region with its own culture, are faced with a similar problem (Colombat, 1991). The issue of deciding which partner's career should take precedence at a given point in time may be even more pressing when the 'trailing spouse' will have to find a job within a new national culture. Relocations can have a negative impact on both family and work (Guerrier, 1990). As one participant in a European workshop on women and place stated, 'I spent the first year of our posting trying to control my aggression towards my partner for forcing me to come here.'

Recent years have seen an increasing number of refusals by dual-career men and women to relocate (Hootsmans and van Royen, 1987; Davidson and Cooper, 1983; IMS, 1987). Even though most companies are still making ad hoc arrangements in Europe, a trend has been signaled towards employer collaboration in seeking to find a position for the employee's spouse (Vlaming, 1991). Young dual-career couples are also taking initiatives themselves to locate matching foreign postings. In doing so, they are switching the framework from reactive to proactive response and helping their companies develop models to address this issue.

Communication

Demographics and bottom-line economics are leading to the discussion of the management of diversity. With the unification of the European Community, cross-cultural factors take on a new importance. A dimension of the cross-cultural discussion largely ignored at present is the difference in communication patterns, both verbal and behavioral, between men and women as well as the foundation for those patterns – a framework of status for men and one of connectedness for women (Schwartz, 1989; Tannen, 1990; Verbiest, 1991). While companies are anticipating difficulties for foreign nationals adapting to a new culture, gender differences have largely been ignored so that male language and behavioral patterns remain the norm.

Even though women are becoming integrated into middle management and technical positions, the misinterpretations arising from these differences block women's opportunities and thus impact negatively on possibilities for equity in dual-career partnerships (Glidden and Kane, forthcoming). In the long term this could develop into a stumbling block for the effective functioning of the organization.

Alternative life/career paths

It is important that corporations do not perceive work and family issues purely in terms of the necessity of making concessions for women. Meaningful changes will need to do more than just allow a bit of leeway for the new workforce to adapt to the current framework of the workplace (Barrère-Maurisson, 1987). They must address the very tenets of the work philosophy that views all structures and facilities in regard to the family man up to his retirement. The idea that we need to 'allow' women time off to have children or even 'allow' fathers some leave for childcare is anathema to change. Corporations need to appraise the life cycles of all employees just as they do the cycles of product lines and revise corporate career paths in relation to those differing phases (Hootsmans et al., 1988b; Friedman and Gray, 1989; Hootsmans, 1990). Gender differences in the life/career paths also need to be addressed (Larwood and Gattiker, 1987; Kamerman and Kahn, 1987; Baruch et al., 1983; Scase and Goffe, 1990).

Life/career planning involves what Hall (1990) describes as the need to decouple age and career opportunities. As people live longer they may extend their working lives, thereby compensating for years spent caring for children or elderly relatives at an earlier stage. The valuing of seniority (see Sekaran, Chapter 3 of the present book; Schleiler, 1991) rather than the expectation that optimum achievement should occur during the stages of maximum family commitment would provide greater age flexibility, enabling women and men to manage work and family peaks sequentially rather than simultaneously.

Conclusion

While major differences exist at present between the starting points in the member states of the European Community, there is nevertheless a certain uniformity in the lack of priority being given to the interface of work and family. Preliminary changes can be seen in corporate attitudes towards childcare facilities, career break schemes and a certain amount of flexibility for family concerns in work-time options as illustrated by the case of Dutch and British Corporations. Real change has not occurred, however, as long as the underlying premise remains to help women adjust to the current framework and to assist managers to accept some diversity. A short-term band-aid approach to benefits merely postpones confrontation.

European unification with the long-term perspective afforded by the Social Charter offers many opportunities for creative leadership. A number of farsighted multinationals and large companies may well take steps to integrate work and family issues into corporate strategic planning. Given present signals, it appears that the majority will wait for further prodding from government or collective agreements and continue their piecemeal approach.

The next few years will be crucial in setting the parameters and pace of developments in the European Community. The timetable, however, will remain different in each of the twelve European Community countries. Management is not alone in bearing responsibility for innovation. An organized, vocal and political force is also needed (Seitchik, 1990). Dual-career couples have a proactive role to play in this. Until their individual successes in negotiating solutions are shared, practice will not advance into policy (Hootsmans and van Royen, 1987). They need to be simultaneously double trouble and potential strength in assisting management to address the complete range of work and family issues for employees at all levels. In the long run economics will have the deciding vote.

References

Barrère-Maurisson, Marie Anges (1987) 'Gestion de la main-d'oeuvre et paternalisme: tradition et modernité dans les stratégies des entreprises', *Economies et Sociétés*, 11: 41–56.

Barrère-Maurisson, A.M., Daune-Richard, A.M. and Letablier, M.T. (1990) 'Le travail à temps partiel plus développé au Royaume-Uni qu'en France' (Part-time work more prevalent in the UK than in France), *Economie et Statistique*, 220 (April): 47–56.

Baruch, Grace, Barnett, Rosalind and Rivers, Caryl (1983) *Lifeprints*. New York: New American Library.

Berry-Lound, Dorothy (1990) *Work and the Family: Carer-friendly Employment Practices*. London: Institute of Personnel Management.

Blanpain, Roger (1990) 'Labour relations in a changing social, economic and technological environment', Presidential address, 8th IIRA World Congress, Brussels, 4 Sept. 1989; *International Journal of Human Resource Management*, 1 (1): 61–71.

Cadden, Vivian and Kamerman, Sheila (1990) 'Where in the world is childcare better?' *Working Mother*, Sept.: 62–8.

Clason, Christine (1990) 'Uitdaging tot gezinsbeleid' (Challenge for Family Policy), in M. de Jonghe and J. von Grumbkow (eds), *Carrières in Tweevoud* (Careers in Duplicate). Heerlen: Open University, pp. 26–43.

Coenen, Frans (1989) 'Telewerken brengt kantoor aan huis' (Telecommuting brings the office home), *Management Team*, 23 Oct.: 80–3.

Colombat, Jacqueline (1991) 'La dimension interculturelle dans le monde du travail: langues, cultures, valeurs', paper presented at the Congrès National des Langues Etrangères Appliquées, 'La Dimension Interculturelle dans le Monde du Travail', Paris, 24–6 Jan.

Commission of the European Communities (1989) *Commission Documents Concerning the Action Program for the Implementation of the Community Charter of Fundamental Social Rights for Workers*. Brussels: COM (89) 568 def.

Commission of the European Communities (1990a) *The Community Charter of Fundamental Social Rights for Workers*. Luxembourg: EEC Bureau, 6/90.

Commission of the European Communities (1990b) *Childcare in the European Communities 1985–1990*. Brussels: Women's Information Service, no.31.

Davidson, Marilyn and Cooper, Cary L. (1983) *Stress and the Woman Manager*. Oxford: Martin Robertson.

Deminent, Marian (1989) 'Topfuncties in Deeltijd' (Part-time positions at the top), *Vrouw en Bedrijf*, Sept.: 24–7.

de Steenwinkel, Saskia (1990) 'Hoe moet het met de kinderen van werkende vrouwen?' (What is to be done with the children of working women?), in M. de Jonghe and J. von Grumbkow (eds), *Carrières in Tweevoud* (Careers in Duplicate). Heerlen: Open University. pp. 58–68.

de Vries, Ineke (1990) 'De magie van flexibilisering' (The genie of flexibilization), *Vrouw en Bedrijf*, Feb.: 25–9.

Emancipatieraad (1989) *Emancipatiebeleid in Macro-Economisch Perspectief*. (Emancipation Policy in Macro-economic Perspective). Den Haag.

Emancipatieraad (1990) *Statistische informatie*. December.

Emancipatieraad (1991) *A Propos*, 4(2): 2.

European Parliament (1990) *1993 und die Beschäftigungssituation der Frauen*. (1993 and the Position of Women in the Labour Market.) Luxembourg: EEC Publications Bureau.

FNV (Federatie Nederlandse Vakbonden) (1989) *De baas past op de kleintjes* (The Boss as Babysitter). Amsterdam: FNV Werkgroep 2000.

FNV Vrouwensecretariat (1990) *Draaiboek CAO-onderhandelingen gericht op de verbetering van de positie van vrouwelijke werknemers* (Handbook of Collective Agreement Negotiations related to the Advancement of Female Workers). Amsterdam: FNV.

FNV Vrouwensecretariat (1991) Interview with staff members A. Pelzer and B. de Jong, April.

Friedman, Dana E. (1986) 'Eldercare: the employer benefit of the 1990s?', *Across the Board*, June: 45–51.

Friedman, Dana and Gray, Wendy B. (1989) *A Life Cycle Approach to Family Benefits and Policies*. New York: Conference Board.

Fuldhauer, Alice M. (1991) 'De dynamiek van de duo-baan' (The dynamics of job sharing), *Elle*, May: 46–9.

Gilbert, Lucia (1985) *Men in Dual Career Families*. Hillsdale, NJ: Lawrence Erlbaum Associates.

Glidden, Priscilla and Kane, Linda (forthcoming) *Sexes in the Workplace: What Men Think of Women at Work and What Women Can Do and Can't Do About It*. New York: New Market Press.

Guerrier, Monique (1990) Keynote address, 'Women on the move', Women's Institute for Continuing Education conference, 18–19 Nov., Paris.

Hall, Douglas, T. (1990) 'Promoting work/family balance: an organizational-change approach', *Organizational Dynamics*: 18: 5–18.

Hansard Society (1990) *Women at the Top*. London: Hansard Society for Parliamentary Government.

Hermanussen, Ria, Molenaar, Frances and v.d. Meijs, Anja (1988) *Emancipatie in bedrijf* (Business and Emancipation). Den Haag: SoZaWe.

Hootsmans, Helen (1986) *Dual Career Partners: A Selected Bibliography 1980–1986*. Amersfoort: VVAO.

Hootsmans, Helen (1990) 'Het bedrijfsleven en de carrières van werkende paren' (Corporations and two-Career couples), in M. de Jonghe and J. von Grumbkow, *Carrières in Tweevoud*. Heerlen: Open University, pp. 69–84.

Hootsmans, Helen (1991) 'The Netherlands – parental rights and employment flexibility: one step forward or two steps backward?', in Alan Gladstone et al. (eds), *Labour Relations in a Changing Environment*. Proceedings 8th IIRA World Congress, Brussels, Sept. 1989. Berlin: Walter de Gruyter.

Hootsmans, Helen and van Royen, Rita (1987) *Verslag enquête partners en levensloop-baanplanning* (Report on the Partners and Life/Career Planning Survey). Amersfoort: Netherlands Association of University Women.

Hootsmans, H., Ottens, A.M. and Pierrot, A.C. (1988a) *Partners en Organisaties: een verkenning van werk en gezinsbeleid en de praktijk.* Amersfoort: VVAO Partners Project. (English version: *Partners and Organizations: A Preliminary Study of Work and Family Policy and Practice.* Amersfoort: VVAO.)

Hootsmans, H., Ottens, A.M. and Pierrot, A.C. (1988b) *Eindverslag partners en levensloopbaanplanning project* (Final Report Partners and Life Career Project). Amersfoort: Partners Project.

Hubregste, L.M. (1987) *Vrouwen in hogere posities* (Women in Higher Positions). Rotterdam: SKIM.

Huws, Ursula, Korte, Werner B. and Robinson, Simon (1990) *Telework: Towards the Elusive Office.* Chichester: John Wiley.

IMS (Institute of Management Studies) (1987) *Relocating Managers and Professional Staff*, Report 139. Sussex: IMS.

Kamerman, Sheila and Kahn, Alfred (1987) *The Responsive Workplace.* New York: Columbia University Press.

Kassalouw, Everett (1990) Workshop: The European Community 1992 Initiatives. IRRA, Washington, 28 Dec.

Kelly, Marcia M. (1988) 'The work at home', *The Futurist*, Nov. – Dec.: 28–32.

Köhler, E. (1988) 'Telework in the European Community: problems and potential', in W. Korte, S. Robinson and W. Steinle (eds), *Telework.* North Holland: Elsevier.

Kops, Hans (1986) 'Incorporating women', *Holland Herald*, Sept.: 73–7.

Kupfer, A. (1988) 'Managing for the 1990s', *Fortune*, 26 Sept.: 46.

Larwood, Laurie and Gattiker, Urs E. (1987) 'A comparison of the career paths used by successful women and men', in B. Gutek and L. Larwood (eds), *Women's Career Development.* Beverly Hills: Sage.

Lewis, Suzan and Cooper, Cary L. (1989) *Career Couples. Contemporary Life Styles and How to Manage Them.* London: Unwin Hyman.

Metcalf, Hilary (1990) *Retaining Women Employees: Measures to Counteract Labour Shortage.* Brighton: Institute of Management Studies.

NEDO and the Training Agency (1989) *Defusing the Demographic Time Bomb.* London: NEDO.

NWW (New Ways to Work) (1989a) 'German employers commission research before introducing job sharing', *Newsletter*, 5(4): 12.

NWW (New Ways to Work) (1989b) *Changing Times, Changing People* (Annual Report 1988–9). London.

NWW (New Ways to Work) (1990) 'The action programme of the Social Charter – rights or rhetoric?' *Newsletter*, 6(3): 8–9.

OECD (1986) *Labour Market.* Paris: Organisation for Cooperation in Economic Development.

Ohren, Margaret (1989) 'Redistributing the rewards of work', paper presented at ENWS Seminar, The Interface of Work and Family, Brussels.

Olmsted, Barney and Smith, Suzanne (1989) *Creating a Flexible Workplace.* New York: AMACOM.

Russel, John (1990) Workshop, The European Community 1992 Initiatives, IRRA, Washington, 28 Dec.

Scase, Richard and Goffe, Robert (1990) 'Women in management: towards a research agenda', *International Journal of Human Resource Management*, 1 (1): 107–25.

Schimmel, Arthie (1989) 'Emancipatiebeleid in positieve actie bij de PTT' (Emancipation policy via affirmative action at the Post, Telegraph and Telephone Company), in *Vrouwen in/en Organisaties*, Amsterdam: Hogeschool van Amsterdam.

Schleiler, C. (1991) 'Foreign affairs', *Across the Board*, Jan./Feb.: 47–50.

Schoemaker, N. and Bartelings, E.M. (1978) *Deeltijd op hoger niveau* (Part-Time Work at Higher Levels). Wageningen: VVAO.

Schwartz, Felice N. (1989) 'Management women and the new facts of life', *Harvard Business Review*, Jan./Feb.: 65–76.

Seitchik, Adam (1990) *Workplace Family Benefits*. Wellesley, MA: Wellesley College Dept. of Economics.

SKON (1991) *SKON kinderopvang: als medewerkers bevallen* (When Employees Give Birth). Utrecht.

Smith, Suzanne (1988) 'New developments in work time options facilitating the combining of work and family responsibilities', USIS, SER and VVAO Seminar, The Hague.

SoZaWe (Ministry of Social Affairs and Employment) (1989a) *CAO Afspraken 1988* (Collective Agreements in 1988). Den Haag.

SoZaWe (Ministry of Social Affairs and Employment) (1989b) *Resultaten inventarisatie vrouwen in technische beroepen* (Results of the Inventory of Women in Technical Occupations). Den Haag.

Tannen, Deborah (1990) *You Just Don't Understand*. New York: William Morrow.

Toffler, Alvin (1981) *The Third Wave*. New York: Bantam Books.

Toffler, Alvin (1990) *The Power Shift*. New York: Bantam.

Triest, Monica (1990) 'Arbeid van vrouwen in Nederland en Belgie' (Women's Work in the Netherlands and Belgium), in M. de Jonghe and J. von Grumbkow *Carrières in Tweevoud* (Careers in Duplicate). Heerlen: Open University. pp. 17–25.

Truman, Carole (1986) *Overcoming the Career Break*. Sheffield: Manpower Services Commission.

Truman, Carole (1991) 'Demographic change and new opportunities for women: the case of employers' career break schemes', in S. Arber and N. Gilbert (eds), *Women and Working Lives. Divisions and Change*. London: Macmillan.

van Luijn, Heleen and Parent, Anneke (1990) *Laatste kans-moeders* (Last Chance Mothers). Delft: Eburon.

van Vonderen, Jose (1989) 'Waar blijft de duobaan?' (What's holding up job sharing?), *Vrouw en Bedrijf* (Woman and Business), Feb.: 43–6.

Verbiest, Agnes (1991) *Het gewicht van de directrice: taal over, tegen en door vrouwen* (The Status of the Female Director: Language about, against and by Women). Amsterdam: Contact.

Vlaming, Henk (1991) 'Twee carrières op één kussen' (Two careers on one pillow), *PW Magazine*, March: 58–63.

VNO (1988) *Vrouwen in Bedrijf (Women in Business)*. Den Haag: Netherlands Employers Association.

Walton, Pam (1990) *Job Sharing: A Practical Guide*. London: Kogan Page.

Watts, Patti (1990) 'A giant step for day care at Stride Rite', *Executive Female*, July/Aug.: 9, 30.

Wijsman, Jeanette (1990) 'Komt er ooit een deeltijdcarrière?' (Will the part-time career ever materialize?), *Intermediair*, 26 (14), April 6.

Winfield, Fairlee (1985) *Commuter Marriage*. New York: Columbia University Press.

12

Can Work Requirements Accommodate to the Needs of Dual-Earner Families?

Alice H. Cook

Dual-earner families are more and more the rule in the industrialized countries as married women move massively into the labor force. Much of the response to this phenomenon has been in the form of family support programs. These have mainly aimed to substitute for some of the wife's traditional work in the home – childcare of all kinds and occasionally programs for care of the elderly.

The women's liberation movement early hoped, even assumed, that with the adoption of equal employment opportunity programs, partnership marriage would come to be the rule in the home. Husbands would as a matter of course see their wives' dilemma and would take over their share of the home responsibilities. This has occurred only exceptionally, chiefly among young couples. In fact, time use studies show pretty clearly and internationally that over the last twenty years husbands continue to spend very little more time on housework when their wives are employed than when they are not (Walker, 1970; Szalai, 1972; Woods, 1976; Goldschmidt-Clermont, 1983; Hochschild, 1989). As previous authors in this volume attest, in spite of some individual and cultural differences, the majority of men continue to put the demands of work above those of family, and to leave home responsibilities almost entirely to their wives, including their working wives.

This behavior is readily explicable. Work in a capitalist (later in a communist) economy has been organized since the Industrial Revolution to demand of workers loyalty to a competitive company (or to the state), demonstrated in a long working day and a full working life (Oakley, 1976). Capitalist employers could make almost any time demands, because they could assume an unpaid wife at home caring for the needs of a fully occupied worker – bearing his children, feeding and nurturing him after his hard day in the mill or office and protecting him against additional demands at home. The communist states to a greater degree substituted state-sponsored institutions to take over some of these family tasks. These views of workers and working life continue to pervade modern work life. They account for deep-going job segregation of men's and women's work, in both kinds of economy. Particularly in capitalist nations they account for the inequalities that flow from this segregation: women's lower wages; the prevalent view that women's first loyalty – in sharp contrast to men's – is to the home and not to the job or career; that an employer's investment in a woman's training for promotion or higher skill will not be repaid in continuous employment; the tolerance of sex harassment; the existence of the glass ceiling for women managers or professional workers; the proposal for a 'mommy track' in corporate hiring of women managers (Schwartz, 1989; BNA, 1989b); and all of the other explicit and subtle differences that have attached to women's work.

Thus, although women in most modern states represent 40 to 48 percent of the workforce, they are working under conditions, attitudes, and customs established by what Kessler-Harris (1982) called 'the domestic code', developed in the nineteenth century when men were 'the breadwinners', and women 'the homemakers'. Women enter a workplace and join a workforce constructed by and for men whose home responsibilities were peripheral to their work lives. Women, however, enter the labor market loaded with all the responsibilities of the home, a state long since described as 'the double burden'.

The family, even when both adults are employed, does not present a model of equality equivalent to that set forth for work life. Part of the reason is that dual-earner families are not all alike. The categorization of Gilbert and Dancer in this volume offers three types: the traditional, modern, and egalitarian, to convey some of the variations in marital role behaviors, which cut across the distinction between dual-career and other dual-earner families.

A woman worker in a traditional family has little reason to hope or expect that when she works she will not carry 'a double burden'. Indeed she may share the traditional view that home is her proper priority. Accordingly, she will seek routine work; resist taking on training on her own or company time, seeing it as implying additional burdens at work; accept intermittent employment; show little concern about joining a union to improve working conditions, or participating in other collective activity. She works because her husband does not earn enough. Her husband does not want her to work, is perhaps even ashamed that she must. When by chance he earns enough more, she will go home again.

Couples who attempt to pursue careers and share domestic work and parenting in an 'egalitarian' fashion or even in 'modern' families, in which parenting is shared but women retain responsibility for domestic chores, pursue greater change in marital roles and relationships, but in the absence of changes in the workplace, they do so at the risk of conflict and pressure.

While this chapter acknowledges the central importance of family support systems, such as child and eldercare and family and medical leave programs, its purpose is to inquire and evaluate whether possible adjustments in work life may be significant in easing the conflict parents experience when they both work. Such adjustments, I argue, can obviate or supplement many family support systems not only for working women but for their husbands, lovers, or companions as well.

Equal opportunity legislation, as it has been introduced in many countries, has uniformly disregarded the male bias in the structure of the labor market (Waring, 1989). Equality in all the aspects of the market – recruitment, hiring, training, promotion, wages, layoffs, unemployment, benefits, and retirement – has meant women's equality with men under conditions men established for men without home responsibilities. If we are to conceive of satisfactory lives that integrate both work and family for both parents, we have to make changes not just in family support, but think as well of work restructuring as conditioned by the demands of family (Gerstel and Gross, 1987; Lee, 1983; Lozano, 1989; Meier, 1979).

Experience with old forms and innovations

Out of sheer necessity, innovations have occurred as a result of pressure from employees and applicants for jobs. These have included time adjustments to work such as flexitime, a somewhat shorter work-week than the previous 40-hour norm, part-time employment, job-sharing, shift work, and contingent work. In addition, we are beginning to debate and experiment with place adjustments as well. The latter rubric emphasizes but is not limited to home-based work, both of employees and subcontractors. We turn now to define, describe, and evaluate such schemes for the degree to which they contribute to the improvement of workers' family life.

Flexitime

Flexitime is one of the most widespread alternative work patterns. Introduced more widely in Europe than in the United States, perhaps one-quarter of workers there are estimated to be covered by some form of it. In any of its many forms, it allows both men and women to vary their arrivals and departures at work by several hours, usually with the provision that everyone works during a stated 'core' period of four or more hours a day. In return, workers agree to make up any time lost below the standard total of weekly or monthly hours. Some systems allow workers to accumulate hours for extra holidays, or to work a few days longer to form a shorter working week. Originally, these adjustments were thought helpful to women in fitting in with children's schedules, but men have also found flexitime a more relaxed pattern, which some use to assist with family schedules, as I learned in interviews in the late 1980s with German public employees who generally operate on these schedules.

To the extent that flexitime is more than a gender-dominated modification of old rules, it has the potential to contribute to equality in labor market practice by allowing both parents to share responsibilities for children's schedules as well as for the performance of some household functions. However, evidence suggests that this occurs only when parents have non-traditional gender expectations (Bohen and Viveros-Long, 1981; Lee, 1983).

Flexitime, moreover, is not easily adaptable to factory and office functions dependent on the integration of individual tasks in assembly-line production, or on those services that must be available around the clock in hospitals, and police forces. Such conditions narrow the possibility of its broadest usefulness.

The shorter work-week

Within the past few years, unions in many European countries and in Japan, though not in the United States, have made the achievement of a shorter work-week their chief goal. In Japan the effort has been made to abandon Saturday work for the leisure of a two-day weekend (see Chabot, Chapter 10 in the present book). It has not yet been uniformly achieved, but a half-day Saturday has become a minimal standard. Other Asian countries are beginning to follow the Japanese example.

In Europe the goal of a shorter work-week has been to reduce the 40-hour week eventually to 35 hours by gradual shortening of hours without loss of pay. This campaign was originally undertaken in the name of reducing unemployment. Throughout the 1980s when German unemployment was double-digit, German metalworkers in the largest union in the world carried through two major strikes with this purpose in mind. While they have won some reduction in hours – in some cases down to 37 or 36 hours per week without loss of 40 hours' pay – studies of the results do not strongly support a positive effect on unemployment (Protzman, 1989).

This lack of effect on unemployment may be attributed in part to the agreement that each works council or regional bargaining unit could determine with individual employers how the new schedule would be enforced. In most cases, reports indicate that the leisure time gained is added to vacation time, when work in any case may be somewhat slacker.

A recent study of alternative schedules in the US assumes that late twentieth-century lifestyles contribute to a rising pressure from workers on employers for 'more leisure' (Pierce et al., 1989). It is possible that such a motivation may better account for the widespread support among employees in other countries for a short work-week than the unemployment rhetoric does. That the metalworkers nevertheless use the unemployment rationale may also cover the fact that men and women workers' differing interests have caused a deep split in the way in which each gender looks at the question. Women, very explicitly and broadly throughout Europe, want shorter days, while men, including union men, want shorter work-weeks or more annual vacations (Petersson, 1989).[1] Where men predominate, the decision has gone to more leisure time. Clearly shorter working days would be beneficial to parents during the years when they have young children.

Part-time work

The remedy a large proportion of working women seek, perforce, particularly in their younger adult years, is fewer hours or days per week. This solution, except in Sweden, is only available in the form of part-time work. In Britain, for example, Martin and Roberts sum up the situation as follows:

> Women who have had children are more likely to work part-time than women who have not, and married women are more likely to do this than non-married women. So it is not marital status *per se* so much as the family roles men and women play within marriage which are important in their consequences for women's employment. (1984: 186)

Among all the possible rearrangements of schedules, women prefer part-time work. Table 12.1 clearly indicates this trend.

Table 12.1   *The share of women in full-time and part-time work in Germany, Sweden, the United Kingdom and the United States, 1973–1983 (as percentage of relevant labor force)*

	1973			1983		
	Total	Full-time	Part-time	Total	Full-time	Part-time
Germany	35.6	30.9	92.0	38.6	30.9	91.9
Sweden	40.8	29.9	87.4	46.3	32.2	84.2
UK	36.5	26.7	92.3	40.9	28.9	89.6
US	38.5	33.3	66.3	43.7	38.5	69.3

Source: de Neubourg (1985: 564)

Among many problems in writing comparatively about part-time work is that it is defined differently in each country, or not defined at all. In some countries any hours per week below 40 are considered part-time; in Sweden, a distinction is made between 'long part-time' at 20–36 hours per week, and 'short part-time', that is less than 19 (see

Sandqvist, Chapter 5 in this book). Laws or agreements usually set a minimum number of hours worked per week, month, or year, for eligibility to health or welfare benefits. But these conditions vary from country to country and in the United States and Canada from state to state.

It is not surprising that in all the industrialized countries women make up the vast majority of part-time workers, though the reasons for this phenomenon appear to differ from country to country. Apparently in Israel, as reported in Chapter 2 of the present book, educated women prefer part-time work, because they can afford to take lower earnings. In other Western countries it is precisely these women who occupy available managerial and professional positions and these rarely allow such a choice. On the other hand, the quasi-professional occupations such as nursing, teaching, accountancy, and librarianship are more amenable to part-time work. At the other end of the economic and educational scale, however, where single parenthood or implacable husbands set the parameters, women have to find any work that will permit them to care for children and household tasks. Part-time work is the only way out. Otherwise, there are not enough hours in the day.[2]

Employers in businesses directly serving the public – banking, retail trade, travel agencies, for example – want maximum service at peak customer hours. These employers may be able, in hiring part-timers, to avoid requirements for rest periods, lunch hours, and coffee breaks because these employees work only four or five hours. They may also be able to impose a lower wage scale, especially if unions are reluctant to organize and represent these part-time workers.

At the same time employers have complained that part-time workers require as much book-keeping and supervision as do full-time workers, and therefore the employment of part-timers, despite other cost savings, is not so great as might appear. Nevertheless, the rapid growth of service industries has in fact contributed to the increase in demand for part-timers. Women in their need have responded by taking up the available part-time openings, despite the lower standards and remuneration often attached to these positions.

Other disadvantages that attach to part-time work beyond low pay and lack of benefits exist but are rarely reported in official records. For example, union membership is often unavailable or is constructed on a second-class basis. To this degree, unions have been said to condone low wages, and have failed to enforce seniority status. Further, part-time workers are usually passed over for on-the-job training programs that might lead to promotion to supervisory positions or higher levels of skill. Furthermore, they often fail to receive regular pay increments.

The reasons for unions' historical reluctance to admit part-time workers to membership or even to condone their hiring were that the inferior conditions offered to part-timers represented a threat to the unions' hard-won standards and pay scales. They also saw part-time workers as difficult to organize and to activate. They therefore found it difficult to deal constructively, with part-time work and workers, at the same time that they recognized their inferior conditions.

Gradually unions in the retail trades began to take a more favourable view, since modern supermarkets and department stores rely heavily on part-timers. Nevertheless, in the USA these unions bargained for their workers, at least in the beginning, as a separate category, working under separate agreements. In these, unions directed their main concern to regularizing wages and hours. In doing so, they have often provided for part-timers' right to be considered first for full-time jobs as these become available. Unions of hotel and restaurant workers, long used to dealing with workers on split shifts, likewise have come to recognize and bargain for part-time workers. Some of these unions have won pro rata participation in benefit programs.

What is lacking in most countries, as a major Canadian study of part-time work points out (Canada Ministry of Supply and Services, 1983), is any legal definition and therefore any significant regularization of part-time work. One result is that national legislation rarely supports part-time employment by linking it to other labor and social legislation. An exception is the individual taxation or extended parental leave policies that the Swedes have instituted. Without such consideration of part-time workers, women have become the major victims of the unfavourable conditions that widely adhere to this kind of work. The consequence is that their temporary preference for it during their young adult years ultimately handicaps their earnings and work careers for the rest of their lives.

Job-sharing

At a time when job-sharing or work-sharing was widely advocated as a means for equalizing tasks and goals in the lives of dual-earners in the late 1960s and mid-1970s, it was seen as a desirable way for workers to share work life and family life at the same time. Even then, scholars interested in this adaptation to both work and family needs found very few persons actually engaged in it (Rapoport and Rapoport, 1978; Grønstedt, 1975; Meier, 1979). In part this was because few opportunities outside of self-employment were available, but in part because few couples saw themselves as able to afford to live on what amounted to a single income. More recently, research has disclosed that most job-sharing, like part-time work, is done by women, who may also share childcare (*Business Link*, 1988). Nevertheless, some couples use job sharing to share work and childcare between them (Lewis and Cooper, 1989).

Job-sharing is somewhat less subject to the exploitation represented in other part-time work. One reason is that many job-sharers work full days – two or three a week – and thus are subject to the protection of wage and hour laws. They may, however, at the same time be subject to restrictions in benefits and training opportunities. Nevertheless, an organization in the UK is campaigning for the introduction of job-sharing in a number of occupations (see Hootsmans, Chapter 11 of this book). In the US, companies located in small towns see job-sharing as a decided help in recruitment (*Business Link*, 1988).

Shift work

Some dual-earners, particularly blue-collar workers who work in industries or services that are scheduled in shifts, have chosen to alternate shifts. This means parents sharing childcare between the day shift and the night or evening shift.

It is done, obviously, at a cost to family life in the hours before and after work. In my own interviews in a few US factories I found that the circumstances that motivate such a choice include the unavailability or unaffordability of childcare as well as the assumption that the arrangement will last only a few years at most. Nevertheless, the women here too pay a heavy price in work overload in the home in order to make the system work.

Alternative work systems have both advantages and disadvantages, while sheer availability of a given system may be the decisive factor in its selection. But alternative schedules are not the only approach to solving work and family conflicts. Alternative locations of work are another possibility.

Alternative locations of work: moving work out of the workplace

This approach seems to cover at least three categories:

1 Volunteer activity, that Daniels (1988) calls 'invisible work'. It plays a particularly significant role for upper middle-class women, although it is by no means limited to them.
2 A growing kind of subcontracting, particularly linked to high-tech industries that is also described as 'invisible'. This has been the subject of a recent US study (Lozano, 1989). This kind of home work has been overlooked and uncounted by the labor market statisticians, because it falls between the accepted definitions of either waged or self-employed work. It is largely carried out by

technicians of both sexes – though males may predominate – who work independently for a limited number of client firms, often their former employers. It is carried on in homes and garages, and may employ others – mainly family members.

3 Waged homework largely carried out by women. In this case, the employer places a machine in the worker's home and pays her by some form of piece work rate.

All three forms of work are variously attractive to women in varying circumstances and with varying backgrounds or social upbringing and education. Contingency work, as type 2 has been called, and home work (type 3) appeal to mothers who find childcare inadequate or too costly for the family to bear. For them, the possibility of working at home, even part time, may seem the only way to meet these equally important demands. But let us look more in detail at each in turn.

Volunteer work   Volunteer work is quite invisible to any labor market institution because no employment relationship involving wages exists, yet, as Daniels makes clear, it can be demanding of time, and even constitute a 'career'. Moreover, this career may have rewards in terms of power and influence that few waged jobs attain. It is, however, not perceived as work, though it may replace work as a major reason for being and for self-definition. In fact, one of the demands of women's groups dealing with problems of widows and divorcees who in late middle age must enter the labor force is to help these women bring volunteer work to the level of visibility and appreciation by making the experience tangible for the world of paid work. Writing a résumé that includes the administrative, organizational, interpersonal, and personnel skills exercised in volunteer activities is one way of using volunteer skills to achieve waged work. These services and skills, when performed by men, tend to enhance their employing firm's public image and the individual's status in the workplace. Women, however, still find it difficult to gain acceptance of this experience when they seek a foothold in the world of 'real work' (André, 1985).

Similarly, women's efforts to achieve recognition of the administrative skills gained in the other 'invisible occupation', housework, meet greater difficulty and even resistance. This problem of achieving labor market equivalency for skills learned in the home confronts women who have taken child-rearing leave from the labor force and then seek re-entry some years later. Their earlier work skills have meanwhile become outdated – think only of the last five years' changes in technology for nurses and secretaries – and the "work" they have done on leave is in no way evaluated positively for their chances of upgrading on the career ladder.

Contingency work: 'invisible'? A very substantial number of workers have broken with the legal and customary requirements of the capitalist system of employment for wages at a workplace, by becoming intermittent, piecemeal subcontractors in their own homes, often for their former employers. In her study of individuals carrying out important segments of work in Silicon Valley, Lozano writes about their circumstances and motivations with a great deal of theoretical as well as practical insight. Despite the fact that they fall outside the categories with which the US Departments of Labor and Commerce operate, they are not a new phenomenon (Ferman et al., 1978; Simon and White, 1982).

The group Lozano studied were for the most part one-time employees of computer firms, who, for a variety of reasons, preferred to cut themselves loose from the constraints of employment in the workplace, and 'to work for themselves at home, on their own time'. Garages and spare bedrooms, kitchens and living rooms become the worksite. No sign announces the one- or two-person enterprise to the public. They undertake assignments when the main firm needs extra or specialized help. They work under a written or verbal contract to complete a specific batch of work by a given time for an agreed-upon fee. Deadlines or quantity of work may make them employers of their own, but their employees are usually family members or neighbors, hired only as needed.

In this particular network, linked as it is to high tech operations, Lozano found more men than women. Nearly all of them earned as much or more than they had earned as employees. Their loss of benefits, their irregular employment, the necessity many of them faced to work to short deadlines and at the risk of having themselves to pay for errors or below-standard production, appeared to be balanced against personal freedom from the rigid hours and bureaucratic requirements of standard employment. Estimates of the number of Americans working in this fashion run between two and seven million (Lozano, 1989: 99).

The advantages to the employer are clear. He or she uses these workers as an informal staff who can be called up when needed and neglected in slower periods. In this regard they are comparable to 'temporary workers' in Japan. They are a buffer against downturns in the business cycle. Unlike in Japan, however, the Western employer of informal workers pays by the piece, losing no downtime and no payment for imperfections, and paying only when the job is perfectly completed. Lozano sees 'informal work at home as [seeming] to offer a cheap and convenient solution to some of the immediate needs of capital, state, and family in the 1980s' (1989: 101).

Home-based work   Homework is even less a new concept than 'informal work'. Reformers in the early twentieth century, especially in the United States, saw it as a severe kind of worker exploitation of immigrant women in the clothing trades. In Europe, where the practice was widespread as 'cottage industry', the remedy adopted was to insist upon inspection and regulation, usually by agents of the Ministry of Labor. In the US, the practice became the subject of state legislation that almost invariably forbade it altogether. Textile and clothing unions strongly supported such measures, seeing homework as essentially a danger to union standards and pay, achieved in and for factory conditions. Their main appeal for support was addressed to consumers of these goods, on the grounds of the unregulated, insanitary conditions in the tenements where the women and child workers lived. Times of course have changed. Yet the alignment of advocates and critics remains much the same. Would-be employers of homeworkers appeal now as then to women who wish to or must care for their own children and yet need an income (Applebaum, 1987; Christensen, 1987).

The work offered today is not limited to artificial flowers or to operations on clothing.[3] An employing firm may place a computer in the employee's home. It then monitors and supervises work through the company's mainframe, and pays by piecework that can be measured even by finger-strokes. Presumably the worker is on her own time. Often, however, work assignments have short deadlines and she is surrounded by home responsibilities.

The employee doing home-based work inevitably finds that childcare and work fit together no better at home than when these occupations are separated by several miles. One solution for such work, and one that is sometimes required by the employer, is to have a child-carer also work in the home. Thus the worker-mother becomes supervisor of both carer and children in addition to her work duties. If so, she is the one who pays in time for the interruptions that inevitably occur. These women testify that work often can be done only when children sleep. Moreover, they are completely isolated from colleagues and from supervisors, except for the instructions or criticisms that appear on the computer screen. They know nothing of the informal agreements that invariably exist among workers in office or factory about customary norms of work, breaks, and pay.

The employer, however, finds such circumstances decidedly advantageous. He or she benefits from the conditions attached to informal work – the worker provides space and power and, if necessary, the hands of children and neighbors or other family members to complete assignments. It is not surprising that many employers can report increased productivity on homework (BNA, 1989a).

Nevertheless, even women alert to this balance sheet may see no better way to combine home and work responsibilities. Offers of 'homework' consequently continue to find grateful takers, who save time and the cost of travel to work, special clothes, and lunch money, all items that take their toll on the budget of the on-site office worker. Even limited ability to control their own working time compensates to some degree for periods of rush work against a deadline.

Part-time work at home For a somewhat higher level of professional or technical workers, the opportunity from time to time to 'take work home', or to have a designated day or two a week when work can be done at home, is almost a godsend. The interruptions at the workplace caused by meetings, casual conversations with co-workers, tasks of staff supervision and the like, leave little time for sustained research or editorial work, for thinking and planning. Work at home, for the brain worker, may be the only or the most desirable solution to 'getting through the in-tray'. In contrast to the arrangements the employer seeks in home-based work, the initiative in this situation is entirely the employee's. The ability to negotiate for such an arrangement is not altogether limited to high status or high professional specialization, but such characteristics certainly help a worker gain this kind of adjustment of schedules.

The mommy track
A short-lived storm was created when Catalyst President, Felice Schwartz (1989), who had been advising American would-be career women and their employers about integrating women into corporate careers, suggested that such employers consider designating a special track – immediately dubbed the 'mommy track' – for women who in placement interviews admitted that they wanted to have children. This track, though previously unnamed but nevertheless real, already existed in many firms, and in many countries as well. Once placed on it, a woman may have a less rigid and demanding work schedule in respect to overtime and travel, but she may never have an opportunity to achieve the status necessary for real upward mobility. Such a response of corporations to working mothers will never ameliorate the handicaps women face either at home or at work (BNA, 1989b).

Future contingencies
European development will take on a new shape, at least in the

Common Market, after 1992 (see Hootsmans, Chapter 11 of the present book). While radical changes affecting the workplace are in progress, we have only marginal indications that the role of women in the new Common Market is an element of the new equations. In addition, in view of recent unexpected changes in all the East European countries, work and work relations seem destined in several countries to take on a more Western look. The possibility in some of these countries, notably Poland and Czechoslovakia, is that we may see the emergence of a completely new system involving a high degree of worker control and of social welfare. Change in some form is inevitable. Will these changes be planned to place family considerations front and center? The adaptations to new systems of employment could offer opportunities to introduce alternative scheduling in the interests both of maximum employment, and of accommodation to family needs. At the time of writing, however, the matter of women's roles and of their effect on work arrangements has not appeared on the agenda.

How one assesses future economic growth determines whether one's view is rose-colored or black. Ten or fifteen years ago, some European economists had already begun to think of the effect of robotization and computerization on the need for workers. They foresaw the possibility of full or nearly full employment as necessarily defined in other than present terms. While their estimates and prognoses varied considerably, they generally foresaw a time when, if there is to be enough work to go around, work-days, weeks, years and lifetimes would be defined in terms of many fewer hours than are standard today (Gorz, 1987; Rehn, 1974). On the other hand, others point out that with the slowed population growth in the industrialized countries, a labor shortage is one of the contingencies to be reckoned with in the years ahead. In such circumstances, women, like men, might find their labor price rising at the same time that concessions in time and place adjustments become part of the employment bargain (Berry-Lound, 1990).

Conclusion

The existence and history of job segregation in the workplace and the home continue to victimize women workers, whether married, single, head of household, or second earner. The evidence of continuing job segregation in the workplace is overwhelming. Indeed its existence remains the basis of the continuing inquiries into the payment of low wages for jobs in which women predominate and hence the inequity which 'comparable worth' is aimed to correct (Roos, 1985).

The evidence for persistent job segregation in the family is equally overwhelming. We have only to ponder the long-accumulated evidence from studies of the male spouse's reluctant and minuscule contribution to sharing housework and childcare to know that women at the end of the twentieth century continue to be relatively unassisted in these tasks (Walker, 1970; Woods, 1976; Berk, 1980; Berk and Shih, 1980; Cowan, 1989; Hunt and Hunt, 1987). When we add the information that ever higher proportions of women will continue in the labor force (Taeuber and Valdisera, 1986), then we recognize that these problems will take a very long time, even generations, to correct themselves. In the meantime the demands of work will fall most heavily on women.

The purpose of this chapter is to see to what degree changes in work schedules and structures could succeed where other approaches have been insufficient. We know from the European agitation for shorter hours that men are prepared to take shortened work schedules in more vacation time or shorter work-weeks, whereas women much prefer shorter days. We also know that women, except in some circumstances in Scandinavia, recognize that they have so far lost this battle.

Flexitime, insofar as it has been introduced, has proved popular with both men and women, and can, under certain conditions, be of help to both parents in accommodating daycare and school schedules as well as children's out-of-school needs to working hours. It does not, however, lessen total hours of work during a given week or month. Moreover, it is not readily applicable to employees in factories or other continuous and integrated work operations.

Part-time work continues to be women's preferred accommodation to compelling family needs. It accounts for the fact that 90 percent of this work is done by women. Job-sharing, one form of part-time scheduling, is also sought more by women than men. This predilection of women is often interpreted as women's preference and therefore their voluntary choice of work schedules (see Lewis, Chapter 1 and Izraeli, Chapter 2 of this book). This view commonly arises in societies that place high value on individualism and individual 'choice'. Certainly those holding such views tend to oppose any social intervention into what they see as the 'privacy of the family' (Brannen and Moss, Chapter 7 of this book). Even if choice is as free as it is often made to sound, definition and regularization of part-time work is necessary to the achievement of standard monetary rewards, eligibility to both governmental and employer benefits, and adjustments to rest periods and meals. Steps in this direction would result in a more nearly living wage for women. It could also result in men more freely 'choosing' this form of work and sharing parental tasks.

As for homework, Lozano has made clear that work free of a bureaucratic relationship is appealing to many men and women. It is also clear that it is a viable way to work for individuals with special skills and special connections to firms needing these skills, even on an irregular basis. But it is important to remember that the most successful practitioners of this way of work life are dependent on a network of family and other co-workers to make the scheme work dependably, and these people have no guarantees whatever against exploitation.

Home-based computer work, like other home-based work, has few protections and regularizations beyond the employer's unilateral terms of efficiency, productivity, or savings. To institute alternative schedules we women need to insist on the priority of family strength and health. Workers under these conditions probably see this kind of employment as temporary, lasting not more than a few years until children reach a more independent age or are going to school. Shift work, somewhat similarly, is not in itself a desirable way to organize family life; at best it fills a gap until better solutions can be found.

On the whole these ways of relaxing the rigidities of work structure are more promising than realistic solutions. Rather than asking whether any one form is cost-effective, the real test is the degree to which it can achieve thoroughgoing accommodation of work to family life, and to gender equality in the home. That remains a puzzling and still unsolved statement of the problem.

Notes

1. Petersson notes that in addition to shorter hours for all workers, Sweden by law allows parents of children under school age, at their own request, to work a 6-hour day (admittedly for a corresponding cut in salary) (see Sandqvist, Chapter 5). German trade union women whom I have interviewed stress their wish for shorter days over other outcomes of gains in shorter working hours. Men, however, do not join them. The shorter day appears to be a lost cause there. Since this chapter was written the German metalworkers have gained an agreement by which they will have achieved the 35-hour week by 1995.

2. After I did research for *The Working Mother: Problems and Programs in Nine Countries* (Cook, 1978), and had interviewed working mothers around the world, my strongest conclusion was that working mothers above all else lack time and sleep. In many countries, particularly in the communist world at that time, part-time work was not available. Nevertheless, these women when asked what changes they would most like to see in their working conditions said, 'Part-time work!'

3. In 1984 the US Federal Department of Labor had already exempted knitted outware from the ban on homework. By mid-1989 it allowed seven other clothing items to be produced in household production. These items included gloves and mittens, jewelry, embroidery, belts and buckles, and handkerchiefs.

References

André, R. (1985) *Homemakers: the Forgotten Workers*. Chicago: University of Chicago Press.

Applebaum, E. (1987) 'Restructuring work: part-time and at-home employment', in Heidi Hartmann (ed.), *Computer Chips and Paper Clips*. Washington, DC: National Academy Press.

Berk, S.F. (1980) *Women and Household Labor*. Beverly Hills, CA: Sage.

Berk, S.F. and Shih, A. (1980) 'Contributions to household labor: comparing wives and husbands: report', in Berk (ed.), *Women and Household Labor*.

Berry-Lound, D. (1990) *Work and the Family. Career Friendly Employment Practices*. London. IPM.

Bohen, B.H. and Viveros-Long, A. (1981) *Balancing Jobs and Family Life. Do Flexible Work Schedules Help?* Philadelphia: Temple University Press.

BNA (Bureau of National Affairs) (1989a) 'Telecommuting enhances workers' productivity, California study shows', *Daily Labor Report*, 22 August, 161: A-3.

BNA (1989b) *The Mommy Track*, Special Report. Washington, DC: BNA.

Business Link (1988) 'Critical Issues: Steelcase offers job-sharing to entire workforce', 4 (2): 6–7.

Canada Ministry of Supply & Services (1983) *Part-time Work in Canada*. Ottawa: Publications Distribution Centre.

Christensen, K. (1987) *A New Era of Home-Based Work: Directions and Policies*. New York: Henry Holt.

Cook, Alice H. (1978) *The Working Mother: Problems and Programs in Nine Countries*. Ithaca, NY: Industrial Relations Press, Cornell University.

Cowan, Alison Leigh (1989) 'Women's gains on the job: not without a heavy toll', *New York Times*, 21 August: A1, A14.

Daniels, Arlene Kaplan, (1988) *Invisible Careers: Women Civic Leaders from the Volunteer World*, Chicago: University of Chicago Press.

De Neubourg, Chris (1985) 'Part-time work: an international quantitative comparison', *International Labour Review*, 124(5): 564.

Ferman, Louis, Berndt, Louise, and Selo, Elaine, (1978) *Analysis of the Irregular Economy: Cash Flow in the Informal Sector*. Ann Arbor, MI: University of Michigan Press Wayne State University Press, Institute of Labor and Industrial Relations.

Gerstel, Naomi and Gross, Harriet Engel (eds) (1987) *Families and Work*. Philadelphia: Temple University Press.

Goldschmidt-Clermont, Luisella (1983) *Unpaid Work in the Household: A Review of Economic Evaluation Methods*. Geneva: International Labour Office (ILO).

Gorz, André (1987) 'S/He who doesn't work shall eat all the same: tomorrow's economy – and proposals from the Left', *Dissent*, Spring: 179–87. (A French version appeared in *Lettre International*, Spring 1986.)

Grønstedt, Erik (1975) 'Work-sharing families: adaptations of pioneering families with husband and wife in part-time employment', University of Oslo, Institute of Sociology, Skriftsserie 22.

Hochschild, Arlie (with Anne Machung) (1989) *The Second Shift: Working Parents and the Revolution at Home*. New York: Viking Penguin.

Hunt, Janet G., and Hunt, Larry L. (1987) 'Male resistance to role symmetry in dual-earner households: three alternative explanations', in Naomi Gerstel and Harriet Engel Gross (eds), *Families and Work*. Philadelphia: Temple University Press.

Kessler-Harris, Alice (1982) *Out to Work: A History of Wage-Earning Women in the United States*. New York: Oxford University Press.

Lee, R.A. (1983) 'Flexitime and conjugal roles', *Journal of Occupational Behaviour*, 4: 297–315.

Lewis, Suzan and Cooper, Cary L. (1989) *Career-Couples: Contemporary Lifestyles and How to Live Them.* London: Unwin Hyman.

Lozano, Beverly (1989) *The Invisible Workforce: Transforming American Business with Outside and Home-based Workers.* New York: Free Press, Macmillan.

Martin, Jean and Roberts, Ceredwin (1984) *Women and Employment: a lifetime perspective*, London: Department of Employment, Office of Population Censuses and Surveys, HM Stationery Office.

Meier, Gretl S. (1979) *Job Sharing: A New Pattern for Quality of Work and Life.* Kalamazoo, MI: W.E. Upjohn Institute for Employment Research.

Oakley, A. (1976) *Women's Work: The Housewife, Past and Present.* New York: Vintage Books, Random House.

Petersson, Gisela (1989) 'Working hours in Sweden: trends and background to the current discussion', *Working Life in Sweden.* New York: Swedish Information Service (Sept.).

Pierce, Jon L., Newstrom, John W., Dunham, Randall B., and Barber, Alison E. (1989) *Alternative Work Schedules.* Boston: Allyn & Bacon.

Protzman, Ferdinand (1989) 'Shorter workweek: a volatile issue for Germany', *New York Times*, 9 October.

Rapoport, Robert and Rapoport, Rhona (with Janice Bumstead) (1978) *Working Couples.* New York: Harper & Row.

Rehn, Gøsta (1974) *Lifelong Allocation of time.* Paris: OECD Directorate for Social Affairs, Manpower and Education.

Roos, Patricia A. (1985) *Gender and Work: A Comparative Analysis of Industrialized Societies.* Albany: SUNY/Albany.

Schwartz, Felice (1989) 'Management, women and the new facts of life', *Harvard Business Review*, February: 65–76.

Simon, Carl and White, Ann (1982) *Beating the System: the Underground Economy.* Boston: Auburn House.

Szalai, Alexander (1972) *Use of Time: A Multinational Study.* Paris: Mouton.

Taeuber, Cynthia and Valdisera, Victor (1986) *Women in the American Economy.* Current Population Reports, Special Studies Series P–23, 146. Washington, DC: US Department of Commerce, Bureau of the Census.

Walker, Kathryn (1970) 'Time spent by husbands in household work', *Family Economics Review*, 4: 8–11.

Waring, Marilyn (1989) *If Women Only Counted.* Chicago: University of Chicago Press.

Woods, Mary (1976) 'Time use: a measure of household production of family goods and services', paper delivered to the American Home Economics Association.

13
Towards Balanced Lives and Gender Equality

Suzan Lewis, Dafna N. Izraeli and Helen Hootsmans

The growth of dual-earner families in country after country opens up new opportunities. It brings economic independence for women and raises the standard of living for families. It also creates new tensions as increasingly inappropriate ascribed gender roles within the family persist, to varying extents, across national boundaries. Where do we go from here? How do we create the opportunities and incentives for dual-earner men and women to achieve a balance between work and family in ways that disadvantage neither sex and strengthen the family? It would not be appropriate for us to set a single agenda for change in diverse cultures. Rather, in this final section we consider what appear to be the conditions under which dual-earner roles and relationships change and some of the questions raised by the consideration of dual-earner families within a cross-national perspective.

A precondition for effective change for dual-earner families is that the discourse on balancing work and family be framed as an issue for both men and women. The recognition in most countries that families need two incomes and that women are needed in the labour force must be balanced by the acknowledgement that men have responsibilities for family work. Organizational and public policies that merely enable women to combine the two domains leave men's roles untouched, perpetuating women's double burden and the lack of fit between family and work life.

Social policies which focus directly on the family and which recognize that men's family roles must change can structure opportunities for men and women to work out a more satisfactory balance between work and family. Sweden provides a model of such a social policy. It is committed not only to equal opportunities in the workplace but also to changing families, with some measure of success. Elsewhere affirmative action programmes and other policies which focus specifically on the workplace are useful but not sufficient to address the work and family issues. The public provision of childcare and care for the elderly are important in this respect but even these are of limited benefit if the care of family members is still widely regarded as women's responsibility.

The emerging issue of eldercare for dual-earner families suggests that a life cycle approach to family policy is called for. The sharing of family responsibilities could be encouraged by the provision of incentives and support for men and women to integrate periods of caring with a career viewed within a long-term perspective.

Employers also have a vital role to play in enabling dual-earner partners to find the right balance between work and family. They must be willing to create alternatives to the male model of work. This model of continuous full-time work constrains men from full involvement in their families and disadvantages women. Women do have special needs but they are only disadvantaged by these needs if male patterns of work are viewed as the norm, from which women deviate. Parents of young children and people with responsibility for the care of elderly or sick relatives also have special needs. They too are disadvantaged only if they are regarded as deviant. In the context of organizational policies which allow flexibility in hours and places of work and in career pathways over time, and make this acceptable for both men and women, the continuous full-time pattern of work may become only one of many genuine options.

The valuing of women's work is another condition for change within dual-earner families. The gender segregation of occupations with women's work attracting lower pay is universal, but some countries, notably in Scandinavia, are making genuine attempts to give equal value and rewards to women's and men's work. Several of the contributors to this volume note that men whose wives earn as much as or more than they do are more likely than other men to participate equally in family work. Women's lesser earning power is often used to legitimize their greater domestic responsibility. The balance of power within families does not automatically shift with women's higher earnings. Nevertheless equal earnings provide women with the bargaining power and men with the incentives to alter the gender arrangements in the home. Women's earnings also empower them to negotiate with other role partners, for example in their relationship with their mother-in-law in extended families in India.

The movement of more women into previously male-dominated areas, especially the field of management, is also important, not only in raising women's earnings, but also in changing the nature of work. There is evidence that when women are equally represented in management or in other occuaptions they bring considerable changes to their work, including a greater insistence on a balanced lifestyle (Lunneborg, 1990). Patricia Lunneborg suggests that men also change under these circumstances and that everyone – women and men, workers and clients – benefits from these developments. The promotion of token women or small numbers of women into management is not sufficient to bring about radical change. Indeed women who construct their realities in a way which enables them to succeed in male-dominated structures, with minimal threats to their identity, frequently do so by adopting male values (Lewis, 1991). Real change in the nature of occupations can occur only when women are well represented.

It is unlikely that the redistribution of power within the family and the workforce will come about without a similar redistribution within wider societies. Token or minority women policy makers can achieve only minimal change in societies because their power and influence are achieved within and dependent upon male-dominated structures. In Norway where women are well represented in government, childcare subsidies and generous parental leave provisions remained a top priority even in the context of spending cuts. Increasing the number of women in politics and other positions of power can help to place and preserve the needs of families high on the public agenda.

A final condition for change is an ethos of openness and willingness to confront taboo subjects, bringing taken-for-granted issues into the public discourse. Taboos contribute to the maintenance of the status quo. For instance the subject of domestic work is taboo in many contexts. Women are expected to get on with this work or to find another woman to do it, but not to discuss this issue at the same level of importance as more weighty (male) concerns. The way in which money is handled is another taboo subject which preserves power differentials. In the workplace the fact that workers have family responsibilities over and above the demands made by employers has for too long been a taboo subject, and even now that many men do restructure their work and family they often have to do so covertly (Hall, 1990).

Issues and questions

Career women in many countries attempt to relieve their double burden and achieve parity in the workplace by conforming to the male ethic of total work involvement and by paying other women, sometimes at low rates, to perform domestic and childcare work, an option which is not available to other women. This can perpetuate gender inequalities within families, both because domestic help is often construed as help for the woman and therefore not associated with changes in men's behaviour, and also because it upholds the male model of work. It enables men and women to adopt patterns of work which assume a full-time helpmate, thus obscuring the need for organizations to change. Class inequalities thus uphold gender inequalities. The link between ongoing class inequality and the perpetuation of gender inequality within families raises the question of whether it is possible to address the issue of achieving balance and equality in families separately from issues of social class and privilege within wider societies.

A second question is whether the nuclear dual-earner family is an ideal to be pursued at all. Can it ever offer real support and possibilities for gender equality? The nuclear family was functional in the context of a gendered division of labour and the separation of work and family domains. The dual-earner family, one of many non-traditional family forms, heralded the reintegration of work and family and some reallocation of gender roles, but in the context of the nuclear family it can create problems of supports for the young, sick and elderly and even for the breadwinners themselves. We have seen that support for the dual-earner lifestyle is embedded in the three-generational extended families in the East. However, these supports bring their own problems and can constrain the pace of change in gender roles within the family. Perhaps the gradual breakdown of the gender allocation of roles opens the way to new possible family forms with more built-in supports, such as extended cross-generational families. In the future we may be debating issues concerning not dual-earner but various forms of multiple-earner families within which flexible de-gendered roles may develop.

This book raises questions with respect to gender equality and diversity among dual-earner families. Can gender equality, defined in terms of a reallocation of family roles, be a universal ideal which transcends cultural tradition? Should egalitarian ideals be modified to take account of strong cultural attitudes? Feminist writers have argued that it is only by modifying traditions to take account of women's needs that the reproduction of inequalities will be halted. At the same time women value the traditions of their respective countries. The constructs of Western feminism are not necessarily acceptable or valid for women in all contexts. While the commonalities in the experiences of dual-earner women in diverse national cultures are apparent in this volume, so are the differences among women whose experiences of gender and family roles are constructed within different historical and socio-cultural frameworks. Contributors to this volume have demonstrated that when there is a clash between cultural and egalitarian values women frequently attempt to reconcile their needs within the boundaries of traditional expectations in non-threatening ways, which also diffuse the tension that might lead to change. The perceived high cost of social change in the West, in terms of family breakdowns and other social problems, is not a price that dual-earner women everywhere are willing to pay. The dilemma for many women concerns not how to alter gender roles in dual-earner families, but rather the relative costs of change and stability, especially where other supports are available to reduce their double burden and other pay-offs exist for the persistence of gendered roles.

What is certain is that the solutions to issues of balance and equality in work and family will be diverse. The way ahead does not lie in uniform change whereby the ideas of certain cultures are imposed upon others without sensitivity to national needs. The Hungarian experience illustrates the futility of this. Rather it lies in open-minded debate about the choices of life scripts open to men and women in dual-earner families in diverse contexts, and in new perspectives for policy which treat work and family as a single integrated social system. Ultimately this may enable us to optimize life choices while retaining respect for diversity and for those aspects of each national heritage which do not disadvantage people by virtue of gender and class.

References

Hall, Douglas T. (1990) 'Promoting work/family balance: an organizational change approach', *Organizational Dynamics*, 18: 5–18.

Lewis, Suzan (1991) 'Motherhood and employment: the impact of social and organizational values', in Ann Phoenix, Anne Woollett and Eva Lloyd (eds), *Motherhood: Meanings, Practices and Ideologies*. London: Sage.

Lunneborg, Patricia W. (1990) *Women Changing Work*. New York: Greenwood.

Index